Making Indiana University

History, Landscape, and a Sense of Place

James H. Capshew

Indiana University Bloomington Libraries Publishing
Bloomington, Indiana

Indiana University Bloomington Libraries Publishing
1320 E. Tenth Street
Bloomington, IN 47405

Published 2025

Cover Image: Joe Lee, 2024; © 2024 James H. Capshew
Cover Design: Adam Mazel

ISBN-13: 979-8-218-79408-8

DOI: 10.5967/m1tv-xc36

Table of Contents

List of Figures

Front Matter

Abstract

This book sheds light on the creation of Indiana University's institutional identity and image over its two centuries of existence by investigating the role of historians, archivists, and others in documenting its historical record. As such, it is an exercise in historiography, or the study of the history of IU history. The first part presents a rationale for an inclusive view of contributors to IU history, including not only historians and archivists but also architects, groundskeepers, and other members of its academic community. Essays on the contributions of the first professor as well as the invention of the genre of Indiana University history provides a useful provenance. The second section supplies a chronological study of the history of IU's distinctive campus design, from its beginning in 1885 to 2020, to illustrate the essential role that place plays in university culture. The third and final part are essays that uncover hidden efforts to sustain the university's historical record in publications, faculty memorials, and historic preservation. By its interrogation of the sources and methods that construct the historical record, this book makes a unique contribution to the study of Indiana University history and culture.

Dedication

For Sheila,
who was present at the sunrise of my scholarship,
returning now for the sunset.
Together...at the last.

Introduction: Past Writers of a Present History

Figure 1: Jordan River

> Institutions of higher learning in fact have a long history of association with the garden, be it the parks and groves of the famous Greek schools, the Roman villa, the bowers of Sainte-Geneviève in medieval Paris, the Italian garden academies of the Renaissance, the British "college garden," or the idyll of the traditional American campus. The question that interests us here is whether there is more to this association than just a matter of setting.
>
> —Robert Pogue Harrison, *Gardens: An Essay on the Human Condition*

A university's natural environment, modified by human intervention, provides more than a setting for higher education. The physical campus becomes part and parcel of institutional image, identity, and integrity. "The singular magic of a place is evident from what happens there, from what befalls oneself or others when in its vicinity," ecological philosopher David Abram has written. "To tell of such events is implicitly to tell of the particular power of that site, and indeed to participate in its expressive potency."[1] By touching the place with hands and eyes, by walking through it and observing the interacting patterns of natural landscape and built environment, by listening to and reading stories about the lore of the place and its denizens, one might activate an ancient and ineffable sensibility. This book explores how history and landscape and place-making contribute to Indiana University (IU)'s institutional identity.

Voices along the Way

Between 1890 and 1977, a handful of books dealing with the narrative history of IU were published. The authors were faculty men, nearly all of whom were retired. These books' content reflected a loose consensus on the dominant themes found in the institution's history. Among them were the value of public education, the worth of individual students, curricular changes responding to social needs, the academic community at the juncture of intellectual ideals and

[1] David Abram, *The Spell of the Sensuous: Perception and Language in a More-Than-Human World* (New York: Vintage, 1996), 182.

practical living, the symbiosis between students and teachers, and the animating ideal of research as the basis for knowledge.[2]

But general narratives are but one form of university history at IU. Casting a wider net, one finds program, department, school, or campus histories; studies of student life; biographical directories of administrative officers and trustees; autobiographies, memoirs, and biographies; and various thematic and topical works. They defy easy summary since they vary widely in tone, approach, and length. Their authorial demography, perhaps not surprisingly, is more diverse in gender, ethnicity, and age—although the vast majority have either worked or studied at IU.[3]

In 2020, Indiana University commemorated its 200th anniversary with a broad and inclusive public history program.[4] One of its goals was to engage critically with past institutional narratives; to reexamine their assumptions, sources, and methods; and to write new, empirically based historical accounts that take a more inclusive and equitable approach that does not privilege one set of historical actors over another. In this way, more voices could be heard as well as new perspectives explored, especially ones that are underrepresented in existing histories.

This book focuses attention on record-keepers (archivists, historians, editors, faculty, and staff) who preserve, make accessible, and interpret written documentation about university programs, events, and people. In addition, because the campus is the physical embodiment of the institution, and it too has a history, physical plant staff (planners, architects, landscapers, gardeners, and groundskeepers) receive consideration as well.

---

[2]Theophilus A. Wylie, *Indiana University, Its History from 1820, When Founded, to 1890, with Biographical Sketches of Its Presidents, Professor and Graduates, and a List of Its Students from 1820 to 1887* (Indianapolis: Wm. B. Burford, 1890); Samuel Bannister Harding, ed., *Indiana University, 1820–1904* (Bloomington: Indiana University, 1904); James A. Woodburn, *History of Indiana University: Volume I, 1820–1902* (Bloomington: Indiana University, 1940); Burton Dorr Myers, *History of Indiana University: Volume II, 1902–1937, The Bryan Administration*, ed. Burton D. Myers and Ivy L. Chamness (Bloomington: Indiana University, 1952); Thomas D. Clark, *Indiana University: Midwestern Pioneer*, 4 vols. (Bloomington: Indiana University Press, 1970/1977).

[3]See "How To Conduct Research at the IU Libraries University Archives".

[4]Office of the Bicentennial, "Indiana University Bicentennial Final Report" (Bloomington: Indiana University, 2020), https://wayback.archive-it.org/219/20240413230003/https://200.iu.edu/doc/IU-bicentennial-final.pdf.

Emplacing the University

Persistent lacunae in IU's historiography are the role of place and the process of place-making as key components of institutional image and historical identity. This is ironic because members of the university community have been touting the beauty of the flagship campus in Bloomington since the late 1800s. In more recent times, outside experts comparing campus design and facilities implementation across the nation judge IU to be in the top rank regularly. How and why did the university develop "America's legacy campus," as a recent book title phrased it, and what were the institutional consequences of possessing a vivid sense of place?[5]

Focusing on place might open new conceptual horizons. It can be argued that the campus itself has a measure of historical agency, albeit a nonhuman one. Its assemblage of natural elements and processes provides a unique environment of opportunities and constraints. From this perspective, the campus serves as the place where the university is enacted and the academic community is, both literally and metaphorically, grounded. It follows that the design and operations of the physical plant are historically important, and so the work of campus planners, architects of structures and landscapes, and caretakers and gardeners assume a renewed significance. Such individuals express their intentions in the media of stone, brick, and wood used for buildings and other campus facilities or in a vegetal palette of trees, shrubs, grasses, and flowers. The choices made by architects of buildings and landscapes are rooted in the rich traditions and disciplines of design, captured at a specific moment, as they shape the physical plant. The resulting visual image and tactile feel of the campus became part of the university's historical identity that cannot be completely conveyed in words.

Sense of place is built on historical and experiential knowledge of a particular locality. Relevant past work includes IU political scientist Lynton K. Caldwell's brief foreword to the encyclopedic survey *The Natural Heritage of Indiana*, in which he distinguishes "natural features are what they are and where they are without regard to human presence" and places "defined by human perception." Thus, "the qualities and characteristics defining a place express not only

[5]See Thomas A. Gaines, *The Campus as a Work of Art* (Westport, CT: Praeger, 1991), for comparative campus analysis; and J. Terry Clapacs, *Indiana University Bloomington: America's Legacy Campus* (Bloomington: Indiana University Press, 2017), for his use of "America's legacy campus."

its biophysical attributes, but also its aesthetic value and historic significance."[6] Near the start of the twenty-first century, three IU professors in the humanities and arts—Will Counts, James Madison, and Scott Sanders—composed a portrait of Bloomington in words and photographs, attempting to capture the special qualities of the community. Explaining their approach and motivation, the preface states, "Good places are shaped by the gifts of nature and by the labor and love of many people over generations. The city of Bloomington, tucked away in the forested hills of southern Indiana, is one such place. Three of us who have worked here, played here, reared children here, and set our roots right down to the limestone bedrock made this book to chronicle and celebrate our home town."[7] In my own previous historical work, I have employed the concept of *genius loci* to shed light on the activities of IU administrator Herman Wells at Indiana University.[8]

Plan of the Book

This volume is divided into three parts. The first deals with origins and beginnings. Chapter 1 locates the nascent institution in a new town in a new state, painting with a broad brush some salient features of the frontier environment and culture. Chapter 2 recounts the story of the first teacher, the Reverend Baynard Rush Hall, and his career. Because much of what we know today about the institution's early history came from his 1843 book *The New Purchase*, he also qualifies as the first historian. Chapter 3 deals with how a distinct genre of historical writing about Indiana University arose in the 1890s in response to significant changes in the university. An 1883 campus fire led to a decision to move the campus to a more promising locale and an 1884 presidential scandal caused a change in leadership that catalyzed serious historical reflection for the

[6] Lynton Keith Caldwell, "Foreword: A Sense of Place," in *The Natural Heritage of Indiana*, ed. Marion C. Jackson (Bloomington: Indiana University Press, 1997), xvi.

[7] Will Counts, James H. Madison, and Scott Russell Sanders, *Bloomington Past and Present* (Bloomington: Indiana University Press, 2002), x.

[8] James H. Capshew, "Indiana University as the 'Mother of College Presidents': Herman B Wells as Inheritor, Exemplar, and Agent" (Bloomington: IU Institute for Advanced Study, 2011), https://hdl.handle.net/2022/14123; James H. Capshew, *Herman B Wells: The Promise of the American University* (Bloomington; Indianapolis: Indiana University Press; Indiana Historical Society Press, 2012).

first time. With deep connections to IU and representing different generations, three individuals—Theophilus Wylie (1810–95), David Banta (1833–96), and James Woodburn (1856–1943)—composed narratives of institutional progress circa 1890 as a response to the move to Dunn's Woods and the fresh leadership of David Starr Jordan. They anchored the university in the collective memory of the community and gave voice to institutional aspirations for the future. The subsequent career of institutional history is sketched, with critical commentary.

Part Two analyzes the design history of the flagship campus at Dunn's Woods. The narrative reveals a remarkable consensus about conserving the native woodland character of the landscape at the beginning and then enduring persistence in extending that vision as the campus grew one hundredfold, from twenty to 2,000 acres. The result of that extraordinary fidelity to local conditions was a cultural landscape of acknowledged beauty and integrity. Chapter 4 opens with the university moving to a new campus in 1885, having outgrown the original Seminary Square location that had served as the site of instruction for sixty years. A fateful decision in the ordinary course of building placement nudged the university community toward a variation of the medieval Gothic quadrangle as the campus design evolved organically. The remnant forest was preserved as new buildings, made of local limestone, were constructed to frame Dunn's Woods in a giant quadrangle. By 1915, two out of four sides of the frame had been completed and a start made on the remaining two sides. Chapter 5 explores the period between 1915 and 1945, when additional lands were purchased and the campus moved beyond the great quadrangle that married the gray stone buildings and the green woods. Further development occurred on Third, Seventh, and Tenth Streets, and Jordan Avenue (now Eagleson Avenue) was built to provide a boundary on the east. The woodland theme was carried through by the preservation or renovation of green spaces as the campus acquired specialized facilities (e.g., athletic stadium), accommodated the proliferation of professional schools (e.g., music, education, business), and started housing students on campus. Attentive members of the academic community noted the delights that the Indiana campus held. The chapter ends with the disruptions caused by the economic woes of the 1930s and the mobilization for the Second World War. Chapter 6 covers 1945 to 1980, a time that saw an exponential increase in the campus footprint, to about 2,000 acres, designed to accommodate tremendous growth in student enrollments, academic programs, and athletic facilities. With this increase in scale, the pace of campus development quickened as well, and the campus grew into its present configuration, roughly divided into zones for academic structures, residential life, and athletic and sports facilities. Chapter 7 analyzes the decades 1980 to 2020, a period characterized by increased attention to historic preservation and focused infill. Renovation and rehabilitation of existing structures began in earnest in the mid-1980s, starting with the repurposing of the old stadium into an arboretum, followed later by the restoration of the buildings comprising the original Old Crescent surrounding Dunn's Woods. At times, the modern physical plant stretched, but did not break, the century-old conservationist ethos that has been transformed in the twenty-first century into a search for environmental sustainability.

Part 3 offers another route into place-making, focusing on narratives and stories that emplace Indiana University into historical contexts. Sometimes references about literal places are absent but implied. The point is that our perceptions and understandings of Indiana University as an institution are shaped and conditioned by historical narrative. Using a biographical approach, Chapter 8 analyzes the little-known career of Ivy L. Chamness (1881–1975), the first (and only) person to hold the title of editor of university publications (1917–52). The chapter focuses on her work on behalf of university history, as editor of the *Indiana University Alumni Quarterly*, as developmental editor for both volumes of the official *History of Indiana University*, and as a contributing historical writer. Because she was a woman in a patriarchal society, Chamness's significant historical contributions were undervalued during her career and subsequently overlooked. The evidence demonstrates that she was the linchpin that kept the practice of IU history going through the mid-twentieth century. Chapter 9 explores the practice of honoring deceased faculty members by memorial resolutions written by faculty colleagues. Highlighting the human quality of the institution, faculty careers of teaching, research, and service are the warp threads of the tapestry that is the university while the students are the weft yarns. The contributions of two key faculty members—chemistry professor Harry Day (1906–2007) and English professor Donald J. Gray (b. 1927)—are examined in their roles as university necrologists. Chapter 10 reexamines the role of IU administrator Herman Wells (1902–2000) in the preservation of the 1835 house built by Andrew Wylie, the first president. Beginning with his first encounters in the 1930s as a young faculty member, Wells developed a lifetime commitment to the historic house, the most significant artifact remaining from the early history of Indiana University. In his lengthy career as president (1937–62) and university chancellor (1962–2000), he was responsible for the university's initial acquisition of the house in the 1940s and was involved with decisions for architectural restoration in the 1960s and its gradual emergence as an operating museum in the 1980s. The history of that relationship is explored at length, echoing themes of materiality and identity.

A brief coda, occasioned by the 2020 global pandemic, allows reflection on the meaning of the term *watershed*, taken literally and figuratively. Used to periodize the 200-year history of Indiana University, it can connect history, landscape, and sense of place in constructive ways.

This book is built around the notion that writing institutional history should be a multivocal, iterative, and cumulative process. Multivocal in the sense that the subjects of analysis are individuals from all strata and positions in the university and that a variety of sources is used. History is never finally done, once and for all. Fundamentally an iterative process, there can only be the latest revision to contend with prior interpretations. New sources and different angles of vision can occasion revisions of old stories and help one comprehend how interpretation changes over time. Institutional history is also cumulative: each work has the potential to enhance our current understanding. This historical accumulation creates practical problems for attempts to comprehensively portray an institution over a long span of time, however. It can be done, but there are reasons that the last comprehensive narrative of Indiana University was written fifty years ago in a tome of 1,500 pages in three volumes.[9]

I hope these chapters remind us that a shared institutional history can be an abundant tapestry that weaves together the stories of students, faculty, staff, alumni, donors, citizens, and visitors even though their individual experiences might vary widely and differ profoundly. The university's campus can be seen as a palimpsest inscribed with a record of interventions and mediations—great and small, temporary and permanent—of both the human and the nonhuman environment. Everyone can learn to observe and recognize the past within the present, to identify how the university

[9] Clark, *Indiana University*, 1970/1977.

expresses its enduring values and goals by its institutional history as well as by its campus landscape, yielding an abiding sense of place. There are benefits to be gained and insights to be gleaned in understanding the past writers of our present history, whether that history is written in ink, chiseled limestone, or the ground beneath our feet.[10]

[10]Eric Sandweiss, "Personal Communication to the Author," June 7, 2024.

Part One: Provenance

> Each age writes the history of the past anew with reference to the conditions uppermost in its own time.
> —Frederick Jackson Turner, *The Significance of History*

Figure 2: First image of the Indiana University seal. Hand-drawn in the manuscript minutes of the Indiana University Board of Trustees, July 21, 1841.

1 First the Forests

Figure 3: Seminary Building

> This was the order of human institutions: first the forests, after that the huts, then the villages, next the cities, and finally the academies.
>
> —Giambattista Vico, *The New Science*

In the beginning, there was the land, covered by a vast deciduous forest. Far from empty, it was full of vegetative life and animals of every size, including humans. Indigenous people lived within this natural abundance—hunting, fishing, and gathering plants for food, shelter, and medicine.

After the Revolutionary War created the United States of America, the Northwest Territory (spanning six eventual states: Ohio, Indiana, Illinois, Michigan, Wisconsin, and Minnesota) was developed in the late-eighteenth century. European migrants moved in to occupy the homelands of native communities. Treaty after treaty gave a legal gloss to systematic genocidal terror as Indigenous peoples were forcibly removed and property rights were retained by the federal government. Ironically, their absence defined the beginning of "the land of the Indians"—Indiana—and left deep scars from a historical trauma yet to be reconciled.

As the white population increased to 60,000 (the threshold to petition for statehood), the state of Indiana was carved out of the Indiana Territory in 1816.[1] The Seventh US Congress granted a township of land (six miles by six miles square, or 23,040 acres) to support a seminary of learning.[2] In 1818, that location became Perry Township in the new county of Monroe. The recently concluded Treaty of St. Mary's ceded Native American lands comprising the central third of the state and was known as the New Purchase. In the southern portion of the New Purchase, Monroe County marked the northern extent of white settlement in the new state.

On January 20, 1820, the Indiana General Assembly passed a bill to establish a state seminary of learning and designated a board of trustees to oversee its operation. The board, headed by physician David H. Maxwell from the new village of Bloomington (population 300), decided to locate the new seminary in Perry Township on

[1] James H. Madison, *Hoosiers: A New History of Indiana* (Bloomington: Indiana University Press; Indiana Historical Society Press, 2014), 49.

[2] See Center on Education Policy, "Public Schools and the Original Federal Land Grant Program: A Background Paper from the Center on Education Policy" (Washington, 2011-04), https://eric.ed.gov/?id=ED518388.

seminary lands, although they could have located it anywhere in the state. They selected a ten-acre site with a spring a quarter mile south of the county courthouse square for the campus of the Indiana State Seminary. Other seminary township lands were sold to provide a meager endowment for the school.

The site was cleared of trees and other vegetation, marking an opening in the wild forest. The trustees hired contractors to build a classroom building and a professor's house. The next order of business was to find an instructor who could teach Greek and Latin, the foundation of the classical curriculum derived from medieval European roots. As it happened, a Presbyterian minister, Baynard Rush Hall, had moved to Monroe County recently, and, as he later boasted, he was "the very first man since the creation of the world that read Greek in the New Purchase!"[3] Finally, preparations were complete, and the seminary opened in April 1825, with a dozen young men comprising the student body and Hall as the sole faculty member.

1.1 Pioneer Bloomington

Getting to Bloomington required overland travel, typically by horseback, stagecoach, or walking. In the frontier village, log cabins abounded, and the rudimentary dirt roads were full of stumps and turned into muddy messes when it rained. Heating and cooking were managed by stove or fireplace, and the provision of firewood was a constant concern. Residents obtained their food by growing vegetables in home gardens and possessing flocks of chickens, which ranged freely. Hunting wild game as well as slaughtering pigs and cows supplemented diets with meat.

As the population slowly grew, the amount of land cleared for the construction of houses and crops increased, and the village became more economically diversified and socially stratified. In 1828, the general assembly raised the seminary to the status of a college—Indiana College—and the trustees offered its presidency to Andrew Wylie, a Presbyterian minister who had been a college president in western Pennsylvania. Wylie took up his duties in 1829, joining a

[3]Baynard Rush (Robert Carlton, pseud.) Hall, *The New Purchase, or, Seven and a Half Years in the Far West*, ed. J. A. Woodburn (1843; repr., Princeton University Press, 1916), 158.

faculty of two and a student body of nearly forty. Plans were drawn up for a new college building to provide additional classrooms, a library, and a chemical laboratory. The first commencement, in 1830, celebrated the achievements of four students who had completed the college course.

In 1833, Cornelius Pering, along with his family, arrived in Bloomington to teach in the nascent Monroe County Female Seminary. An Englishman, he immigrated to the United States the year before. His observations of Bloomington were keen, and he described the small settlement in words and drawings. He noted the ubiquity of tree stumps, including on the rustic unfinished campus: "You will observe that the land has been recently cleared, and that the stumps of the trees are not yet entirely rotten. Trees are always cut down with the axe a foot or two from the ground and the stumps left to rot, which they do in eight or ten years."[4]

The first professor, Baynard Hall, who had left in 1832, lamented the wholesale clearing of the land for the campus. Looking back in 1843, he wrote, "That a most sumptuous area had already been marred by the ignorance and cupidity of planners and builders; and among other irremediable evils, not a grove of forest trees had been left standing on the campus."[5] The great hardwood forests of Indiana were only beginning to be exploited for economic gains at that time, and little attention was paid to other values, including their aesthetic beauty.

1.2 Original Campus

In 1835, President Wylie and his wife, Margaret, moved their large family into an imposing two-story brick house located near the college on a twenty-acre farmstead. One of the finest houses in the county, it was a marker of their social status. Meanwhile, the new College Building experienced prolonged delays in construction and was finally opened in 1836. The three-story brick structure was set on a foundation of limestone. Its design was inspired by "a picture of a New England cotton factory [found] on a bolt of muslin

[4]Cornelius Pering, "The Pering Letters of 1833," *Indiana University Alumni Quarterly*, no. 20 (1933): 420.

[5]Hall, *The New Purchase, or, Seven and a Half Years in the Far West*, 1916, 71.

in one of the stores of Bloomington" seen by one of the trustees.[6] It housed the chapel, ample recitation rooms, and rooms for the Athenian and Philomathean student literary societies.

In 1838, with the campus as a going concern in the small town of 1,500, the college was legislatively transformed yet again, into Indiana University, with plans for schools of medicine and law to be established.[7] That year, the Boarding-House was erected, incorporating the professor's house in its structure. It provided accommodation for thirty to forty students, and residents could grow their own vegetables on the campus.[8] (A small laboratory building was also planned but would not be erected until 1840.) Now the campus claimed a physical plant of four buildings—Seminary Building, professor's house, Boarding-House, and College Building. The teaching staff remained small, however, reaching a low of three instructors in 1839.[9] Chronically poor finances and lack of demand for higher education maintained the institutional status quo of basic subsistence.

The pace of change gained momentum in the 1850s. President Wylie died in 1851, at sixty-two, because of a woodchopping accident. He had led the infant institution for over two decades, ensuring its survival in the face of sectarian controversies and political pressures. His successors were men of the cloth, as the university was led by Protestant ministers until 1884.

The railroad came to Bloomington in 1853, revolutionizing transportation around the state and beyond. Coincidentally, the railroad tracks were placed along the west boundary of the campus and brought noise, smoke, and danger to a formerly peaceful locale.

Three years after Wylie died, disaster struck the physical plant. The main College Building was destroyed by fire in 1854, along with the library and administrative records. The small academic community organized the Society of the Alumni to mobilize support for university rebuilding, and the local government, as well as residents, contributed financially. The old Seminary Building and the small

[6]John W. Cravens, "Buildings on the Old and New Campuses of Indiana University: II: Six of the Buildings on the Old Campus," *Indiana University Alumni Quarterly* 9, no. 2 (1922): 158.

[7]See Woodburn, *History of Indiana University*, 1940, 118.

[8]Cravens, "Buildings on the Old and New Campuses of Indiana University," 1922, 159.

[9]Woodburn, *History of Indiana University*, 1940, 120.

Laboratory Building were pressed into service for classroom space as trustees made plans for a new building.

The plan for the new University Building represented a departure from the past practice of the trustee board acting as building designers. Instead, the board hired a professional architect, the Irish-trained William Tinsley, who practiced in Cincinnati and Indianapolis. The edifice followed a Gothic style modified for college buildings, with brick as the main material, highlighted by handsome stonework made of locally sourced limestone on the windows and entry doors. The new University Building opened in 1855 and featured an image of the university seal, adopted in 1841, carved into the limestone.[10]

By 1860–61, the faculty had grown to nine men, including the president.[11] Debate over the Civil War roiled the IU campus as well as the town of Bloomington from 1860 to 1865. Some students enlisted in the Union Army; some fought for the Confederacy. Passionate arguments animated the two literary societies as they debated the causes of the war and whether secession was allowable under the US Constitution.[12]

In 1869, the university lost its bid to become the recipient of a federal land grant to teach agriculture and engineering through the Morrill Act when the Indiana General Assembly accepted gifts from Tippecanoe County and John Purdue to establish an agricultural college in West Lafayette.

Curriculum expansion and increasing enrollments drove the trustees to the decision to build another major building on the campus—Science Hall—to accommodate a natural history museum, a chemical laboratory, the library, and the departments of philosophy, zoology, comparative anatomy, and law. The new science building, completed in 1873, was constructed of brick and trimmed in limestone. Indianapolis architect B. V. Enos designed the structure in collegiate Gothic style, to harmonize with the 1855 University Building.[13] These two large academic halls, at right angles to each

[10]See James H. Capshew, "Memo University Seal" (Reference file: University Seal, Indiana University Archives, March 1, 2019).

[11]Woodburn, *History of Indiana University*, 1940, 267.

[12]Steven E. Towne, "Indiana University During the Civil War," *200: The Bicentennial Magazine* 1, no. 2 (2018): 18–19.

[13]Cravens, "Buildings on the Old and New Campuses of Indiana University," 1922, 162.

other, were the principal buildings on the campus site. The old Seminary Building and the Laboratory Building had been torn down in 1858, and the Boarding-House in 1864; some of the material found reuse in other structures in Bloomington.[14]

Prompted by growing enrollments, the 1880s saw much change at Indiana University. Women students became more numerous after their initial admission in 1867, and a few African American students began to attend. Curricular reforms resulted in the expansion of courses of study: ancient classics, modern classics, and science. The faculty, in 1885, numbered twenty-four men.[15]

In July 1883, a lightning strike ignited a blaze in Science Hall, and the building, with its library, museum collections, and university records, was destroyed and its contents a total loss. Despite the fact that the fire destroyed nearly half of the physical plant, the members of the university community were not as disheartened as they had been following the 1854 College Building fire. The university was larger and stronger, with an active alumni group, and the state had just started annual appropriations for university operations only months before. The board of trustees, headed by David Banta, a former circuit court judge, moved quickly to stabilize the situation and explore options. Some trustees thought it might be a suitable time to move the campus away from the railroad, and the board looked at several sites. The trustee board decided to buy twenty acres of the Dunn family farm on the eastern outskirts of town. That woodlot became the campus at Dunn's Woods. The new Dunn's Woods campus was ready in 1885, presided over by a new president, the former biology professor David Starr Jordan, who oversaw major changes in the curriculum that accompanied the move.

[14]Cravens, 159–60. The former campus was bought by the City of Bloomington in 1967 and subsequently redeveloped. The northeast corner of the property was designated Seminary Park and received local historic site status in 1976.

[15]Indiana University, "Annual Catalogue of the Indiana University for the Academical Year 1885–86" (Bloomington: Indiana University, 1886), 9–11.

2 The First Historian

Figure 4: Baynard R. Hall

> Human beings participate in history both as actors and as narrators. The inherent ambivalence of the word "history" in many modern languages, including English, suggests this dual participation. In vernacular use, history means both the facts of the matter and a narrative of those facts, both "what happened" and "that which is said to have happened." The first meaning places the emphasis on the sociohistorical process, the second on our knowledge of that process or on a story about that process.... The inability to step out of history in order to write or rewrite it applies to all actors and narrators.
>
> —Michel-Rolph Trouillot, *Silencing the Past: Power and the Production of History*

Few people today are familiar with the Reverend Doctor Baynard Rush Hall (1798–1863), the inaugural instructor at the progenitor of Indiana University—the Indiana State Seminary of learning. The school was chartered by the state legislature in 1820, and Hall served as principal from its opening in 1825. When the tiny institution was elevated to Indiana College in 1828, it acquired its first president, Andrew Wylie, who also served as an instructor. In 1832, Hall left the institution following an administrative struggle with President Wylie. The thwarting of his ambitions motivated Hall to write a lightly fictionalized account of his Bloomington career, *The New Purchase, or, Seven and a Half Years in the Far West*, published in 1843 in two volumes.[1]

In addition to its endurance as a vivid description of pioneer life in southern Indiana, the book serves as a uniquely valuable source on the early history of Indiana University. IU's historiography has been shaped by Hall leaving and Wylie staying for the rest of his career. Thus, the first written accounts of institutional history describe the "faculty war" ending with the termination of Hall. Ever since, the historical role of Hall has been impoverished, relegated to the margins of IU's institutional saga.

Hall thus was not only the first instructor, teaching Greek and Latin in the classical curriculum, but also the first historian of the

[1] Hall, *The New Purchase, or, Seven and a Half Years in the Far West*, 1916. The New Purchase referred to the 1818 acquisition by the United States of the central third of Indiana from the resident Miami tribe and others living in the territory in the Treaty of St. Mary's, conducted in Ohio during September and October 1818. Monroe County and Bloomington were organized in 1818.

institution. To be sure, he narrated history in a partisan manner, outlining what he saw as Wylie's mistaken approach, but the factual details about college life have been generally accepted. Indeed, early IU historians wove Hall's recollections, sometimes without attribution, into their narratives. As living memory faded over time, Hall's book became an increasingly important historical source. Because his activity as a historical narrator has been neglected, a closer examination of his foundational role in the university's historiography might yield deeper understanding.

2.1 From the Metropolis to the Frontier

A Philadelphia native, Baynard Hall received his bachelor's degree from Union College in Schenectady, New York, in 1820. He then attended Princeton Theological Seminary in New Jersey, obtaining a certificate in 1823, and received a license to preach from the Presbyterian ministry. Hall and Mary Ann Young were married in 1820, in Danville, Kentucky. Their two young children died in 1824. Propelled by a mixture of frontier fascination and personal tragedy, Baynard Hall and his wife left Philadelphia in April 1824, bound for Owen County, Indiana, where other members of the Young family had settled. Baynard was twenty-six, and Mary Ann was twenty-eight. Completing their journey by stagecoach in May, they arrived in Owen County, near the northern limit of white settlement in the new state.[2]

Meanwhile, the Indiana State Seminary of learning was being organized by a board of trustees. Endowed with a federal land grant, the trustees located the school in Bloomington, a new settlement established in 1818. The campus was carved out of the forest a few blocks south of the Monroe County courthouse. A two-story brick Seminary Building went up, as well as a professor's house, as ten acres of land were cleared for the school.

In November 1824, Hall was hired by the trustees as the sole instructor a few months before the seminary opened. Newspaper advertisements described the young instructor: "Mr. Hall is a gentleman, whose classical attainments are perhaps not inferior to any in the western country; and whose acquaintance with the most

[2]See Dixie Kline Richardson, *Baynard Rush Hall: His Story* (Indianapolis: Dixie Kline Richardson, 2009).

approved methods of instruction in some of the best universities in the U. States, and whose morals, manners, and address render him every way qualified to give dignity and character to the institution."[3]

The description of the campus was similarly embellished: "[The buildings] are erected on an elevated situation, affording a handsome view of Bloomington the county seat...and also a commanding prospect of the adjacent country which is altogether pleasant and well calculated for rural retreats; and as it regards the healthiness of its situation, we hazard nothing in the assertion, that it cannot be excelled by any in the western country."[4]

The Indiana State Seminary of learning opened for classes in April 1825, with Hall welcoming around ten young men. Hall continued to serve as an instructor for the infant institution until 1832. In those seven years, student enrollment increased from ten to forty. The faculty was expanded to two in 1827, with the addition of John Harney to teach mathematics, and to three in 1829, with the hiring of Andrew Wylie to serve as president of the institution, now known as Indiana College, as well as to teach mental and moral philosophy, political economy, and literature.

Hall left the college under a cloud in 1832, as did Harney, because of personal differences with President Wylie. Harboring bitter disappointment, Hall and his wife traveled back east. Never returning to the scene of his professional origination, the classical scholar spent the rest of his life teaching and preaching at a series of schools and churches in Pennsylvania, New Jersey, and New York.[5]

Hall became a published author in 1836 with a Latin grammar textbook, which was reviewed harshly.[6] In 1843, Hall published his second book, detailing his time in Indiana. *The New Purchase* chronicled how pioneer Hoosiers cultivated life on the frontier, including colorful descriptions of daily activities of subsistence, transport, social mores, and religious observance.[7] The book's title was the common name of the middle third of Indiana, after resident

[3]Richardson.

[4]Richardson.

[5]Richardson, 180ff.

[6]Baynard Rush Hall, *Exercises, Analytical and Synthetical; Arranged for the New and Compendious Latin Grammar* (Bedford: Harrison Hall, 1836); reviewed by Alfred Addis, "Latin Grammars," *The Literary and Theological Review* 6, no. 21 (1839): 59–66.

[7]Hall, *The New Purchase, or, Seven and a Half Years in the Far West*, 1916.

Indian tribes ceded their land to the United States in the Treaty of St. Mary's. The book has defied easy literary categorization: written as a nonfiction composition, it was presented as a quasi-fictive work.[8] It contains aspects of autobiography, memoir, and travelogue, leavened with personal diatribes directed against Wylie.

To tell his side of the story, Hall adopted an unusual approach. The cutting satire that bordered on defamation in his statements pertaining to Wylie motivated Hall to invent names for characters and places in *The New Purchase.* Since he was both the narrator and the chief protagonist, he devised twin alter egos, identifying pseudonyms for the author, Robert Carlton, Esq., and for the professor, Reverend Charles Clarence. Carlton was also given the role of trustee (which Hall was not).

The preface is a dialogue between Carlton and Clarence about history, fiction, and truth. Regarding the contents of the book, Carlton estimates "that the Truth is eight parts out of ten, the Fiction only two:—that the Fiction is mainly in the colouring and shading and perspective...in the aggregation and concentration of events, acts, actors...that the Chronology of the whole and the parts is in need of some rectification."[9]

In discussion about its title, Carlton suggests to Clarence, "Whereabouts? or Seven and a Half Years in a New Purchase of the Far West; being a Poetic Dream at Sun Rise, with a Prosaic Reflection as Sun Set—a Novel-History, and a Historic-Novel." Clarence objects, shortening the title to the published version. In the same vein, Carlton wants to add a "little scrap" of Latin—*alter et idem* ("one and the same") and *per multas aditum* ("through many paths").

As a historical memoir, *The New Purchase* has had singular value as a narration of the early years of the institution by a main historical actor. But the fictive names of individuals and places, and the lack of a dependable chronology of events, have created interpretive problems. Evidently, Hall was determined to publish an account where the line between fact and fiction was vague, one that contained accurate descriptions of the places and people he encountered during his sojourn on the frontier of settlement but also infused with his private opinions and feelings. Perhaps he took this literary approach

[8]The book was referred to as "quasi-fictive" by *The Oxford Companion to American Literature* in 1983.

[9]Hall, *The New Purchase, or, Seven and a Half Years in the Far West,* 1916, xvii.

in order to process and redeem his young adulthood—and to protect himself from potential charges of libel. At its publication, *The New Purchase* was read as an account of pioneer life in Indiana. For the people of Bloomington, it also contained a fascinating account of the early operation of the seminary and college, still less than two decades old. Some in Bloomington were scandalized by Hall's airing of the college's dirty laundry; others might have been secretly gratified. In the eastern market, the book sold well, and the initial run of one thousand copies eventually sold out.

2.2 An Urtext

In *The New Purchase,* Hall described the situation that led to his eventual termination. The three faculty members—Hall, Harney, and Wylie—shared much in common, including an allegiance to the Presbyterian faith and a belief in the power of classical education. Harney and Hall were more traditional, however, and hewed to the method of rote learning, whereas Wylie was more open to expanding the classical curriculum. They also differed on questions of managerial authority and student discipline. With the coming of Wylie, who was older and had more administrative experience, battle lines soon emerged.

For the nearly four years of the seminary's operation, Hall and Harney had accomplished the simple administrative tasks required. However, after the infant institution became a college, Wylie came in as president (fleeing an untenable situation at Washington College in western Pennsylvania) and took over administration. Complicating matters, Wylie brought several students along with him, and friction developed between students already in residence—so-called "natives"—and the Pennsylvania transfers, termed "foreigners."

In keeping with his satirical intent, Hall invented the name "Bloduplex" for Wylie, to signify "a person that could blow hot and cold with the same breath," and introduced him with a rhetorical flourish: "We now introduce a very uncommon personage, a most powerful prodigious great man, the first of the sort beheld in the New Purchase—the very Reverend Constant Bloduplex, D.D.—in all the unfathomable depths of those mystic letters."[10]

---

[10]Hall, 477, 480.

In describing Wylie's scholarly accomplishments, Hall wrote:

> His talents were good; his acquirements respectable especially in Classics, Antiquities, History, and Literature in general; —still they were not uncommon. In Mathematics and Sciences, we cannot state his attainments; and simply because we never discovered them—yet he must have gotten beyond arithmetic, since Clarence [Hall], in return for aid in Greek, did gratefully assist the Doctor in Algebra. Harwood [Harney], indeed, thought the President's attainments in such matters inconsiderable; but then Harwood was Professor of Mathematics and may have expected too much. At all events the President set no great value on these matters, making himself merry at Clarence's expense, on accidentally discovering that this gentleman was studying Mathematics under the guidance of his friend Harwood, while Harwood read Latin and Greek with Clarence.[11]

Underscoring Wylie's exaggerated portrait, Hall explicitly stated: "We must say that Bloduplex is really a fictitious character!"[12]

Hall went on to analyze the character of the president:

> As a companion, no man *could* be more agreeable than our President. It was this led our young Professors to unbosom [*sic*] in his presence—and even when, in an unguarded moment, the President remarked—*proton pseudos*, to imagine all sorts of wickedness and chicanery in all others; and then to combat all with such weapons as he fancied they were using or would use against him![13]

The verbal portrait was not all negative: "Doctor B. was an excellent preacher, and a still better lecturer, whether is regarded the matter or the manner: and some of his pulpit exhibitions were surpassingly fine."[14] Admiring his adroitness in "ecclesiastical combats," Hall explained that Wylie's success was due to his "Phrenological organization."[15] "My own opinion is, President B. owed most of

---

[11]Hall, 486.
[12]Hall, 488.
[13]Hall, *The New Purchase, or, Seven and a Half Years in the Far West*, 1916, 486–87. *Proton pseudos* refers to a wrong assumption or error in premise.
[14]Hall, 487.
[15]Hall, 487.

his victories—and some of his defeats—to his Wonderful Religious Experience! which in the stereotyped crying places always when *first* heard inclined *weak* believers to his side!" But upon repetition, most people saw through the act, the narrator averred.[16]

Alter ego professor Clarence analyzes why the president dislikes the professors, enumerating a list of probable reasons:

> 1. His jealousy of equals, and suspicious and untrustful temper: 2. His determination for a very low grade of studies—especially in Mathematics, and even in Classics,—he being resolved to level down and not up: 3. His love of ease, and wish to get along with a relaxed, or rather no discipline: 4. His using discipline as an instrument of avenging himself on students disliked by him: 5. His domineering and tyrannical temper: 6. His prying disposition, by which he was led to have spies in the professors' classes, and to watch when they came and went to and from duties. &c.: 7. His desire to make room for former pupils and relatives: 8. His erroneous theology.

Summarizing the list of grievances, the text continues:

> Hence, without consulting his peers, nay, contrary to their known wishes and earnest remonstrances, he tried to discipline students at will and to suspend and dismiss; he permitted some to be graduated, and who now hold imperfect diplomas, signed with his sole name: and he *commanded* what the Professors should and should not do, and what teach, and how, answering their arguments with insult and derision, and threatening to stamp them and the trustees also under his feet! He pretended to think, and dared to assert, that the discipline of a College was of right a President's special duty, —and teaching, the Professors'. And, therefore, he rudely, on several occasions, contradicted his Faculty in public, and aimed to consider and treat them as boys![17]

Continuing in the same vein, Hall ended the section with speculation about the president's motivations, including the possibility of

[16]Hall, 487–88.

[17]Hall, *The New Purchase, or, Seven and a Half Years in the Far West*, 1916, 489.

mental illness. In addition to criticism of Wylie, the text describes the organization and operation of the seminary, which became increasingly valuable historical source material.

After he introduced the major characters, Hall narrated a mystery that was the proximate cause that led to his termination: In his recitation room before class, Hall found an unsigned letter tucked into his pocket edition of Virgil and read it. It accused him of being an indolent and ineffective teacher and advised the professor to resign. The letter was sealed with wax that bore the imprint of Wylie's desk key, so Hall naturally thought that the president was the author. His colleague Harney and his wife, Mary Ann, agreed with that surmise after they read the letter. They compared older letters written by Wylie for corroboration and discovered "the most remarkable similarity, as to the hand—the style—the words—the expressions—was apparent: nay, in some things, was an identity."[18]

Harney advised Hall not to resign, however, without seeing President Wylie first. Hall described their meeting:

> The letter was taken by the President, but *not read all carefully and indignantly over*, as by the others! And yet, at a glance, he learned all its items, and that so well, as to talk and comment on them! But still, after what he designed should pass for a searching scrutiny, in a moment he exclaimed,—"I *know* the hand writing—it is *Smith's*!"
> "How you relieve me, Doctor Bloduplex," said Clarence; "Harwood was right to prevent me from sending in my resignation.—I shall continue—"
> "Mr. Clarence," replied the President, "Smith, *I* know, is your bitter enemy; and I am *told* you have many more, and especially among the *young gentlemen* that came with me: now, this shows a state of great unpopularity, and *I do candidly advise, all things considered, that you had better resign!!*"
> "Doctor, pardon me, my first belief is returned—I know the author of this letter, and it is *not* Smith."

Later in the passage, Hall shared his strong impression that Wylie wrote the letter:

[18]Hall, 493.

> "Dr. Bloduplex, from my inmost soul I do hope you may remove my suspicion,—but I much fear that you yourself are the author of this letter!"
> "I!—the author! how could you ever entertain so unjust a suspicion?"
> "God grant, sir, it be unjust—but I will give you the grounds of my suspicion."
> "Name them, sir,—I am curious and patient."
> Here Clarence went over all that the reader has been told, but to a much wider extent, and with many arguments and inferences not now narrated; and then spread out the Doctor's own letters, to be compared with the anonymous one. Upon which the Doctor said:
> "Well, Mr. Clarence, there is no resemblance between them, or but very little."
> "But is there not *some*? Has not the writer tried to imitate your hand—your style—your very grammatical peculiarities?"
> "It does, maybe, seem a little so—"
> "It does, indeed, Doctor Bloduplex; and now look here!—*the seal is stamped with the key of your desk!*"
> Here the President coloured; of course in virtuous indignation and surprise at such roguery, and in some little confusion exclaimed:—
> "The wicked dogs! they have *stolen* the *key* of my desk!"
> Clarence was here affected to tears; that one the other day almost loved and trusted as a father could be by him no longer so regarded....
> "Only assure me, Doctor, on your word of honour and as a Christian that *you* did not do this base action, and even now will I burn this letter in this very fire—(it was a cold day)—before your face."
> "Mr. Clarence," said he "I solemnly declare I did not write this letter; but stay, do not burn it—let me have it and I will try and find the writer."

Still mystified by the poisonous letter, Hall narrated both his disbelief and his surprising reaction:

> Of course, then, the letter was not written by the Reverend Constant Bloduplex, d.d.—for he had the best right to know; and he *said*, solemnly, that it was not. Yet Clarence, "all things considered," did that very week

> send his resignation to Dr. Sylvan [trustee president David Maxwell]; offering, however, to remain till the meeting of the Board. At that the Board offered him nearly double salary to remain some months longer till a suitable successor could be found; to which proposal Clarence acceded.

This then is the story that Hall narrated in *The New Purchase*, in which he was the primary protagonist.

The next year, 1831–32, Hall continued teaching temporarily, and the mystery of the anonymous letter persisted. Harney became embroiled in public controversies with Wylie over student behavior. Things escalated so much that the two men were involved in a physical altercation in which Wylie pushed Harney off a log spanning a mudhole. Eventually Wylie convinced the board of trustees to terminate Harney for insubordination. So, at the end of the 1831–32 school year, the original two professors left, and the administration was faced with finding replacements. The author of the anonymous letter did not come forward, leaving a chasm of silence surrounding the initiatory event that triggered the termination of the original faculty.

2.3 A Complex Historiography

Most of what we know about the early history of the Indiana State Seminary and Indiana College derives from Hall's account in *The New Purchase*. There are no extant sources that bear on Wylie's or Harney's reactions to Hall's testimony in the book. Although Hall had ample motivation to tell his side of the story about his conflict with the president, there is little reason to believe that he exaggerated or made false claims about it. As a writer, Hall usually left clear evidence of the facts of the matter at hand and his interpretation of them. But his deliberate scrambling of chronology and his penchant for combining separate acts have left readers puzzled. What emerges in *The New Purchase* is a protagonist trying to integrate various aspects of his personality and come to grips with his young adulthood by narrating his personal experiences, including his emotional reactions.

In a figurative sense, taken as a metaphor for those pioneering times, *The New Purchase* is a tale of ambition, intrigue, and disenchantment. Each of the protagonists—Hall, Wylie, and Harney—attempted to gain purchase on new opportunities as the state of Indiana made halting steps toward public higher education. Although our perspective is obscured by the passage of nearly two centuries, each of these men, full of passion and hope, made their way to the frontier hamlet of Bloomington to shape an infant institution. The outcome of their contest for influence meant that their names are differentially remembered, but all of them acquired some return for their investment of time and energy.[19]

Using *The New Purchase* as an archival source for interpretations of IU's past has generated a complex and interesting historiography. Although the college was expanded and renamed Indiana University in 1838, its history remained confined to oral tradition until Hall's book was published in 1843. David Maxwell and Andrew Wylie continued their administrative service into the 1850s, although faculty turnover was high. The deaths of Wylie in 1851 and Maxwell in 1854 were blows to the institution, removing two key individual mainstays. Over time, the details of their accomplishments were obscured, and collective memory enshrined the two men as founding figures. Following the College Building fire in 1854, Hall published a revised edition of *The New Purchase* in 1855, omitting the invective against Wylie and with it some descriptions of the institution.

After his departure from Bloomington in 1832, Hall held a variety of teaching posts at small academies in Pennsylvania, New Jersey, and New York, often in combination with serving local Presbyterian congregations. He had a remarkable career as an author, with six books published in the two decades between 1836 and 1855.

[19] One early example is found in Charles Blanchard, ed., *Counties of Morgan, Monroe, and Brown, Indiana: Historical and Biographical* (Chicago: F.A. Battey & Co., 1884), 478:

> President Wylie's connection with the college proved very advantageous, not only to that institution, but to Bloomington and Monroe County. He was famed for his learning all over the East and South, and soon students from distant States came to Bloomington to place themselves under his instruction. But the sudden and permanent popularity of President Wylie led to bitter jealousy on the part of Profs. Hall and Harney, who no doubt envied him his good fortune, and wished for the possession of his place and honors. The unpleasantness ceased with the permanent departure of Hall and Harney, in 1832. The college flourished greatly under the management of President Wylie, and its influence was soon felt upon the community.

As mentioned previously, the first, in 1836, was a Latin grammar textbook "for the use of primary schools, academies, and colleges." Seven years later, *The New Purchase* came out. It became his most successful book and, perhaps, his most personally gratifying.

His rate of publication then dramatically increased, with another three titles in seven years. In 1846, Hall published another blend of personal quasi-fictive narrative: *Something for Every Body: Gleaned in the Old Purchase, from Fields Often Reaped.* Using the same pseudonyms (Robert Carlton, Esq., and Reverend Charles Clarence) and a dialogue structure, the book was an exchange of letters between Hall's twin alter egos, talking about how to live a godly life. Dixie Richardson, Hall's biographer, called the book "an exuberant exposition of Hall's opinions and observations on numerous subjects: theology, medicine, capital punishment (a gallows at the edge of town indicates the community provides its citizens safety), temperance, contemporary trends (unlike Brooklyn writer Walt Whitman, Hall scoffs at phrenology) and in the process he added more of his own history."[20]

Two years later, Hall published a nonfiction title, *Teaching, a Science: The Teacher an Artist*, in which he expressed his views on pedagogy, noting in the preface, "This book is not an experiment, but an experience."[21] In 1852, riding the wave of interest created by the publication of *Uncle Tom's Cabin* by Harriet Beecher Stowe, Hall released *Frank Freeman's Barber Shop*, a novel featuring both Black and white main characters.[22]

Upon publication of the revised edition of *The New Purchase* in 1855, Hall was coming to the end of a remarkable period of literary productivity. It had been a dozen years since its original publication, and New Albany, Indiana, publisher John Nunemacher stoked Hall's hopes for a revival of interest in the work. After Wylie's death in 1851, Hall felt it was unseemly to mention their conflict and so excised nearly 130 pages that gave details about the story, omitting much of the description of the state seminary and college.[23]

[20] Richardson, *Baynard Rush Hall*, 208.

[21] Baynard Rush Hall, *Teaching, a Science: The Teacher an Artist* (New York: Baker; Scribner, 1848), v.

[22] Baynard Rush Hall, *Frank Freeman's Barber Shop* (New York: Scribner, 1852).

[23] In correspondence about the second edition, Hall stated, "In the work here and there certain words and expressions that have caused me often much sorrow in remembrance, and I would have given many dollars if they could

Illustrations were added, the subtitle was shortened to "Early Years in the Far West," and the original preface was replaced with a new one, written and signed by B. R. Hall, "Author, *Pro. Tem.*" The frontispiece featured an engraved portrait of Hall, identified simply as "The Author." Never resisting a didactic opportunity, Hall translated the Latin quotations that appeared on the title page: "'*Alter et idem*' means,—'*pretty much of a muchness*,' or in better Saxon—'*Six of one and half a dozen of the other.*' ['*Per multas aditum sibi sæpe figuras repperit*' means]—'*Being crafty he catches with guile.*' And these are the *freest* translations we are at liberty to give."[24] Appearing in a single volume, the second edition of *The New Purchase* did not attract many new purchasers interested in reading about frontier days in southern Indiana.

On the first of January 1863, during the Civil War, the Emancipation Proclamation was issued. Hall was living in Brooklyn at the time, working at the Park Institute School and assisting with services at the Dutch Reformed Church. Later that month, Hall died a few days before his sixty-fifth birthday. His passing merited an obituary in the *New York Times*:

> As an author, as well as a teacher, he gained a wide reputation. Dr. Hall was distinguished by high intellectual culture and refinement, by delightful conversational powers, to which an incessant current of humor lent animation and brilliancy, and to which the cordial kindness of his nature gave geniality. His life, influenced by the strongest religious convictions, as well as by inherent charity, was spent in labors of beneficence which were only interrupted by his final illness.

---

have been blotted out. And more especially there would be so manifest an unkindness in reprinting a vast amount of what pertains to the late President of a certain college, that I would nearly as soon consent to have a finger taken off as to continue that" (Baynard Rush Hall, "Letter to John Nunemacher," May 13, 1855).

Hall reminded Nunemacher that "all of the chapters and passages in the second volume relative to Dr. Bloduplex (President Wylie) are by all means to be discarded.... This gentleman richly deserved all that was done to him some years ago, but he is now in the other life, and I hope in a better one" (Hall; David D. Banta, "History of Indiana University: IV. The 'Faculty War' of 1832," *Indiana University Alumni Quarterly* 1, no. 4 (1914): 369–86)

[24]Baynard Rush Hall, *The New Purchase; or, Early Years in the Far West*, 2nd ed. (New Albany, IN: Jno. R. Nunemacher, 1855).

In addition to misspelling his middle name as "Rust," the obituary included a mischaracterization in the recitation of his positions: "Pastor of a Church and President of a College in Bloomington, Ind. for some years."[25] The first IU professor passed into historical memory, joining the first president and the first trustees board president.

2.4 Gathering the "Historical Catalog"

In 1881, the IU Board of Trustees asked longtime professor Theophilus Wylie to prepare a written "historical catalog" for the university. The university had been granting diplomas for a half century, and there was a felt need to summarize the history of the institution in a permanent document. Hired in 1837, Wylie was the seventh person appointed to the faculty; he was also Andrew Wylie's cousin. Wylie started writing to alumni and former faculty to gather information. Trustee David Banta, a former judge and county historian, became president of the trustee board in 1882, and he also started writing to former members of the university's academic community for information.[26]

Among the people Professor Wylie contacted was his relative Andrew Wylie Jr., the eldest son of the former president and an 1832 graduate of Indiana College. He served as a federal judge of the Supreme Court of the District of Columbia. Professor Wylie was seeking information about Judge Wylie's father and inquired about the anonymous letter that Professor Hall referred to in *The New Purchase*: "I have never thought it possible that he could have written it, & I would [inquire if?] you know certainly that & positively that it was not written by him, not as I know it [from?] being morally certain that he did not & could not have written it. Please inform me, so that from positive knowledge I might contradict it. I do not mean in the published catalogue, for I think it would be better to ignore all disagreeable things in such a publication."[27]

---

[25]"Obituary: Baynard Rust [*sic*] Hall," *New York Times*, January 27, 1863, 5.

[26]D. D. Banta, *A Historical Sketch of Johnson County, Indiana* (Chicago: J.H. Beers & Co., 1881); William McCaslin and D. D. Banta, *History of Johnson County, Indiana* (Chicago: Brant & Fuller, 1888).

[27]Theophilus Wylie, "Letter to Judge Andrew Wylie," July 18, 1881. IUA/C202/B5/F Letters relating to history.

Banta wrote to Matthew Campbell, a member of the class of 1834 and a former instructor in IU's Preparatory Department, who replied in detail about his memories. Regarding the anonymous letter, he wrote, "I know that Judge Wylie (who now strongly resembles his father tho' he was nothing like him 50 years ago) w[oul]d acknowledge the anonymous letter as his own. And yet I judge he never so acknowledged it to his father. Ask him."[28]

Unbeknownst to Campbell, Banta had received a letter from Judge Wylie a short time earlier, admitting that he was the author of the anonymous letter.

> Washington Dec 17, 1882
> D.D. Banta, Esq.
>
> Dear Sir: Your letter date 7th inst. was duly received and would have had earlier attention but for the pressure of official and other duties. The anonymous letter to which you refer was written by me without the knowledge, suggestion, remotest hint, or suspicion on the part of my Father. I was at that time a boy of sixteen years. The anonymous note to Mr. Hall contained no more than the almost universal opinion of the students. He was indolent, careless, superficial and shamefully neglectful of his duties. Both he and Mr. Harney had been professors in the college for several years previous to Father's election as its first president, and were jealous of him, on that account, as well as for other obvious reasons. The letter was the deed of a boy, a small affair, and ought to have been so regarded. Mr. Hall & Mr. Harney, however, declared that it was my Father's hand, disguised, would accept no denial, would hear no explanation, and refused consent that an investigation should be made by the faculty. Father offered to have every student examined, on honor, and pledged himself that whoever should be found to have written the letter he should be expelled. Hall & Harney declined to have the investigation made, but continued to circulate this false charge throughout the state, along with others equally unfounded. Father became indignant, and thenceforth treated them as personal enemies and

[28]Matthew Campbell, "Letter to David Banta" (Indiana University Archives/C112/B1, December 25, 1882).

> wilful [*sic*] slanderers. It was an ill considered [*sic*] thing on my part to write such a letter, but every word of it was true, and I had no idea that it was to create so much trouble. After the trouble was created[,] I felt impelled to come out and avow its authorship, but was restrained from so doing, by the consideration that such an avowal would be used by H. & H. as proof that their charge was substantially true, and that the letter, if not written by the hand of Dr. Wylie, was written by his son, at his dictation; and I retained the secret for years afterwards, even from my Father. I do not now pretend to claim that my conduct in this respect was either wise or brave. A man of mature mind and experience would have adopted the other course. I do not know whether or not my Father even ever prepared such a written account of the matter as that you refer to: I never saw, or heard of it, if he did. I have always regarded, as do now look upon the affair as beneath the serious consideration of sensible people, except for the slander to which it gave rise to and the annoyance it gave to my Father, whose nature revolted at the suggestion of a meanness and was ever at warfare with all sorts of pretenders and rascals.
>
> [Signed]
> Andrew Wylie

With the letter in hand, Banta confirmed the identity of the anonymous writer of the letter that had led to Hall's termination a half century before. Surviving records do not tell whether he shared the knowledge with Theophilus Wylie and other individuals, but he suppressed the information when he prepared a speech on "The Faculty War" presented ten years later.

In mid-July 1883, amid a driving rainstorm, Indiana University suffered another calamity as Science Hall was struck by lightning and consumed by the resulting fire. Science Hall housed IU's extensive scientific collections, including the Owen Cabinet of natural history and Professor David Jordan's fish specimens, as well as the library and administrative records—nearly all of which was destroyed. Unlike the 1854 campus fire, it did not cripple the university, but it was the proximate cause of relocating operations to a more commodious site on the eastern outskirts of Bloomington. About a year later, a new president was chosen. The new Dunn's Woods campus was ready in 1885, presided over by the former biology professor Jordan, who oversaw major changes in the curriculum that accompanied the move.

The loss of another tranche of university records made the historical catalog project more difficult but increased motivation for its completion. Professor Wylie and trustee president Banta continued to push forward in the tedious gathering of data from the alumni body. Wylie reached emeritus status in 1886, and though now in his mid-seventies, he remained dogged in his pursuit of the project. Banta was working closely with the new president, Jordan, making pleas for more state support and trying to improve the university. An important way to document the past, the historical catalog was seen as a necessary background to the current revivification, which added the promotion of research to the existing goals of equipping students with useful skills in the context of liberal arts education.

While research continued for the historical catalog, in 1889 President Jordan announced a day dedicated to the founders of IU—called Foundation Day. Its centerpiece was a historical address by Banta, who soon would retire as trustee president to take up the deanship of the IU School of Law. In keeping with the oral tradition and hewing to the storyline promoted by David Maxwell, the inaugural leader of the trustees, Banta started with "The Seminary Period (1820–1828)," which dealt with the state's first effort to provide higher education.[29] Reading from a text prepared for the occasion, he described the legislative history of the Indiana State Seminary of learning and its first instructor:

> While the General Assembly was legislating the seminary into existence, a young man, destined to be its first professor and to stay with it through its seminary life, and to be with it when it passed up into the Indiana College, and finally to leave that college a disappointed and embittered man and write a book maligning his enemies and making sport of his friends, was taking his last year's course of lectures at Union College, under the celebrated Dr. Nott. This young man was Baynard R. Hall. After receiving his first degree at the commencement of 1820 at Union, he went to Princeton where he

[29]See Howard F. McMains, "The Indiana Seminary Charter of 1820," *Indiana Magazine of History* 106 (2010): 356–80.

> studied theology, after which he was ordained a minister of the Presbyterian church. Returning to Philadelphia, his natal city, at the close of his theological studies, he married and soon after set out with his bride for the New Purchase.[30]

Banta mentioned Hall several times during his speech and used information derived from *The New Purchase*, sometimes without attribution. He also speculated, without evidence, that Hall came to Indiana because of the seminary.

On the following Foundation Day, in 1890, Banta continued with the early history of the institution, "From Seminary to College (1826–1829)." He detailed its legislative history and the coming of Andrew Wylie as its inaugural president. Members of the class of '90 presented *Scenes from the New Purchase*, an original play adapted from *The New Purchase.* Composed of four scenes depicting Hall's sojourn: travel from Louisville to Bloomington, his hiring by the board of trustees, the first meeting of the first class, and the protest over Harney's religious faith (Presbyterian) being the same as Hall's. The play featured handmade costumes, and a prologue read by Samuel B. Harding, a history professor.[31]

The historical catalog, titled *Indiana University, Its History from 1820, when Founded, to 1890*, was finally ready for publication in 1890. Banta contributed the chapter "The Indiana Seminary," which was shortened from his Foundation Day address. In it, he described the first professor:

> The choice could hardly have fallen upon a worthier man. His academic education he had received at Union College and his theological at Princeton. He was an excellent classical scholar and a persuasive and sometime eloquent preacher. As a teacher he was enthusiastic, faithful and painstaking. Into the frontier life of the White River settlement, in which his lot was cast for a time after he first came to the State, he entered with a zeal that soon brought him to know all its peculiarities,

[30] David D. Banta, "History of Indiana University I: The Seminary Period (1820–1828)," *Indiana University Alumni Quarterly* 1, no. 1 (1914): 3–24, quote on 13.

[31] See the description of the second staging of the play twenty-five years later, at the 1915 alumni reunion: "The 1915 Commencement," *Indiana University Alumni Quarterly* 2, no. 3 (1915): 282, 286–87.

> a knowledge that stood him many a good turn while at the head of the State seminary.[32]

Banta described the frontier skills Hall acquired and his interest in pioneer ways.

Two years later, in 1892, Banta presented his fourth Foundation Day address, entitled "The 'Faculty War' of 1832."[33] He described the main protagonists—President Andrew Wylie, Professor Baynard Hall, and Professor John Harney—and concluded with a summary of their characters: "Men admired the tall, graceful, grave, stately-stepping, and dignified Wylie. Men loved the blue-eyed, jolly, laughing, easy-going Hall. Men feared the erect, precise, nervous, heavy-jawed, firmly-stepping, neatly dressed, military-looking Harney."[34]

Banta went on to narrate a key element of the story—the anonymous letter: "Some time toward the close of the collegiate year of 1830–1831, probably in September—which was nearly two years after Dr. Wylie came—Professor Hall found in his 'pocket Virgil, left as usual on the mantel of his recitation room,' an anonymous letter, which taxed him the very plain language with the same charges current among the 'foreign' students—incompetency and neglect of duty—and demanded his resignation."[35]

Hall was convinced that Wylie wrote the letter, and his colleague Harney agreed, but Wylie "solemnly and indignantly denied its authorship."[36] Banta stated unequivocally, "And yet Dr. Wylie did not write that letter. It was written by a Pennsylvania student, 'without,' as he himself says, 'the knowledge, suggestion, remotest hint or suspicion' on the part of Dr. Wylie."[37] Banta quoted Hall's account of his resignation in *The New Purchase* but went on to discuss Hall's actual letter, which he saw as part of the "old record"

[32]Wylie, *Indiana University, Its History from 1820, When Founded, to 1890, with Biographical Sketches of Its Presidents, Professor and Graduates, and a List of Its Students from 1820 to 1887*, 38–46, quote on 43.

[33]Banta, "History of Indiana University: IV. The 'Faculty War' of 1832"; quote on 373. Republished in Woodburn, *History of Indiana University*, 1940, 78–97.

[34]Woodburn, *History of Indiana University*, 1940, 82. They were all dead by that time, so he relied on other sources.

[35]Woodburn, 84.

[36]Woodburn, 85.

[37]Woodburn, 85. Banta quoted from Andrew Wylie Jr.'s letter but did not identify him by name.

that was destroyed by the 1883 campus fire and in which Hall cited dissatisfaction.[38]

For his general storyline, Banta depended on the description of the episode in *The New Purchase*, even quoting the book without citation, but augmented by his inquiries the decade before. He did not reveal the plain truth that the junior Andrew Wylie, now a federal judge, had written the letter, only that a "Pennsylvania student" was the author. Obliquely, he did disclose Matthew Campbell's understanding that Wylie, a fellow classmate in the 1830s, was the writer.[39]

Thus, Banta's narrative became the latest writing on the subject, incorporating Hall's 1843 account but providing a new interpretation that emphasized its effect on the university. Judging that "neither side was without fault," he eschewed assigning blame but concluded "their personal controversy worked a grievous wrong to the institution."[40] This rewriting of institutional history obliterated Hall's original motivation by incorporating his account for new purposes.[41]

2.5 Into the Twentieth Century

In 1902, the *Indianapolis News* published a retrospective review of *The New Purchase* with fresh insight into its historical value:

> As a volume curiously expository of early Indiana, it is also a volume curiously expository of Dr. Baynard Rush Hall. Regarded as a literary boomerang, the printed word far outranks the pen or the sword....To the painful surprise of Dr. Hall and his New Albany publishers, the new edition of "The New Purchase" created no furor in the book world, East or West. The book, however, sold

[38]Woodburn, 85.

[39]Banta described Campbell: "who was a student here at the time the letter was written, and who for forty years kept the secret of the writer." Woodburn, 84. "Forty years" probably refers to the publication of *The New Purchase* in 1843 and the 1882 receipt by Banta of letter from Andrew Wylie Jr. admitting authorship. That raises the intriguing questions of who else knew the secret in the 1830s, how it was spread following the 1882 letter, and why it remained hidden in the archival files for decades.

[40]Woodburn, 96–97.

[41]Cf. Merton's dictum, "obliteration by incorporation." See Chapter 3.

> slowly for almost half a century; and now a copy of the 1855 edition is almost as unobtainable and as great a book curio as one dated 1843. With all its faults, and in spite of Indiana's resentment of its unjust caricature, the human interest of "The New Purchase" will long maintain it, as Dr. Hall pronounced it, an "Indiana classic."[42]

With no mention of its role as an early account of the origins of Indiana University, the review underscored its value in American literary and social history.

In 1913, IU historian James Woodburn published a commentary on *The New Purchase*, inaugurating another phase in its literary historiography. Appearing in the *Indiana Magazine of History*, it was an address prepared for the History Society of Wabash College and was also read before other county history groups. Woodburn emphasized Hall's connection to the new state seminary and his literary ambitions before launching into a review of frontier life as depicted in the volume. He spoke about Hall's descriptions of native speech patterns, social life, amusements, and politics, among other topics. Despite the presence of "the benighted and the indifferent," Woodburn spoke about the pioneer spirit that Hall brought to life: "But let us remember that among the rank and file of struggling Hoosiers in the new commonwealth there were others who hailed the prophecy and the promise of a better day; who gave of their toil and meagre substance to truth, to religion, to learning and education, and who were ready to dedicate to the upbuilding and higher intelligence of their State, their lives, their fortunes and their sacred honors."[43] In keeping with Woodburn's professional commitments, he advised the audience of students and residents in his conclusion: "One of the uses of history is to remind us not only of our unpaid obligation to the past, but of our never-ending obligation to the future."[44]

As IU enrollments had grown steadily since the late nineteenth century, the ranks of alumni had followed suit. To increase communication with that constituency, the *Indiana University Alumni*

[42]Emma Carleton, "About the New Purchase," *Indianapolis News*, May 16, 1902, 10.

[43]James A. Woodburn, "Local Life and Color in the New Purchase," *Indiana Magazine of History* 9, no. 4 (1913): 215–33, quote on 233.

[44]Woodburn, 233.

Quarterly was launched in 1914. It contained a mix of university news items, feature articles, and alumni notes. It soon became the journal of record for contributions to IU history, with the help of Professor Woodburn and the editor, Ivy Chamness. Banta's annual addresses on Foundation Day, presented from 1889 to 1894, were published in the first six issues of the *Alumni Quarterly*, including "The Seminary Period" and "The 'Faculty War' of 1832," further disseminating his version of the story.[45] Woodburn followed with eight articles, published from 1915 to 1917, dealing with the university's history from 1840 to 1860.[46]

Meanwhile, Professor Woodburn convinced Princeton University Press to republish the 1843 edition of *The New Purchase*, long since out of print, as a contribution to the 1916 centennial commemoration of Indiana's statehood. Woodburn wrote an introduction to the volume and some explanatory footnotes. He enthused, "This work has been pronounced 'one of the best books ever written concerning life in the West,' " adding, "There is certainly no more valuable book on early Indiana." Woodburn quoted his erstwhile colleague Banta, who praised it as "the best and truest history of pioneer life and pioneer surroundings in Indiana that can anywhere be found. Hall evidently entered with zest into the life and scenes about him, and he writes graphically of all he sees and hears."[47]

In his discussion of the book's publishing history, Woodburn noted that the 1855 revised edition omitted 130 pages, including mention of Hall's conflict with Wylie. In the interests of historical completeness, the decision to republish the original 1843 version was made, "college quarrel, personalities and all, without change or expurgation," the editor explained.[48] Woodburn concluded his paean to *The New*

---

[45]Banta, "History of Indiana University I"; David D. Banta, "History of Indiana University: II: From Seminary to College (1826–1829)," *Indiana University Alumni Quarterly* 1, no. 2 (1914): 142–65; David D. Banta, "History of Indiana University: III: The New Departure (1829–1833)," *Indiana University Alumni Quarterly* 1, no. 3 (1914): 272–92; Banta, "History of Indiana University: IV. The 'Faculty War' of 1832"; David D. Banta, "History of Indiana University: V: From College to University (1833–1838)," *Indiana University Alumni Quarterly* 2, no. 1 (1915): 5–17; David D. Banta, "History of Indiana University: VI: Perils from Sectarian Controversies and the Constitutional Convention (1838–1850)," *Indiana University Alumni Quarterly* 2, no. 2 (1915): 99–110.

[46]Woodburn, *History of Indiana University*, 1940.

[47]Hall, *The New Purchase, or, Seven and a Half Years in the Far West*, 1916.

[48]Hall, xii. Calling the conflict between Professor Hall and President Wylie the "college quarrel," Woodburn eschewed Banta's "war" metaphor.

Purchase and its author: "The general truthfulness of the book, the integrity and sincerity of its author and the great value to history of Hall's descriptions and portraitures are now recognized by all and I do not hesitate to say that his book will ever remain what Hall richly deserved that it should prove to be, an imperishable Indiana classic."[49]

Woodburn's edition, with a valuable key to characters and places, became a standard. It was reviewed by at least eight periodicals, ranging from Boston's *Transcript* to the *Times Literary Supplement.* Woodburn read the introduction at the 1916 annual meeting of the Ohio Valley Historical Association.[50] The *Indiana Magazine of History* soon published a review of Woodburn's edition of *The New Purchase*:

> There is only one sufficient argument for a new edition of the story, but that argument is enough. As a picture of pioneer life in Indiana it is unequalled, and must necessarily always remain so. Mr. Hall qualified for writing the story by entering fully into the pioneer life around him. He saw and was broad-minded enough to appreciate the sterling character of the settlers. He was also frank enough to point out the unattractive features. The picture is not a burst of sunlight on the snow but a mixture of light and shadow, the light tempered with humor and the shadow tempered with sympathy.

The only criticism was that the author's notes were mixed in with the editor's notes.[51]

Meanwhile, one of Woodburn's IU colleagues, Logan Esarey, published his massive two-volume *History of Indiana* in 1915. Encyclopedic in scope, the publication reviews the literature of the state, identifying Hall as the author of a penetrating study of early Indiana. In a concise summary, Esarey wrote: "The lure of the West was in his blood. He had visions of doing great deeds for humanity in this land of miracles. He followed this dream, about 1822, into

[49] Hall, xii.

[50] James Albert Woodburn, "The New Purchase," in *Proceedings of the Tenth Annual Meeting of the Ohio Valley Historical Association*, ed. Harlow Lindley, vol. 6, 1 (Indiana Historical Society Publications, 1916), 43–54.

[51] "The New Purchase or Seven and Half Years in the Far West," *Indiana Magazine of History*, n.d. unsigned review of Hall, *The New Purchase* (1916), quote on 354.

the wilderness of Indiana, locating on the frontier near the present town of Gosport. His book, *The New Purchase, or Seven and a Half Years in the Far West*, narrates his experiences there and at Bloomington. As a critical study of the pioneers it stands without a rival."[52] He quoted David Banta's 1888 assessment that it was "the best and truest history of pioneer life and pioneer surroundings in Indiana that can anywhere be found." Harking back to the contemporaneous New Harmony experiment, Esarey concluded on an elegiac note: "Nevertheless, like Robert Owen, Hall was unable to realize his beautiful vision and returned a disappointed man."[53]

2.6 The Lincoln Inquiry

In the 1920s, *The New Purchase* came under fire precisely because of its catholic treatment of all sectors of frontier society. The Southwestern Indiana Historical Society, formed in 1920, had an ongoing "Lincoln Inquiry," seeking to establish the salience of Abraham Lincoln's life in southern Indiana from 1816 to 1830. In 1923, at a luncheon meeting of the society, President John Iglehart explained the aim of the research program on Lincoln's formative years in southern Indiana: "Since American democracy was not of New England or of Atlantic Coast civilization, but was born in the northwest territory, the history of pioneer Indiana assumes a new importance; particularly because of its effect on Lincoln."[54] But "the history of the people of southern Indiana has never been written," he lamented.

---

[52]Logan Esarey, *History of Indiana* (Indianapolis: W. K. Stewart Co., 1915), 1112.

[53]Esarey, *History of Indiana*. In a footnote, Esarey evaluated: "The volume does not rank high in literary merit, but the descriptions are vivid, faithful and historically just." In 1919, another historian of Indiana, Jacob P. Dunn, published a massive multivolume compendium, *Indiana and Indianans: A History of Aboriginal and Territorial Indiana and the Century of Statehood* (Chicago and New York: American Historical Society, 1919), in which Hall's career at the state seminary and college is briefly noted in volume two, pages 873–874.

[54]John E. Iglehart, "Correspondence Between Lincoln Historians and This Society," in *Proceedings of the Southwestern Indiana Historical Society*, Bulletin No. 18 (Indianapolis: Indiana Historical Commission; Wm. B. Burford, 1923), 63–88, https://hdl.handle.net/2027/inu.32000001722687, quote on 64.

Iglehart cited sources of literature that contributed to the historical image of Indiana, complaining that they presented a skewed picture because they did not focus on the "better class of people."[55] He singled out for criticism *The New Purchase* by Hall, freshly available in the Woodburn edition. Rather than providing a new perspective, he cited the old criticism mounted by the Indianapolis *Sentinel* nearly seventy years previously in its review of the 1855 edition: "The original design of the work was principally to hold up to public indignation and ridicule the late Rev. Dr. Wylie, president of the University, with whom the author has a disagreement, which led to his leaving the college, and also the late Governor Whitcomb, General Lowe, and others."[56]

Iglehart claimed that the book "breathes a contempt for western character" and that Hall was "unable to adjust to himself to pioneer life and to become a part of it." Iglehart continued to make assertions that were unsupported by evidence in Hall's biography or the book:

> The eastern states opposed the addition of new states to the Union, and there existed a fear of the development of an agricultural democracy on account of which theological students like Hall came West in part to preserve the religious and intellectual *status quo* of these older states. Such a thing was impossible and therefore Hall failed. Hall was wrecked on the shoals which even today confront every eastern man who for the first time comes West as a minister or teacher among western people—shoals which a tactless and narrow-minded man cannot successfully navigate. It cannot be denied that his viewpoint of the people is that of a leading actor in the play of early Indiana life where he failed to succeed and he makes no effort to disguise his bitterness as a bad loser.[57]

Iglehart also put forward another specious claim, regarding the circumstances of Hall's termination from Indiana College nearly a century earlier: "It was libelous in the extreme, full of express malice against leading men more successful than Hall was, who, upon the facts shown in the book, could do nothing less than

---

[55] Iglehart, 68.
[56] Iglehart, 68–69.
[57] Iglehart, 69.

discharge as teacher."[58] Apparently, Iglehart objected to Hall's slice-of-life approach, which was inclusive of all classes in pioneer life and made copious use of colloquial expressions.[59]

After retiring in 1924, James Woodburn moved to Ann Arbor with his wife. He remained in touch with the IU administration, headed by his old friend President William Lowe Bryan, who encouraged him to continue his work in IU history. In 1936, Woodburn authored an entry for Baynard Rush Hall in the *Dictionary of American Biography.*[60] In 1940, he published *History of Indiana University: Volume I, 1820–1902.*[61] With no overarching storyline or integrated approach, the contents represent three distinct periods of composition. The first six chapters were written by David Banta, forming the text of his 1890s Foundation Day addresses about the early history of the institution, reprinted from their original publications in the *Alumni Quarterly* in 1914 and 1915. Next were eight chapters authored by Woodburn dealing with the university in the 1840s and 1850s, republished from issues of the *Alumni Quarterly* dating between 1915 and 1917. The last eight chapters were composed by Woodburn in the 1930s and display a mix of institutional history peppered with personal anecdotes.

The Woodburn volume became an extremely valuable reference to IU's past, displaying stories of IU's nineteenth-century existence filtered through the lens of two alumni authors (Woodburn and Banta) who were also faculty members. That authorship also accounts for some of the volume's shortcomings, including the lack of overarching themes, the favoring of description over analysis, and the shortage of critical or comparative perspectives. The book also highlighted the dearth of primary source materials due to the campus fires of 1854 and 1883. Woodburn, who might have been aware of Andrew Wylie Junior's instigating role in the removal of Baynard Hall, chose not to reveal that secret and published Banta's 1892 account of the "faculty war" of 1832 without amendment.

---

[58]Iglehart, 69.

[59]John Iglehart died in 1934. In her 1938 summary of the Lincoln Inquiry, Bess V. Ehrmann, *The Missing Chapter in the Life of Abraham Lincoln* (Chicago: Walter M. Hill, 1938), 17 does not mention *The New Purchase* by name but by implication when she criticizes "certain novels dealing with the uncouth, illiterate pioneers in the Hoosier state."

[60]James A. Woodburn, "Baynard Rush Hall," in *Dictionary of American Biography*, 1936.

[61]Woodburn, *History of Indiana University*, 1940.

In the 1940s, literary analysts rediscovered Baynard Hall and *The New Purchase*, especially in the context of review articles and bibliography. Discussing early literary developments in Indiana, Agnes Murray noted that settlement patterns northward from the Ohio River confined literary production before 1850: "Baynard Rush Hall's *New Purchase* was the sole distinguished work written in the newer area of southern Indiana."[62] Robert Hubach, in a review of nineteenth-century literary visitors to Indiana, highlighted Hall's sojourn in the new Hoosier state: "One authority states that it stands unrivaled as a critical study of the pioneers," with a footnote citing Banta's earlier judgment.[63]

As IU expanded because of the Second World War, a great building program was launched, including student residence centers. In searching for appropriate names, the university decided to cull from the ranks of early trustees, students, and faculty members. Thus, in 1949, Baynard Hall's name graced a small unit—Hall House—of the Joseph A. Wright Quadrangle.[64]

In 1950, IU history professor R. Carlyle Buley, in his Pulitzer Prize–winning study *The Old Northwest*, gave an insightful description about the author of *The New Purchase*, which Buley called "a unique study of pioneer life in and around a college town":

> Hall has been criticized for a condescending and supercilious attitude and, at times, biting pen, but considering that this Easterner with a classical-theological education was dumped into the middle of the backwoods to teach Latin and Greek, that he found himself more or less accidently embroiled in an academic-theological imbroglio, it is rather to be wondered at that his treatment of persons and life was as sympathetic as it was. It is not necessary to read between the lines to detect that Hall came to like the surroundings and people more than he, himself, may have realized; at any rate he delivered

62 Agnes M. Murray, "Early Literary Developments in Indiana," *Indiana Magazine of History* 36 (1940): 327–33, quote on 331.

63 Robert R. Hubach, "Nineteenth-Century Literary Visitors to the Hoosier State: A Chapter in American Cultural History," *Indiana Magazine of History* 45 (1949): 39–50, quote on 40.

64 Indiana University Board of Trustees, "Minutes of the Board of Trustees of Indiana University, 21 October 1949–22 October 1949" (Bloomington: Indiana University Archives & Indiana University Libraries Digital Collections Services, October 21, 1949), https://purl.dlib.indiana.edu/iudl/archives/iubot/1949-10-21.

himself "right smart" amount of firsthand material. His book, along with Mrs. Kirkland's, would be on any list of a half dozen necessary for a picture of the life of the period.[65]

In the late 1950s, the multivolume *Bibliography of American Literature* contained a directory featuring nearly 300 authors of significance in American literature. Hall was among the authors included, and *The New Purchase* and several other works were mentioned.[66]

As a biographical subject, Hall emerged again in 1966, during the Indiana sesquicentennial year. Brief excerpts from *The New Purchase* were published in the *Indiana Magazine of History*, introduced by editor Donald Carmony, IU history professor, and assistant editor Herman J. Viola, a history doctoral student.[67] In their brief commentary, Carmony and Viola noted Hall's affiliation with the state seminary and his vivid descriptions of pioneer life.

Four years later, Hall's institutional career was discussed in *Indiana University: Midwestern Pioneer* by Thomas D. Clark.[68] A respected University of Kentucky historian, Clark had an extended appointment at IU as a visiting professor to research and write a new history of the institution for its 1970 sesquicentennial. Hewing to the existing historiography, Clark did not break new ground with his narrative of the Indiana State Seminary of learning and the contretemps that led to the discharge of its original faculty members in 1832. He noted, however, "Hall was to have an enduring say. In *The New Purchase* he detailed the quarrel with genuine discredit to Wylie."[69] Clark suggested the root of the problem lay in different approaches to teaching, with Wylie less wedded to rote learning than Hall or Harney.

[65]R. Carlyle Buley, *The Old Northwest: Pioneer Period, 1815–1840*, vol. 2 (Bloomington: Indiana University Press, 1950), 557.

[66]Jacob Blanck, *Bibliography of American Literature*, vol. 3 (New Haven: Yale University Press, 1959), 341–43.

[67]Baynard Rush Hall, Donald F. Carmony, and Herman J. Viola, "The New Purchase: Or, Seven and a Half Years in the Far West," *Indiana Magazine of History* 62, no. 2 (1966): 101–20.

[68]Thomas D. Clark, *Indiana University: Midwestern Pioneer: Volume I: The Early Years*, 4 vols. (Bloomington: Indiana University Press, 1970).

[69]Clark, 45.

2.7 More Recent Scholarship

Scholars of literature and language continued to find *The New Purchase* useful. In 1983, Hall merited an entry in the *Oxford Companion to American Literature*, now in its fifth revision but still under the editorship of James Hart, who first assembled the compendium in 1941. The brief entry mentioned *The New Purchase* (1843) and *Frank Freeman's Barber Shop* (1852).[70] In 1985, the *Dictionary of American Regional English* cited *The New Purchase* a total of 353 times.[71] As Hall's book aged, it found new importance as a historical source to reconstruct pioneer life in southern Indiana as well as linguistic patterns in the Hoosier dialect.

In 2004, Thomas Conway sought to explore the culture of early Indiana, from 1816 to 1830, when Abraham Lincoln was a boy. He stated, "Perhaps the best source of Hoosier culture was a novel, *The New Purchase*, written in 1843 by Baynard Rush Hall under the pseudonym of Robert Carlton. Hall arrived in southern Indiana in 1823 and left the year after Lincoln did."[72] Conway admired "Hall's sharply observant eye" in discerning "the ethos and charm of the pioneers who settled in the 'Big Woods,' " so different from other areas of settlement:

> What was fascinating, especially to sensitive outsiders like Hall, was that a distinct culture had evolved, unlike the world of eastern rustics. Although it was unlikely that he would ever meet the young Lincoln, he did meet and also describe Lincoln-like prototypes. Undoubtedly, since Lincoln was a Hoosier, the language that he spoke among his family and friends was the dialect of the community in which he and his ancestors had grown. Such people had their distinct vocabulary and modified values. This is what Hall discovered and about which he wrote.[73]

The article goes on to discuss "the lost language" of frontier people and problems of historical interpretation. Conway noted that "Hall

---

[70]James D. Hart, 5th ed. (New York: Oxford University Press, 1983), 307.

[71]Frederic G. Cassidy, ed., *Dictionary of American Regional English* (Cambridge, MA: Belknap Press of Harvard University Press, 1985).

[72]Thomas G. Conway, "Finding America's History," *Journal of the Illinois State Historical Society* 97, no. 2 (2004): 92–106, quote on 93.

[73]Conway, 93.

frankly liked the frontier types he describes, and he tried to become a member of their community," unlike other accounts that patronized or caricatured early Hoosiers.[74] He summarized, "Perhaps the stellar work of its genre, Hall's fictionalized memoir of his years in pioneer southern Indiana is the most outstanding source for the culture and, especially, the idiom of the American Backcountry folk."[75] The literary historiography of *The New Purchase*, at least in studies of American language, had moved considerably from the defensive reactions of the Lincoln Inquiry of the 1920s.

In 2009, journalist and genealogist Dixie Kline Richardson published a biographical study, *Baynard Rush Hall: His Story.*[76] Decades after an early encounter with *The New Purchase*, she was determined "to set the record straight" because "the man and the book have been misunderstood, misjudged, and misread."[77] This unlikely champion presented a detailed reading of Hall's life, with critical yet sympathetic insight, and established a helpful personal and family context. Richardson's close reading of archival sources led to the 1882 letter of Andrew Wylie Jr. to trustee president David Banta and disclosed the rest of the story of the "faculty war" that Banta had hidden in 1892.[78]

In 2012, historian Keith Erekson examined the Lincoln Inquiry conducted by the Southwestern Indiana Historical Society in the 1920s and 1930s. Citing the criticism originally leveled by John Iglehart against Baynard Hall and his book nearly a century before, Erekson paraphrased Iglehart's opinion:

> Society workers contended with more widely read novels—in particular Baynard Rush Hall's *The New Purchase* (1843) and Edward Eggleston's *The Hoosier Schoolmaster.* Hall came to Indiana from Philadelphia to teach at the seminary in Bloomington (later Indiana University). When the school passed him over for the position of president, he responded first by feuding with school officials and then by returning to the East, where he wrote a thinly veiled memoir that castigated his former neighbors. Iglehart branded the book "cowardly libel"

[74]Conway, 101.
[75]Conway, 97.
[76]Richardson, *Baynard Rush Hall.*
[77]Richardson, i.
[78]Richardson, 166–68.

> because it "breathes a contempt for western character" and because the author "makes no effort to disguise his bitterness as a bad loser."[79]

Erekson simply embellished Iglehart's unsupported assumptions about why Hall composed *The New Purchase* and ignored other contemporary views, such as Logan Esarey's, which praised Hall's book.[80]

2.8 Conclusion

An irony persists at the heart of Baynard Hall's career at Indiana College. Were it not for Hall's hard feelings and outrage directed toward President Wylie that motivated the writing of *The New Purchase*, we would not have his vivid descriptions of Bloomington and the early years of what became the state university. After Wylie died, Hall demonstrated a measure of charity and excised the criticism of the president in the revised edition of 1855—along with much of the material pertaining to the college. Luckily, when James Woodburn supervised the republication of *The New Purchase* in 1916, he went back to the original text. The narrative remains a monument of personal hurt transformed into literary art.

It was not until later generations that faculty publication became common and then expected of IU professors. With a half dozen books to his credit, Hall outstripped his Indiana contemporaries and most of his nineteenth-century successors. His posthumous reputation rests mainly on *The New Purchase*, an eyewitness account of what he saw, heard, and felt living in southern Indiana from 1824 to 1832. As the first historian of what became Indiana University, understanding his career as a historical figure as well as his historical perspective in all its complexity ought to make us grateful for his life as well as his narrative. We are still learning from Baynard Rush Hall.[81]

---

[79]Keith A. Erekson, *Everybody's History: Indiana's Lincoln Inquiry and the Quest to Reclaim a President's Past* (Amherst: University of Massachusetts Press, 2012), 26.

[80]See discussion earlier about Esarey's judgment of *The New Purchase.*

[81]This essay has concentrated on Hall's best-known book, *The New Purchase*, but scholars have paid attention to another work, *Frank Freeman's Barber Shop*, a novel published in 1852 as a rejoinder to Harriet Beecher Stowe's *Uncle Tom's Cabin.* A mention in 1922 stated: "It is undoubtedly an important

early study of the psychology of the Negro" (Jeannette Reed Tandy, "Pro-Slavery Propaganda in American Fiction of the Fifties," *South Atlantic Quarterly* 21.1, no. 1 (January 1, 1922): 41–50, https://doi.org/10.1215/00382876-21-1-41; Jeannette Reed Tandy, "Pro-Slavery Propaganda in American Fiction of the Fifties," *South Atlantic Quarterly* 21.2, no. 2 (April 1, 1922): 170–78, https://doi.org/10.1215/00382876-21-2-170; quote on 173). A re-examination was launched by Thomas A. Gossett in *Uncle Tom's Cabin and American Culture* (Dallas: Southern Methodist University Press, 1985). More recent discussions include Joy Jordan-Lake, *Whitewashing Uncle Tom's Cabin: Nineteenth-Century Women Novelists Respond to Stowe* (Nashville: Vanderbilt University Press, 2005); Diane N. Capitani, *Truthful Pictures: Slavery Ordained by God in the Domestic Sentimental Novel of the Nineteenth-Century South* (Lanham, MD: Lexington Books, 2009); Erica Burleigh, *Intimacy and Family in Early American Writing* (New York: Palgrave Macmillan, 2014); and Sarah N. Roth, *Gender and Race in Antebellum Popular Culture* (New York: Cambridge University Press, 2014).

3 Inventing IU History

Figure 5: Theophilus Wylie (top), David Banta (bottom), James Woodburn (right)

> It will be seen that during the first generation of its history the Indiana University endured a continuous struggle.... Yet under its first president, during its first quarter of a century, it continued to do respectable and thorough college work. Under the advancing and more liberal policy of the last twenty years on the part of the State toward her institutions of higher learning, the institution, from being only a training school in the classics and mathematics, is rapidly pushing into the work of the university proper, and offers growing opportunities for advanced and original investigation.
>
> —James A. Woodburn, *Higher Education in Indiana*

Between 1883 and 1885, a series of unforeseen and startling events set Indiana University on the long road to its current distinction as an American research university. Shedding its prior identity as an ordinary classical collegiate institution, the new campus with its fresh leadership provided energy to pursue ambitious educational goals and higher aspirations for its academic community. IU got in step with national trends in higher education, characterized by widespread university-building fueled by increasing student enrollments, a focus on research, and renewed commitments to serve society. To make sense of these changes as well as to further encourage the pursuit of lofty goals for the institution, the distinct genre of Indiana University history was invented in the 1880s by a trio of faculty working on individual projects, with some overlap and collaboration. History-making, through historical narratives, was a driving force as the university community confronted its previous sixty-odd years and envisioned a new path forward.

The quest to assemble a formal university history was made public with an announcement in the May 1883 issue of the *Indiana Student*. David D. Banta, president of the IU Board of Trustees, asked for help from the alumni and former students "who have any old documents, such as class programs, catalogues, addresses of professors and presidents, or other papers pertaining to the University," mentioning especially the 1854 or 1855 catalog of the Athenian Society.[1] Banta issued this request to assist longtime professor Theophilus Wylie in preparing the first "historical catalog" of the university. Student life at the small institution located on Second Street and College Avenue centered around class recitations and the self-governed

[1] *Indiana Student* 9, no. 7 (May 1883): 166–67.

literary societies, including the Athenian Society and its chief rival, the Philomathean.

The following month, the 1883 IU commencement featured an alumni reunion and the award of an honorary LLD (Doctor of Laws degree) to Andrew Wylie Jr., the eldest son of the first president, Andrew Wylie. The son, a member of the class of 1832, the third graduating class, had become a lawyer and was an associate judge of the Supreme Court of the District of Columbia in Washington, DC, appointed by President Abraham Lincoln.

The alumni society, first constituted in 1854 in the wake of the campus fire, had been revived a couple of years previously after years of organizational neglect and recently had made efforts to lobby the Indiana General Assembly for increased support for the university. Their efforts paid off in March 1883, when legislation was passed that established a permanent endowment fund from the state.[2]

In July 1883, a catastrophic fire struck the deserted campus, burning the newest of the two main buildings, Science Hall, only ten years old. Since there were no eyewitnesses and a heavy rainstorm at the time, a lightning strike was assumed to be the cause. The building was a total loss, and the thirteen-thousand-volume library, collections of fossils and of fishes, physical and chemical apparatuses, and faculty books and papers were among the items destroyed.[3]

The fire set into motion actions by the IU Board of Trustees that would have far-reaching effects on the small collegiate institution. By August, trustees were debating whether to relocate the university. Some already thought that the ten-acre campus was inadequate, being hemmed in by the railroad on its western boundary since 1853 with its noise, vibration, and clutter. The fire became another argument to move. Bloomington, with its 3,000 citizens, was growing and had ample land for sale. The trustees looked at eleven parcels and decided to move the university to the eastern outskirts of the town, to a twenty-acre woodlot on the Dunn family farm.

---

[2]The Society of the Alumni was organized in 1854 to provide moral and financial support in the wake of the College Building fire. See Janet Carter Shirley, *The Indiana University Alumni Association: One Hundred and Fifty Years, 1854–2004* (Bloomington: Indiana University Alumni Association, 2004).

[3]Woodburn, *History of Indiana University*, 1940, 332–35.

3.1 From Seminary Square to Dunn's Woods

Dunn's Woods, purchased by the trustees for $6,000, became the site of the new campus. In September, the commissioners of Monroe County made a $50,000 donation toward construction costs to rebuild the university.[4] The next month, science professor David Starr Jordan, away on a collecting expedition, wrote to IU president Lemuel Moss: "I am glad to hear of the general brightness of the prospects of the institution. The Dunn's Woods project I do not quite understand, but the location is certainly better among those great maples. I hope that you will let none be cut down, except when their removal is absolutely necessary."[5]

The trustees hired Indianapolis architect George W. Bunting to design three buildings, two of brick and one of wood, and plans were submitted in November 1883. Ground was broken in April 1884 at the new campus, hopefully renamed University Park, and construction commenced using recycled bricks from the burned building. Meanwhile, professors and students soldiered on at the old campus, the ruins of Science Hall a daily sight.

Change was not limited to the built environment; it also extended to the university's leadership. In the first semester of the 1884–85 year, a group of six students plus the janitor, Thomas "Uncle Tommy" Spicer, drilled a small hole in the floor above one of the rooms in the surviving university building. There were rumors of an affair between President Moss, a Baptist minister and a married man, and the young professor of Greek, Katharine Graydon, a single woman. Through the spy hole, the students observed the two kissing and caressing and reported it to the trustees.[6] The trustees, duty bound to launch their own investigation of this serious violation of social norms, set a hearing date for November 11. Graydon submitted her resignation letter on November 5, followed three days later by Moss. The trustees called off the investigation immediately, likely relieved that the university would not have to air its dirty laundry

[4]Wylie, *Indiana University, Its History from 1820, When Founded, to 1890, with Biographical Sketches of Its Presidents, Professor and Graduates, and a List of Its Students from 1820 to 1887*, 84.

[5]David Starr Jordan, "Letter to Lemuel Moss," October 7, 1883. IUA/C73/B1/F Jordan, David Starr.

[6]Later, a picture was staged with the seven "Moss Killers," displaying a wood drill, keyhole saw, and a hatchet on the wall behind.

in public after all.[7] The trustees appointed seasoned professor of languages Elisha Ballantine as acting president.

The trustee board immediately launched a search for a new president. Several candidates were considered from a list containing forty-seven names, but in the end, the trustees chose biology professor David Starr Jordan, a prominent ichthyologist on the faculty since 1879, as the seventh president of Indiana University.[8] Trained at Cornell University and influenced by its progressive president, Andrew Dickson White, Jordan was a staunch Darwinian and an avowed proponent of the research ideal. He was a popular professor, taking students on natural history rambles in the area surrounding Bloomington and pioneering weeks-long expeditions to Europe, called "summer tramps," to sample aspects of natural as well as cultural history.

Jordan took office on the first day of January 1885, announcing: "I believe our University is the most valuable of Indiana's possessions. It is not yet a great University, it is not yet a University at all, but it is the germ of one and its growth is as certain as the progress of the seasons."[9]

The IU trustees, headed by Banta, had faced three major challenges in the previous eighteen months: the burning of the best building on campus, the decision for a wholesale removal to a new site, and an unanticipated change of presidential leadership. Further changes were afoot in the expansion of the curriculum to embrace scientific fields, the reorganization of the faculty into departments, and the institution of the "major" course of study for students. As President Jordan explained, "The highest function of the real University is

[7]Minutes of the IU Board of Trustees, November 1884. Graydon tried to retract her letter of resignation the following month, but the trustees refused to consider it. Indiana University Board of Trustees, "Minutes of the Board of Trustees of Indiana University, 06 November 1884–11 November 1884" (Bloomington: Indiana University Archives & Indiana University Libraries Digital Collections Services, November 7, 1884), https://purl.dlib.indiana.edu/iudl/archives/iubot/1884-11-07.

[8]Indiana University Board of Trustees, "Minutes of the Board of Trustees of Indiana University, 16 December 1884–19 December 1884" (Bloomington: Indiana University Archives & Indiana University Libraries Digital Collections Services, December 1884), https://purl.dlib.indiana.edu/iudl/archives/iubot/1884-12-16.

[9]*Days of a Man, Being Memories of a Naturalist, Teacher, and Minor Prophet of Democracy*, vol. 1 (Yonkers-on-Hudson, NY: World Book Company, 1922), 295.

that of instruction by investigation, and a man who cannot and does not investigate cannot train investigators."[10]

To some longtime faculty members, the pace of change provoked apprehension. Theophilus Wylie, granted emeritus status in 1886, wrote in his diary: "New arrangements, new studies, new teachers, new modes of teaching, give me much anxiety."[11] Some others might have shared Wylie's disquiet, but students were voting with their feet to come to the new University Park, as enrollments surged after 1885.

To improve faculty quality in the face of limited financial resources, Jordan began filling vacancies with professors from eastern institutions, but most "failed to adapt themselves, appearing to feel that coming so far West was a form of banishment." So, he took a page from Hoosier agricultural heritage and populated the faculty with homegrown talent. He started the Specialist's Club for gifted students, and he promised talented recent IU graduates "professorships when they had secured the requisite advanced training in the East or in Europe."[12] Among the many alumni he inspired to become Indiana faculty stalwarts were Joseph Swain, William Lowe Bryan, Carl Eigenmann, James A. Woodburn, David Mottier, and William Rawles.[13]

In the fall of 1885, classes opened on the new campus. The three new buildings—Wylie, Owen, and Maxwell (later renamed Mitchell)—contained classrooms, laboratories, and offices. The old College Building at Seminary Square was still being used for the IU Preparatory Department and large gatherings. Events of the previous two years "uprooted the institution, and the new campus opened in 1885 without a sense of history," as historian Howard McMains later noted.[14]

---

[10]Jordan made this statement in his 1888 report as a trustee of Cornell University; quoted in W. T. Hewett, *Cornell University: A History*, vol. 1 (New York: University Publishing Society, 1905), p. 286.

[11]"Diary Entry" (Indiana University Archives, September 6, 1885).

[12]*Days of a Man, Being Memories of a Naturalist, Teacher, and Minor Prophet of Democracy*, 1:295.

[13]Jordan, 1:295–96; Cf. Capshew, "Indiana University as the 'Mother of College Presidents': Herman B Wells as Inheritor, Exemplar, and Agent."

[14]"The Indiana Seminary Charter of 1820," 359.

3.2 Inventors of IU History

As Indiana University worked through significant changes in the 1880s, a trio of faculty were working, separately and together, to craft the saga of the institution. Each brought different talents and angles of vision to the task of making sense of the recent changes. To be sure, the university had survived serious threats to its welfare, even its existence as an institution, almost since the beginning of instruction, but things were different this time. Nearly every aspect of the university—physical plant, curriculum, leadership, state relations—was affected. In the face of a period of major changes, there was an inevitable distinction to be made between the time leading up to the period and the time since. In simple terms, there was a clear "before" and "after." That distinction, whether explicitly acknowledged or not, became the main armature around which the trio of faculty historians shaped their narratives about IU.

The first, in terms of seniority and length of faculty service, was Theophilus Wylie (1810–95). A younger half-cousin of the first president, Andrew Wylie, he was hired to teach natural science and chemistry in 1837. He taught many other subjects over his long teaching career as well. Wylie also served a variety of administrative posts, including librarian and president *pro tem* of the small university. Thus, he was in a good position when the board of trustees asked him, in 1881, to prepare a historical catalog documenting the history of IU for its first six decades. He was appointed IU vice president in 1882 but resigned from this position in June 1884 to free up more time for historical research and asked Banta for assistance.[15]

The second member of the trio was David D. Banta (1833–96), a former Indiana circuit court judge who became an IU trustee in 1877, serving as board president from 1882 to 1889. He was appointed dean of the newly revived law school in 1889, serving until his death in 1896. He received two degrees from IU: a Bachelor of Science in

[15]Indiana University Board of Trustees, "Minutes of the Board of Trustees of Indiana University, 04 June 1884–11 June 1884" (Bloomington: Indiana University Archives & Indiana University Libraries Digital Collections Services, June 7, 1884), https://purl.dlib.indiana.edu/iudl/archives/iubot/1884-06-04; cf. Burton Dorr Myers, *Trustees and Officers of Indiana University 1820–1950*, ed. Ivy L. Chamness and Burton D. Myers (Bloomington: Indiana University, 1951), 484–85.

1855 and a Bachelor of Laws in 1857. Banta, a successful lawyer and judge, was a self-trained historian, completing a history of the Presbyterian Church in Franklin, Indiana, in 1874. As president of the IU Board of Trustees, he was a key figure during the momentous transition in the university's campus location and leadership from 1883 to 1885.

The trio's last member, James Albert Woodburn (1856–1943), represented yet another, more recent, generation. Son of faculty member James W. Woodburn (1817–65), he had been baptized at seven months by Theophilus Wylie at Bloomington's Presbyterian church.[16] The younger Woodburn had been educated in Bloomington schools and attended IU, receiving a Bachelor of Arts in 1876 and a Master of Arts in history in 1885. In 1879, he began teaching in the IU Preparatory Department and later became a member of President Jordan's Specialist's Club for future faculty members. Securing a leave of absence from IU in 1886, Woodburn pursued a doctorate in history from Johns Hopkins University, studying in the famous seminar guided by Herbert B. Adams. In his absence, in 1888, he was promoted to associate professor of history at IU. After writing a dissertation examining the history of higher education in Indiana, he earned his Doctor of Philosophy in 1890.

Both Woodburn and Banta were IU alumni, and each became acquainted with Theophilus Wylie as college students. Starting in 1879, the trio spent sixteen years on the IU staff together until Wylie's death in 1895, followed a year later by Banta's passing. All were steeped in the traditions of the Seminary Square campus, but each had a different viewpoint based on their personal observations and associations. Wylie was in the final phase of his long teaching career and now embarking on a laborious accounting of all the people who had belonged to the university since 1820—students, faculty, presidents, and trustees. Banta, as president of the trustee board, played a key role in steering the university's course in the turbulent mid-1880s. Pressed into service as the dean of the newly revived law school in 1889, he became a senior faculty figure too. Woodburn, nearly a half century younger than Wylie, was just starting his professorial career, albeit with a family background that had been connected to IU since the late 1830s.

[16]Theophilus Wylie, "Diary Entry" (Indiana University Archives, June 28, 1857): "Baptized James Albert, sone [*sic*] of James & Martha Woodburn[.] Weather warm, summer like."

3.3 Toward a Historical Catalog

When he started the historical catalog project in 1881, Wylie thought it would take him about three years. The intent of the work, according to the trustees' request, was to showcase the university's contribution to the state and the nation through the impact of its faculty and alumni. Taking on what he acknowledged as "a very big task...if it is done as it ought to be," Wylie sent out multiple rounds of postcards and letters soliciting information from former faculty and students as he endeavored to compile exhaustive lists and biographical portraits of professors, presidents, trustees, and students, both graduates and nongraduates, since the university's beginning in 1820 as the state's seminary of learning.

Wylie's painstaking work was frustrated by the loss of university records and papers by the 1854 campus fire and the more recent burning of Science Hall in 1883. He sifted through surviving documents, year by year, for the comings and goings of students and faculty.[17] His wide correspondence with alumni yielded a wealth of materials to replace missing records and other relevant information.

The lack of sufficient documentation and understanding concerning IU's past was illustrated by a historical conundrum addressed by the trustee board in March 1884. In the midst of making plans for the new campus at University Park (and a few months before the Moss scandal broke), a point of clarification was raised about another, seemingly minor matter: "The question of date on the University Seal was brought to the notice of the Board. After discussing the old date (1830) and the date of the organization of the Indiana Seminary (1820), the organization of the Indiana College (1828), and the Indiana University (1838), it was agreed by general counsel to fix the date of the seal at 1820, the other devices to remain as in the former seal."[18] Without relevant records to disclose the reason why 1830 was on the seal, the trustees apparently decided it was a

[17]Wylie, *Indiana University, Its History from 1820, When Founded, to 1890, with Biographical Sketches of Its Presidents, Professor and Graduates, and a List of Its Students from 1820 to 1887*, 3.

[18]Indiana University Board of Trustees, "Minutes of the Board of Trustees of Indiana University, 04 March 1884–25 March 1884" (Bloomington: Indiana University Archives & Indiana University Libraries Digital Collections Services, March 25, 1884), https://purl.dlib.indiana.edu/iudl/archives/iubot/1884-03-04.

simple mistake and removed the last X from MDCCCXXX. After the trustees changed the seal to correspond with the founding date of the institution's earliest progenitor, the Indiana State Seminary, the trustees moved on to more pressing business.

Trying to piece together IU's history during extensive institutional change was not easy for Wylie. On the verge of teaching on the new campus in September 1885, Wylie confessed his anxiety to his daily diary.[19] In 1886, after successfully completing his final year of teaching in the new surroundings of University Park, Wylie was granted emeritus status for his forty-seven years of service.[20] He was a creature of the old campus, retaining his emotional connection to Seminary Square. His living situation reinforced those ties. He had been living in Wylie House, the former home of the first president, for a quarter century and raised a large family there. Wylie persevered with his research and extensive correspondence with members of the university clan for several years after the center of campus life moved to Dunn's Woods. As the scope and complexity of the historical catalog continued to evolve, Banta, who had done some research and writing about the university himself, became both a contributor to the volume and a member of the trustee committee supervising its production.

3.4 Creating a Foundation Narrative

By the mid-1880s, the university had survived for sixty years, with over 1,200 graduates. Stories of the institution's past, leavened with folklore, had evolved into an informal oral tradition, passed from generation to generation. A main source of this oral tradition was physician David H. Maxwell, the first president of the board of trustees; the oral tradition was further amplified by his son, James Darwin Maxwell, also a trustee.

From Jefferson County, the senior Maxwell was a delegate at the convention that wrote Indiana's first state constitution in 1816. That document mentioned that the state would provide, at some

[19] "Diary Entry," September 6, 1885.

[20] Wylie first came in 1837, then spent two and a half years at Miami University in 1852–54, and then returned to IU.

point in the future, "a general system of education, ascending in a regular gradation from township schools to a State university."[21]

Maxwell, with his wife and young son, moved to Monroe County in 1819, a year after the county was organized at the northern limit of white settlement. In 1820, the Indiana General Assembly passed an act to establish a state seminary of learning, to be organized by a board of trustees. Maxwell was among the original trustees and was elected president of the six-member board. In 1828, when the state legislature established Indiana College, new trustees were appointed, including Maxwell. He continued as board president for the next decade. In 1838, the Indiana General Assembly passed "an act to establish a university in the State of Indiana" and a reconstituted board of trustees to oversee it.[22] Maxwell was not among the original members of this twenty-one-person board, although he was appointed the following year, serving until 1852. He died weeks before the 1854 fire that destroyed the College Building.

His son, James Maxwell, also a physician, was an IU alumnus and served the board of trustees as their appointed secretary from 1838 to 1855 before becoming a trustee himself from 1861 to 1892, the year of his death.[23]

Both Maxwells, father and son, lived in Bloomington and were familiar figures in town and on the IU campus at the end of College Avenue. Their combined service as trustees spanned seventy years, from the very beginning of the institution in 1820 into the early 1890s. The main outlines of the oral tradition emphasized the institution's continuity and created a narrative of linear progress. It ignored the inconsistent actions of the Indiana General Assembly and elided the real distinctions between seminary, college, and university in favor of a *post-hoc* vision of inevitable advancement.

Until his death in 1854, Maxwell was a regular figure on campus. Banta, who graduated in 1855, "remembered him with great respect" and "must have listened to Maxwell's version of the foundation narrative many times." His son, James Maxwell, was also a familiar

[21]Wylie, *Indiana University, Its History from 1820, When Founded, to 1890, with Biographical Sketches of Its Presidents, Professor and Graduates, and a List of Its Students from 1820 to 1887*, p. 14. Maxwell was not a member of the education subcommittee that wrote that section of the Indiana Constitution.

[22]Wylie, 21.

[23]James Maxwell served as trustee board president from 1862 to 1865 during the Civil War.

sight until his death in 1892, and no doubt reiterated his father's story.[24] Indeed, all members of the trio who invented IU history had ample occasions to hear the origin story from a Maxwell—father or son or both.

When Banta, now the revived law school dean, was chosen to present the inaugural Foundation Day address in 1889, he spoke on the Indiana Seminary, crystallizing the informal oral tradition informed by Maxwell into historical doctrine. The story was that David Maxwell, acting as an unofficial lobbyist to the legislature meeting in Corydon in December 1819, pressed for the location of a seminary of learning in Monroe County. With the support of Governor Jonathan Jennings, a bill authorizing the creation of a state seminary was narrowly passed on January 20, 1820. Banta admitted in his narrative that "no record, no tradition even, remains to tell the story of what he did, to secure legislative action on behalf of a State school." Maxwell's subsequent actions as a trustee over the next thirty years led Banta to declare that "he was the Father of the Indiana University."[25]

For the next five years, Banta gave Foundation Day addresses, elaborating on the history of the institution to 1850. With this official imprimatur, the origin story became further solidified as a linear chronicle of Indiana State Seminary (1820–28), Indiana College (1828–38), and Indiana University (since 1838).

After a decade of effort, Wylie's historical catalog was finally published in 1890, under the title *Indiana University, Its History from 1820, When Founded, to 1890, with Biographical Sketches of Its Presidents, Professors and Graduates, and a List of Its Students from 1820 to 1887.* It contained an abbreviated chapter from Banta on the Indiana seminary, as well as a chapter on the university's legislative history written by Robert S. Robertson, a trustee. The bulk of the book was filled with biographical sketches of students, professors, presidents, and trustees with short narrative sections covering the collegiate department and law school.[26]

Meanwhile, James Woodburn was away in Baltimore, on a leave of absence from IU to work on a Ph.D. in history. Shortly after

---

[24]McMains, "The Indiana Seminary Charter of 1820," 361.

[25]"History of Indiana University I," 9.

[26]Wylie, *Indiana University, Its History from 1820, When Founded, to 1890, with Biographical Sketches of Its Presidents, Professor and Graduates, and a List of Its Students from 1820 to 1887.*

Banta delivered his first Foundation Day address in January 1889, Woodburn wrote to him about IU history. Banta replied, "Anything in my paper you find of service to you in your monograph you are welcome to use." Banta talked about the Hoosier pioneers who "were much in earnest in their desire for educational advancement" but they faced three main obstacles: "In the first place the great poverty of the people and in the second the physical obstacles such as unprecedented sickness prevailing generally and the difficulties incident to a region so densely wooded as was Ind.; and in the third place want of models. Every thing [*sic*] had to be worked out of the green and it required the labor of 50 years to get the field ready."[27]

Later that year, Woodburn finished his historical monograph, *Higher Education in Indiana*, and in 1890 received his doctoral degree. His mentor, Herbert Adams, was editing a series of studies, Contributions to American Educational History, for publication by the US Bureau of Education. Woodburn's dissertation found a place in the series and was published by the bureau in 1891—his first publication with Ph.D. appended to his name.[28]

Woodburn hewed to the existing foundation narrative in his two chapters on the evolution of Indiana University, writing about the historical progression of seminary, college, and university in an unproblematic way. The view from the present was reinforced by eight illustrations of the buildings of the new campus at Dunn's Woods and only one from the old campus at Seminary Square, still in use for the preparatory department. He also singled out the contributions of David Maxwell: "In the establishment of institutions, it seems that the life and services of some one man are paramount and essential. In the establishment of the Indiana Seminary Dr. David H. Maxwell was the essential man."[29]

The lack of institutional records, exacerbated by two great campus fires, combined with the perceived need to account for the university's history in the 1880s, led to agreement among the three faculty members about the foundation narrative. For over a century,

---

[27]"Letter to James Woodburn" (Indiana University Archives, February 9, 1889).

[28]James Albert Woodburn, "Higher Education in Indiana," ed. Herbert B. Adams, Bureau of Education, Circular of Information No. 1, 1891: Contributions to American Educational History (Washington: Government Publishing Office, 1891).

[29]Woodburn, 77. Comma added.

subsequent historians of IU have uncritically echoed that judgment about the institution's origins and early development.

More recently, contemporary scholars are indebted to historian Howard McMains's revisionist account of the early history of the institution that would become Indiana University. He examined the historical construction that the charter of the Indiana State Seminary was foretold in the state's constitution, thus "laying the bottom rail" for Indiana University, as every previous IU historian had written. McMains explained, "The constitution had not...contemplated the seminary charter; the seminary charter had not contemplated the university." But David Maxwell connected the two together: "His narrative inserted the institution into the very origins of the state and linked constitution, seminary, and college into a seamless development...[and] also made a university in Bloomington seem inevitable."[30] By carefully reexamining both surviving documents and the political and social context, his article lends support to the contention that the foundation narrative created in 1889–91 was not a straightforward piece of historical reporting but an account shaped first by David Maxwell to lend legitimacy to the notion that the seminary was the seed of the university and then by subsequent historians to provide a comforting sense of institutional progress to the circumstances of their present day.

3.5 A Case of Collective Amnesia

The process of constructing a foundation narrative for the institution required a selective reading of past evidence. With the destruction of records and the limits of human memory, the dates of certain key events were lost to history or misremembered, at least for a time. One example occurred at the time IU's origin story was being solidified. Recall that in 1884, the board of trustees, headed by David Banta, believing the University Seal to be misdated, changed the date on the seal from MDCCCXXX (1830) to MDCCCXX (1820). They thought it was a simple misdating of the seminary's founding. Eight years later, Banta, now dean of the law school, reinforced that decision in his 1892 Foundation Day address, "The

[30] "Laying the Bottom Rail" was the title of chapter 3 in Clark, *Indiana University*, 1970, p. 25. McMains, "The Indiana Seminary Charter of 1820", pp. 378–379.

'Faculty War' of 1832." In his introduction, he spoke of inscriptions as historical evidence:

> There is one inscription very close to us that falsifies the truth of history. It is over the east front entrance of this College building. It states that the Indiana University was founded in 1830, and for the benefit of those who may not happen to know better, let me say that there is not a word of truth in that statement. The Indiana Seminary was chartered on January 20, 1820, the day we commemorate....I know of no excuse for the false record inscribed in the stone over the College door, and I know not whether it was the result of ignorance or of mistake. There is nothing connected with this institution which was founded in 1830.[31]

Banta devised a likely story to support the trustees' 1884 interpretation that it was a simple mistake. Conveniently, it reinforced the narrative of linear progress from the seminary.

But 1830 did mark a historic date for the small collegiate institution: it was the first year that Indiana College granted degrees. After ten years of planning and five years of classes, four students finally finished the requirements for a baccalaureate degree in 1830. Now the institution had begun to have success in its raison d'être. In the eleven years following, another sixty-five students received their degrees. In total, eight classes (1830–37) were awarded degrees from Indiana College.[32]

---

[31]"History of Indiana University: IV. The 'Faculty War' of 1832," 370; see also Woodburn, *History of Indiana University*, 1940, 483, which repeats this interpretation uncritically.

[32]Degrees awarded from Indiana College, 1830–37, and Indiana University, 1838–41:

- 1830: 4
- 1831: 4
- 1832: 5
- 1833: 3
- 1834: 4
- 1835: 4
- 1836: 8
- 1837: 10
- 1838: 10
- 1839: 7
- 1840: 5
- 1841: 5

On February 15, 1838, the Indiana General Assembly elevated Indiana College to Indiana University. Section 4 read: "The said trustees shall cause to be made for their use, one common seal, with such devices, and inscription thereon, as they shall think proper, under and by which all deeds, diplomas and certificates and acts of the said corporation shall pass and be authenticated."[33] Several months later, in September, President Andrew Wylie received the following instruction from the board of trustees: "Resolved That Pres't Wylie be requested to procure a Seal for the University, with such engravings and devices as he may think appropriate, and also a [printing] plate for Diplomas."[34] In 1841, the trustee board approved the original university seal, with the date MDCCCXXX, with no further discussion.[35] Diplomas were the primary documents affixed with the seal, but it was also carved on the stone portals of the second College Building in 1855 after the first College Building was destroyed by fire.[36]

Paying attention to context, there is a good argument that the seal's original date was no error. The seal had a symbolic function and was featured on diplomas for certification and validation. In its early years, the institution was small and precarious. After the 1838 name change, it was still a small struggling college for many years, but its aspirations had enlarged as it met with success, year after year, in slowly increasing the number of its graduates. The 1841 trustees well knew that the true mark of institutional accomplishment was the completion of the recurring cycle of higher education—and there had been one dozen graduating classes at the time the seal was approved.

---

[33]Indiana University Board of Trustees, "Minutes of the Board of Trustees of Indiana University, 15 February 1838" (Bloomington: Indiana University Archives & Indiana University Libraries Digital Collections Services, February 15, 1838), https://purl.dlib.indiana.edu/iudl/archives/iubot/1838-02-15.

[34]Indiana University Board of Trustees, "Minutes of the Board of Trustees of Indiana University, 24 September 1838–27 September 1838" (Bloomington: Indiana University Archives & Indiana University Libraries Digital Collections Services, September 27, 1838), https://purl.dlib.indiana.edu/iudl/archives/iubot/1838-09-24.

[35]Indiana University Board of Trustees, "Minutes of the Board of Trustees of Indiana University, 19 July 1841–24 July 1841" (Bloomington: Indiana University Archives & Indiana University Libraries Digital Collections Services, July 21, 1841), https://purl.dlib.indiana.edu/iudl/archives/iubot/1841-07-19.

[36]In 1908, the portals were removed and integrated into the structure of the Rose Well House on the Dunn's Woods campus.

Four decades later, the context had changed substantially. In the immediate aftermath of the Science Hall fire that led to the purchase of Dunn's Woods, the 1884 trustees were newly concerned about institutional history. Where was the university headed? Where had it been? Stories about the inevitable advancement of Indiana University from its precursors, Indiana State Seminary and Indiana College, provided a comforting narrative of linear progress in the past during a time of an uncertain present.

Moreover, annual commencements had become an ordinary feature of the campus calendar, involving dozens of graduates in the 1880s rather than the handful of the 1830s and 1840s. Interest had moved to the consideration of the institution's statutory origins—the 1816 congressional land grant and the 1820 legislative act creating a seminary of learning. But some basic facts about the university's operation, such as the date of the original University Seal or the date when classes started, were misremembered, and lost to collective memory for a time.[37]

3.6 Lack of Primary Documentation

Determining key facts in IU's chronology has been hampered by a lack of primary documentation. Many early university records did not survive the campus fires. A prime example is the confusion about the date classes began at the state seminary. With primary sources unavailable, some university histories have claimed that classes began in 1824, and some have claimed 1825. In 1890, Banta used 1824 in his abbreviated essay "The Indiana Seminary," published in *Indiana University, Its History from 1820, When Founded, to 1890*, by Theophilus Wylie.[38] When Banta's manuscripts were published in full in the *IU Alumni Quarterly* in 1914–15, editor Samuel Harding changed a couple of 1825 instances to 1824. In a long footnote, James Woodburn discussed the ambiguity in the 1940

[37]See Jeremy L. Hackerd, "The Complex History of the Date Classes Began at the State Seminary of Indiana" (Indianapolis: Indiana Historical Bureau, June 30, 2008). Background Report on the State Historical Marker ("State Seminary of Indiana" marker) for Seminary Square, Bloomington, Indiana State Historical Marker Program.

[38]Wylie, *Indiana University, Its History from 1820, When Founded, to 1890, with Biographical Sketches of Its Presidents, Professor and Graduates, and a List of Its Students from 1820 to 1887*, 38–46, quote on p. 43.

History of Indiana University, Volume I: 1820–1902.[39] He cites registrar John Cravens, who told him that "he had found seemingly good authority for two dates—1824 and 1825." Woodburn agreed with Cravens: "For the benefit of future historians, the evidence for both dates is presented here."[40]

Woodburn goes on to discuss various primary sources from outside university records, concluding with a citation of David Maxwell's 1828 report to the legislature. The document never explicitly dated the beginning of instruction but can be interpreted as supporting the 1824 date. Woodburn's final comment implied agreement: "Perhaps on this evidence we can rest our case."[41] There things rested for three decades until 1970, when Thomas Clark published the first volume of *Indiana University: Midwestern Pioneer.* Based on careful study, including an unearthed newspaper notice issued by the board of trustees, he determined that the beginning of classes at the seminary was 1825.[42]

In 1984, university archivist Dolores Lahrman assigned her assistant, Bruce Harrah-Conforth, to research the question again. He wrote "The Beginning of Classes at Indiana University 1824 or 1825? A Study of Evidence" the following year. He argued for 1824, based on counting backward from David Maxwell's 1828 report to the legislature that stated the institution had existed for four years. He dismissed the primary source that Clark cited in support of the 1825 date, claiming that it merely announced the first day of classes for a particular term, not the first day of classes ever at the seminary.

Meanwhile, the City of Bloomington planned to renovate Seminary Park and include important IU dates carved in limestone. In February 1987, Lahrman wrote to President John Ryan informing him of the city's plan and lamenting the inconsistent dates for the opening of classes. Since the publication of Clark's official history, there were some IU offices using 1824 and some 1825.

Rather than search for additional primary sources and do further historical research, the board of trustees accepted Harrah-Conforth's report as definitive and passed a unanimous resolution "acknowledging 1824 as the year and May 1 as the anniversary date of

[39]*History of Indiana University*, 1940, 16–17.
[40]16 fn 10.
[41]16 fn 10.
[42]*Indiana University*, 1970, 30.

the beginning of classes at the State Seminary."[43] An IU news release was issued immediately: "The resolution passed today by the trustees officially resolves that controversy and establishes 1824 as the date to be used in all future university publications."[44] It was not clear whether anyone noticed the irony of overturning a date determined by a reputable historian in the most recent official IU history in favor of a single, ambiguous document by a former trustee who was widely known as "the father of Indiana University" in the origin story first set down in the 1880s.

A month later, the eighty-four-year-old university chancellor and former president Herman Wells sent President Ryan a note, copying archivist Lahrman: "I disagreed with Clark's finding when he made it, and so told him. I am happy, therefore, that further research has revealed that 1824 is the proper date."[45] Lahrman responded to Wells with thanks, saying "it means a great deal to us to know that you have been for a long time in agreement. I was apprehensive about undertaking the research, since I love and respect Dr. Clark and hate to risk offending him, but it seemed that we had to try to determine the facts."[46] In his reply, Wells congratulated Harrah-Conforth on his research and Lahrman for initiating action.[47]

In 2008, Indiana Historical Bureau researcher Jeremy Hackerd made another run at the vexed issues of dating the beginning of classes. In charge of the Indiana Historical Bureau Historical Marker Program, Hackerd exercised due diligence when the City of Bloomington and Indiana University proposed a state historical marker to commemorate the site of the Indiana State Seminary. He carefully studied the historiography of the issue, reexamined old evidence, gathered new information, and produced an authoritative study. Hackerd concluded:

> Determining the beginning date for classes at the State Seminary of Indiana has challenged historians for decades.

[43]Indiana University Board of Trustees, "Minutes of the Board of Trustees of Indiana University, 07 March 1987" (Bloomington: Indiana University Archives & Indiana University Libraries Digital Collections Services, March 7, 1987), https://purl.dlib.indiana.edu/iudl/archives/iubot/1987-03-07.

[44]Indiana University, "IU Trustees Approve 'Official Year' of University's First Classes" (Indiana University Archives, March 7, 1987). News Release.

[45]Herman B. Wells, "Letter to John Ryan" (Indiana University Archives, April 7, 1987).

[46]*The History of Mitchell Hall, 1885–1986* (Bloomington: Indiana University Archives, 1987).

[47]"Letter to Dolores Lahrman" (Indiana University Archives, May 13, 1987).

> The use of newly located primary sources and a reevaluation of interpretations of early standard sources have resulted in the need to correct the official Indiana University timeline. Study of the biography of Baynard Rush Hall—the first teacher, newspaper notices issued by the State Seminary's Board of Trustees, and Presbyterian church records substantiate April 4, 1825, as the date classes began at the State Seminary of Indiana in Bloomington.[48]

Thus, the mystery that dates to the early history of the institution found a satisfactory resolution. Ironically, the 1880s marked the invention of IU history as a literary genre and the creation of difficult problems with the university's chronology.

3.7 Suppression of Historical Evidence

The two examples cited above were unintentional errors exacerbated by scarce records and faulty memories. Another, more serious case of distorting the university's history involved David Banta suppressing a key fact as he recounted the story of the "faculty war" of 1832, as presented in his 1892 Foundation Day address.[49] As mentioned in Chapter 2, the conflict between Andrew Wylie and Baynard R. Hall began with an anonymous letter left for Hall at the end of the 1830–31 school year. The note eventually led to Hall's resignation. In the spring of 1832, Professor Harney began having public conflicts with President Wylie, which led to his dismissal by the trustee board in the fall. Thus, at the close of Indiana College's seventh year, the original faculty were gone, and the president and trustees had to recruit new teaching staff.

Banta learned the identity of the author of the anonymous note when he received a letter from Andrew Wylie Jr. in 1882 admitting authorship but chose to not reveal it in his Foundation Day address a decade later. Banta never revealed his reasons for suppressing Andrew Wylie Jr.'s name from his account of the faculty war, but

---

[48]Hackerd, "The Complex History of the Date Classes Began at the State Seminary of Indiana." Background Report on the State Historical Marker ("State Seminary of Indiana" marker) for Seminary Square, Bloomington, Indiana State Historical Marker Program.

[49]Banta, "History of Indiana University: IV. The 'Faculty War' of 1832."

one can surmise some possibilities. To begin with, both men were judges, with the expectation that their actions should exhibit probity, restraint, and wisdom. What would be gained by exposing a major institutional scandal that occurred sixty years earlier? Better to keep the secret within a small group of elder figures, perhaps.

The 1882 letter from Wylie to Banta was in the university archives for over a century, but the secret it contained was not revealed publicly until a biography of IU's first professor, *Baynard Rush Hall: His Story*, was published in 2009 by Dixie Kline Richardson.[50] Future historians of IU will need to take account of the fact that a student—the president's son, no less—started a process that led to the separation of the original teaching staff from the institution. The episode should be renamed the "war against the faculty" rather than the "faculty war" possibly. Regardless, conflicts between the administrative staff and instructional personnel were present from the start.

3.8 A Variation on the Theme

After the various efforts by Wylie, Banta, and Woodburn to construct a common foundation narrative for the university, a dozen years later another approach to IU history was tried. After rejecting an invitation to prepare an exhibit on Indiana University for the 1904 Louisiana Purchase Exposition in St. Louis, President William Bryan explained: "It was determined to prepare a book which should set forth in permanent form, for those interested, the salient features of the history and current status of the University. Out of this determination arose the present volume."[51] The book functioned along the line of a university viewbook, providing information for the interested public.

Edited by Samuel B. Harding, professor of European history, the book had three parts. The first, authored by William Rawles, professor of economic and social science, was a concise "Historical Sketch," laying out IU's legislative history and organizational evolution. The works of the faculty trio were cited at least once, with Woodburn

[50] For a brief account of the secret, see also James H. Capshew, "New Light on an Old Story: The Secret of the Faculty War," *200: The Bicentennial Magazine* 1, no. 1 (2018): 6–8.

[51] Harding, *Indiana University, 1820–1904*, vii.

being quoted several times. The second part was a close study of the "Development of the Course of Instruction" by Lewis Carson, assistant professor of philosophy. Based on surviving IU catalogs, his text documented the expansion of the curriculum from ancient classics to modern languages and the sciences. The final part was a cumulative bibliography of publications authored by present faculty members, past faculty members, alumni, and students. Librarian William A. Alexander supervised its compilation. Both Rawles and Carson eschewed promotional language and provided sober assessments of their respective subjects. Following the scholarly model pursued by Woodburn in his earlier study of IU history, their writing contrasted with Wylie's focus on the academic community or Banta's storytelling style.

The hybrid volume ritually invoked the past as a prologue to the university's current aspirations. The number of pages for each section reveals something about the institution's self-presentation. The first, containing a brief overview of its development for the last century, was 32 pages (9 percent). The second section, dealing with curriculum, was 160 pages (46 percent), with three-quarters of that (35 percent of the book) about "departments as now constituted." The final part, consisting of a bibliography of publications, was 153 pages (44 percent), subdivided into current faculty (28 pages), former faculty (26 pages), and alumni (98 pages). Curriculum and instruction, departmental organization and facilities, and intellectual production through scholarship are the key themes of the volume as the university presented itself to the wider world. History was a relatively minor theme used to understand the contemporary scene and to implicitly support the university's aspirations for the future.

3.9 Perseveration: The Ritual Use of History

In 1914, when the first issue of the *Indiana University Alumni Quarterly* came out, Woodburn—remembering that the historical addresses of the late law school dean Banta had never been published in their entirety—arranged with the editor of the new periodical, fellow history professor Samuel Harding, to have them appear. Banta's examination of "The Indiana Seminary" appeared on page one, signaling the journal's intent to cover all aspects of alumni experience, past and present. That 1889 address, given at the first Foundation Day, had first been published in Wylie's historical catalog in 1890. The following five issues of the *Alumni Quarterly* published Banta's subsequent addresses from 1890 to 1894, each for the first time, in a "History of Indiana University" series.[52] Later in 1914, Ivy Chamness began working as assistant editor of university publications and was soon drawn into editing the *Alumni Quarterly* as well, succeeding Harding.[53]

Between 1915 and 1917, Woodburn took up where Banta's narrative ended and published a series of eight articles in the *Alumni Quarterly*. Under the general title "Sketches from the University's History," he covered the 1850s at IU in detail. Consequential events included the employment of Professor Daniel Read, the death of President Andrew Wylie, and the 1854 campus fire. He included information about student life, the trustees, and the faculty and curriculum.[54]

In 1921, Chamness edited *Indiana University, 1820–1920: Centennial Memorial Volume*.[55] The first one hundred pages collected

[52]Banta, "History of Indiana University I"; Banta, "History of Indiana University," 1914; Banta, "History of Indiana University," 1914; Banta, "History of Indiana University: IV. The 'Faculty War' of 1832"; Banta, "History of Indiana University," 1915; Banta, "History of Indiana University," 1915.

[53]See Chapter 8.

[54]James A. Woodburn, "Sketches from the University's History I: College Men and College Life about 1850," *Indiana University Alumni Quarterly* 2 (1915): 249–69; James A. Woodburn, "Sketches from the University's History II: College Men and College Life About 1850 (Continued)," *Indiana University Alumni Quarterly* 2 (1915): 409–27; James A. Woodburn, "Sketches from the University's History III: Faculty and Curriculum about 1850," *Indiana University Alumni Quarterly* 3 (1916): 20–37; James A. Woodburn, "Sketches from the University's History IV: Daniel Read, Professor of Ancient Languages, 1843–1856," *Indiana University Alumni Quarterly* 3 (1916): 127–48; James A. Woodburn, "Sketches from the University's History V: Death of President Wylie: A Year of President Ryors and Election of Dr. Daily: Death and Services of Dr. David H. Maxwell," *Indiana University Alumni Quarterly* 3 (1916): 347–59; James A. Woodburn, "Sketches from the University's History VI: The Vincennes Suit and the Fire," *Indiana University Alumni Quarterly* 3 (1916): 489–500; James A. Woodburn, "Sketches from the University's History VII: Dark Days after the Fire: Courage in Adversity," *Indiana University Alumni Quarterly* 4 (1917): 1–11; James A. Woodburn, "Sketches from the University's History VIII: The Board of Trustees Sixty Years Ago; Student Reminiscences," *Indiana University Alumni Quarterly* 4 (1917): 117–28.

[55]Ivy L. Chamness, ed., *Indiana University, 1820–1920: Centennial Memorial Volume* (Bloomington: Indiana University, 1921).

all of Banta's articles published in the *Alumni Quarterly* and republished them as "History of Indiana University," with the article titles serving as chapter headings. Part II included the addresses delivered at the Centennial Educational Conference held at IU in May 1920, under the title "The American University: Today and Tomorrow." The last part republished a lengthy account of the Centennial Commencement, written by Chamness for the July 1920 *Alumni Quarterly.*

In 1940, Woodburn finally published History of *Indiana University, Volume I: 1820–1902*, when he was eighty-four years old.[56] The book was divided into two parts. The first six chapters were authored by Banta and reprinted, for the third time, the material published in 1914–15 and republished in 1921. The second part was authored by Woodburn and contained sixteen chapters, half reprinted from the 1915–17 *Alumni Quarterly* series and half new material. At the end, addenda were added that contained a miscellany of archival correspondence and notes that only became known when the manuscript was in page proofs.

Banta, who died in 1896, was the chief beneficiary of the emerging practice of perseveration in IU history publishing. He was the first out of the gate among the trio who invented IU history, delivering an oral address on the Indiana State Seminary of learning in 1889 at the first Foundation Day. His subsequent addresses were published many years after his death, in the first issues of the *Alumni Quarterly* in 1914–15. Then the six articles became part of the 1921 *Centennial Memorial Volume.* They were reprinted yet again in 1940 as the opening chapters of Woodburn's *History of Indiana University* volume. Banta's name has become indelibly associated with IU history.

This insistent repetition might have been justified because each new student generation should have an opportunity to become acquainted with the institution's history, but that argument was never made explicitly. Closer to the truth was the implicit assumption that Banta's narrative would function as the foundation story, and there was no need for further work on the early history of the university. In fact, many people were interested in the university's story, but few had the interest and skill to write institutional history. Perseveration of Banta's account through repeated republication was sustained for fifty years, from 1890 to 1940, a period of tremendous

[56]Woodburn, *History of Indiana University*, 1940.

growth and change in the university. The impulse that animated Banta, Wylie, and Woodburn to invent IU history in the 1880s had faded, replaced by the ritual invocation of Banta's stories of the early institution, including the creation of the state seminary, the coming of President Andrew Wylie, and the conflict that led to the departure of the original professor, Baynard Rush Hall.

3.10 Postwar Developments

In office since 1937, President Herman Wells had a deep appreciation for the past, filtered through his overriding concern for the improvement of the university. He inherited two institutional history projects that began under the previous administration of President Bryan. One was Woodburn's *History of Indiana University* project, finished in 1940. The other was a project that resulted in a biographical directory, *Trustees and Officers of Indiana University, 1820–1950*, published in 1951.

In the early 1940s, the Wells administration authorized research for a second volume of *History of Indiana University*, to cover the thirty-five-year administration of President William Lowe Bryan from 1902 to 1937. Bryan, still very much alive, was pleased that the author was Burton Myers, the emeritus dean of the Bloomington medical school and a valued colleague. Myers was also tasked with bringing the long-delayed trustees book project to completion.

Spending the better part of a decade researching and writing until his death in 1951, Myers hewed close to the institutional records of the IU trustees and the president's office. The result was a dry official chronicle more than an interpretive narrative. In 1952, *History of Indiana University, Volume II: 1902–1937, The Bryan Administration* was published. The massive volume also contained information reaching back to IU's beginning in the nineteenth century. Whatever its literary deficiencies, the book remained an invaluable reference source and a permanent contribution to IU's historiography.[57]

Through the 1950s and 1960s, Indiana University experienced great institutional growth in students and faculty, proliferation in academic programs and facilities, and a remarkable rise in national

[57] See Chapter 8.

standing among research universities. After twenty-five years, the Wells administration ended in 1962, and the trustees bucked a seventy-five-year-old tradition of hiring from the inside and selected Elvis J. Stahr, a former secretary of the army, as president. Maintaining the university's trajectory set by Bryan and Wells, Stahr oversaw the continued expansion of IU's educational footprint around the state as well as gains in faculty research productivity and creative scholarship. As the university's 150th anniversary approached in 1970, Stahr appointed Thomas D. Clark, University of Kentucky history professor (and one of Stahr's former teachers), as visiting professor in 1967 to prepare a new narrative history of Indiana University.

Clark, an experienced regional historian, took on this task with gusto, examining voluminous primary sources, reading the existing historiography, and conducting numerous oral history interviews. Not since Woodburn's 1891 dissertation research had a professional historian critically explored IU's past—and there was a lot of material after 150 years. The most recent history volume—Myers's (1952)—ended its coverage in 1937, prior to the Second World War and the tremendous postwar expansion.

Eventually Clark's project expanded to three volumes of narrative history and a sourcebook of documents. The first volume of *Indiana University: Midwestern Pioneer*, published during the IU sesquicentennial year, was the first retelling of the early history since Banta. The second volume, published in 1974, focused on the long presidency of Bryan and his consequential administration. The final volume came out in 1977, taking the story of IU from 1937 to 1968, covering the presidential administrations of Wells and Stahr. The volume garnered excellent reviews, both from the local press and from history of education scholars.[58]

[58]Volume I reviews: Maynard Brichford, *Journal of the Illinois State Historical Society (1908–1984)* 64, no. 3 (1971): 355–56, http://www.jstor.org/stable/40190803; Daniel W. Hollis, *The Journal of American History* 58, no. 1 (1971): 201–2, https://doi.org/10.2307/1890153; James Nolan, "Indiana University History," *Courier-Journal*, January 17, 1971; Winton U. Solberg, *Indiana Magazine of History* 67, no. 3 (1971): 268–69, http://www.jstor.org/stable/27789750. Volume II reviews: J. David Hoeveler, "Higher Education in the Midwest: Community and Culture [Reviewed Volumes One and Two]," *History of Education Quarterly* 14, no. 3 (1974): 391–402, https://doi.org/10.2307/367940; Maynard Brichford, *Journal of the Illinois State Historical Society (1908–1984)* 68, no. 3 (1975): 297–99, http://www.jstor.org/stable/40191173; Merle Curti, *The American Historical Review* 80, no. 3 (1975): 518–19,

The Clark volumes recast the history of Indiana University in a long narrative arc of 150 years. For the most part, it followed the foundation story first circulated in the 1880s when institutional history was mobilized as a university asset, adding a few details but not challenging the existing framework. Clark was kind to his predecessors. A key strength of Clark's work was linking the deep and the more recent past into a single whole, although few readers had the stamina to read 1,500 pages over three volumes. Symbolically, the publication represented a turning point, when IU history, written by a professional historian recruited from beyond the institution, made its scholarly debut. It also inspired new work and gave it a richer context. To cite but one example: In 1980, Herman Wells published an autobiography, *Being Lucky: Reflections and Reminiscences*.[59] The book "was, in equal parts, an engaging autobiography, a manual of higher education management, and an artful spoof of his stellar career."[60] Readers of both volumes can get a considered view of how Wells transformed the university by perusing Clark's history, and some flavor of Wells charm and personality that drove his relentless quest for educational improvement through his memoirs. Not since David Starr Jordan published *Days of a Man: Being Memories of a Naturalist, Teacher, and a Minor Prophet of Democracy* in 1922 had a former IU president engaged autobiographically.[61]

The Clark volumes remain an impressive scholarly monument as well as an inviting target for revisionist accounts. In the eighty years between the invention of IU history as a literary genre and the

---

https://doi.org/10.2307/1850710; Patricia Albjerg Graham, *Indiana Magazine of History* 70, no. 2 (1974): 180–82, http://www.jstor.org/stable/27789965; Daniel W. Hollis, *The Journal of American History* 61, no. 2 (1974): 515–16, https://doi.org/10.2307/1904023; John Ed Pearce, "The Middle Years of Indiana University: A Review," *Courier-Journal*, November 18, 1973. Volume III reviews: Merle Curti, *The American Historical Review* 83, no. 4 (1978): 1101, https://doi.org/10.2307/1867836; Daniel W. Hollis, *The Journal of American History* 65, no. 3 (1978): 836–37, https://doi.org/10.2307/1901512; William C. Ringenberg, *History: Reviews of New Books* 6 (1978): 148; Francis P. Weisenburger, *Indiana Magazine of History* 74, no. 4 (1978): 367–68, http://www.jstor.org/stable/27790338. Volume IV reviews: George W. Knepper, *Indiana Magazine of History* 75, no. 1 (1979): 95–96, http://www.jstor.org/stable/27790359.

[59] Herman B Wells, *Being Lucky: Reflections and Reminiscences* (Bloomington: Indiana University Press, 1980).

[60] Capshew, *Herman B Wells*, 332.

[61] Jordan, *Days of a Man, Being Memories of a Naturalist, Teacher, and Minor Prophet of Democracy*.

publication of *Indiana University: Midwestern Pioneer*, accounts of IU's past have played various roles for the institution and have contributed to the university's identity and integrity. Since the 1970s, a comprehensive IU history has not been attempted, much less written. Perhaps two centuries are too long to cover in sufficient detail or the currents of fashion for microhistory run too swiftly. One can count on, however, institutional history playing a key role in the university's public persona and contributing to the self-understanding of its diverse community.

Part Two: The Campus at Dunn's Woods

Consult the genius of the place in all.

—Alexander Pope, *Epistles to Several Persons*, "Epistle IV: To Richard Boyle, Earl of Burlington"

Figure 6: A bird's eye view of the campus in 1897, a dozen years after the move to Dunn's Woods. From left to right, Maxwell Hall, Carpenter Shop (demolished), Owen Hall, Assembly Hall (demolished), Power Plant (demolished), Wylie Hall, Kirkwood Hall, Mitchell Hall (demolished). © **Jack H. Smith. Image from the IU Archives.**

4 Establishing University Park

Figure 7: Owen Hall (left), Wylie Hall (right)

> Places are fusions of human and natural order and are the significant centres of our immediate experiences of the world. They are defined less by unique locations, landscape, and communities than by the focusing of experiences and intentions onto particular settings. Places are not abstractions or concepts, but are directly experienced phenomena of the lived-world and hence are full with meanings, with real objects, and with ongoing activities. They are important sources of individual and communal identity, and are often profound centres of human existence to which people have deep emotional and psychological ties.
>
> —Edward Relph, *Place and Placelessness*

By the 1880s, Indiana University had occupied the Seminary Square campus for nearly sixty years. Carved out of the forest that was Bloomington in the 1820s, the campus had accommodated a succession of buildings that served the academic needs of the tiny collegiate institution. The ruins of Science Hall, destroyed in the 1883 fire, lay next to the College Building, itself rebuilt in 1855 after an earlier fire. The site had had hard usage and "no attention was given to beautifying the campus," but some trees and shrubs had sprung up on their own after the initial clearing.[1]

The IU Board of Trustees was pleased to be getting away from the dirty clatter of the railroad abutting the campus, away from the industrial machine and back into the peaceful quiet of the woods. Hoosier attitudes had changed since the Seminary Square campus was cleared of trees in frontier Bloomington. Six decades of increasing use of Indiana's forests led to a growing realization that they were not an inexhaustible natural resource, and they deserved conservation for the future. In fact, one of Bloomington's largest employers was the Showers Brothers Furniture Company, which made wooden bedsteads and other furniture.[2] Overall, forests provided essential materials for shelter, fuel, and food, and their magnificent forms dwarfed any manmade structures until the mid-nineteenth century.

[1]Kate M. Hight, "Reminiscences," *Indiana University Alumni Quarterly* 24, no. 4 (1937): 455–60, quote on 455.

[2]Carrol Krause, *Showers Brothers Furniture Company: The Shared Fortunes of a Family, a City, and a University* (Bloomington: Indiana University Press, 2012).

The contrast between Dunn's Woods and the original site was stark, and the move was accompanied by a new appreciation of landscape beauty. Although wood still provided many of the raw materials for daily life, no longer was the forest regarded as an obstacle to civilizing forces, symbolized by a clearing in the wilderness. In a time of widespread deforestation in the state, now the presence of trees was seen as a welcome amenity, a moral counterweight to industrial society, where one could regain a measure of peace and equilibrium by contact with nature. The university's recent purchase was not virgin forest by any stretch, but the unimproved farm woodlot did have mature trees that prompted an aspirational designation as "University Park" by the trustees in June 1884.[3]

The ideas of Frederick Law Olmsted, landscape designer of Central Park in New York City, were spreading around the nation, including to universities and colleges. It was his belief "that the location and design of the campus played an essential role in the students' educational experience" of equal importance with the academic curriculum: "The properly designed campus was part of the civilizing mission of the college or university, educating the taste and sensibilities of students."[4]

The new site contained twenty acres of a gently sloping hill, generally oriented west toward the town, with a small brook. Before the university acquired the land, it was used by local townspeople "chiefly for the practice of outdoor speeches, solitary strolls, and clandestine meetings" with the tacit approval of the property owners.[5] Decisions were made to construct the principal buildings toward the back of the lot, in the northeast corner, oriented at right angles to each other and to have their main entrances facing the woods. Two halls were built of brick recycled from the ruins of Science Hall, and a smaller wood-frame building completed the initial tableau. In keeping with the thirty-year tradition of employing consulting architects, the university hired Indianapolis architect George W. Bunting to design all three.

Ground was broken in spring 1884, and by June, the trustees had chosen building names. The larger of the brick buildings was

[3]The designation of "University Park" died out by 1890.

[4]David Schuyler, "Frederick Law Olmsted and the Origins of Modern Campus Design," *Planning for Higher Education* 25, no. 2 (1996–1997): 1–10, quote on p. 10.

[5]Clarence L. Goodwin, "The *Indiana Student* and Student Life in the Early Eighties," *Indiana University Alumni Quarterly* 17, no. 1 (1930): 155.

designated Wylie Hall, in memory of the first president, Andrew Wylie, and in honor of Theophilus Wylie, a longtime professor. A plaque of gratitude for the financial aid from Monroe County was to be placed in the interior.

The other brick structure was named Owen Hall, for the brothers Robert Dale Owen, David Dale Owen, and Richard Dale Owen, sons of social reformer Robert Owen, famous for a utopian social experiment in New Harmony, Indiana. Still living, Richard was a retired IU professor of natural sciences. His brothers, both deceased, had achieved prominence in their careers.[6]

Given the university's poor financial situation, the trustees simply desired to replicate existing programs and facilities on the Dunn's Woods campus, albeit with new buildings. With the increasing interest in scientific subjects and their demands for laboratory and museum space, Wylie and Owen Halls were devoted to science.

The *Student* newspaper described the remaining structure: "The third, a poor little frame, is used for chapel; [and] stored away in its attic are four or five little rooms, about 12 x 16, where the student must get his philosophy, political economy, literature, languages, & etc."[7]

The city of Bloomington was supportive of the site of the new campus and desired to honor the most distinguished member of the faculty in March 1884: "Since the location of the new University buildings have been known, the citizens, and especially those on 5th street, have been talking of naming that thoroughfare Kirkwood Avenue, in honor of our distinguished townsman, Prof. Kirkwood. Last Friday night a petition was properly presented to the Council, and by a vote the name was so changed. The new University buildings now front on Kirkwood Avenue, if you please."[8]

Soon after campus was opened for classes in 1885, the setting of University Park was highly praised by a local newspaper: "The forest trees in the new college campus now present a scene of true magnificence. Never was there a lovelier scene than the one presented there last Sunday October 1885. It was a lovely Indian summer

[6]Brother Robert was an Indiana politician and statesman, and brother David was a well-known American geologist.

[7]*Student*, February 1886, cited in Clark, *Indiana University*, 1970, 228.

[8]*Bloomington Telephone* 7, no. 46 (March 29, 1884): 1; see also Frank K. Edmondson, "Daniel Kirkwood—'Dean of American Astronomers'," *Mercury* 29, no. 3 (2000): 27–33, quote on p. 32, who mistakenly dated it as 1885.

day, and the earth, the air, the clouds, the sky, and the roseate tints of the stately forest streets seemed to vie with each other in presenting a scene of gorgeousness never excelled by nature."[9]

The contrast between the old and the new campuses became a theme that would resonate and provided a temporal marker of IU history—that is, before or after the move to Dunn's Woods.[10]

4.1 A Sylvan Park

By 1888, after the initial flurry of construction, the trustees wanted to improve the grounds in University Park. To remedy the muddy dirt paths on campus, brick walks leading into the campus and to the buildings were in place by the summer of 1889, and boardwalks were elevated over the low ground in the woods.[11] For advice on planning, they contacted landscape architect Olof Benson, who had been involved in the design of Chicago's Lincoln Park, and arranged a site visit.[12] He spent over a week mapping out the twenty-acre campus and submitted a planning sketch and a report.[13]

Benson, in keeping with the idea of working with nature popularized by Olmsted and his design of Central Park in the 1850s, extolled the native trees growing on the old farm woodlot. Taken by the charm of "graceful groves of round-headed trees on gracefully sloping hillsides," he advised prospective landscape gardeners to highlight the "characteristics of a place and enhance its beauties." He urged protecting the green space for the future: "Everything should be in keeping with the 'Stately Groves.' Nothing should be planted on the

[9]Bloomington *Saturday Courier* cited in Clark, *Indiana University*, 1970, 228.

[10]Naturally, the trustees were concerned with maintaining and protecting the new physical plant. In 1885, they hired John W. Stuart as the janitor of the new campus to be responsible for the heating and lighting systems of the three new university buildings as well as general upkeep. His caretaking extended to campus grounds surrounding the new buildings. He was required to give "his entire attention and time including vacations" to the job. Indiana University Board of Trustees, "Minutes of the Board of Trustees of Indiana University, 03 June 1885–10 June 1885" (Bloomington: Indiana University Archives & Indiana University Libraries Digital Collections Services, June 10, 1885), https://purl.dlib.indiana.edu/iudl/archives/iubot/1885-06-03.

[11]Clark, *Indiana University*, 1970, 228; Clapacs, *Indiana University Bloomington*, 46–47.

[12]See bio of Olof Benson.

[13]The report is in the IU Archives, but the sketch has disappeared. Hearsay located it on an office wall in Maxwell Hall as late as 1916.

grounds, either buildings or trees, that *will belittle* these Patriarchs of the Forest."[14] He went on to give further suggestions, like planting evergreens as a backdrop to the large deciduous trees.

Benson's written report was accompanied by a beautifully rendered hand-drawn, colored sketch of the campus, with potential building sites, walkways and roads, and planting areas identified. A large plot next to Wylie Hall was deemed a suitable site for the main university building, a couple of locations on Third Street were endorsed for buildings of manual training and a physical laboratory, and west of Owen Hall had space for another large building.[15]

Students appreciated the campus as well. In 1889–90, future author Theodore Dreiser spent a year at IU as an eighteen-year-old first-year student. He had been working in the "smoky, noisy city" of Chicago before coming down to Bloomington "where all was green and sweet." He remembered:

> The college campus, while it contained but a few humble and unattractive buildings, was so strewn with great trees and threaded through one corner of it (where I entered by a stile) with a crystal clear brook, that I was entranced. Many a morning on my way to class or at noon on my way out, I have thrown myself down by the side of this stream, stretched out my arms and rested, thinking of the difference between my state here and in Chicago.[16]

Although he did not continue as a student, his year on campus was restorative, and he reported, "my outlook and ambitions were better."[17]

Benson's recommendations affirmed the wisdom of building on the perimeter of the plot. Soon a library building was planned to the west of Owen Hall. Completed in 1890 and named for the Maxwell

---

[14]"Description of the Plan of Improvement of University Park" (Indiana University Archives/C77/B1, 1884).

[15]"Ideas Concerning Campus Plans Change Considerably with Time," *Indiana Daily Student* 41, no. 98 (February 11, 1916): 3.

[16]*A Hoosier Holiday* (New York: John Lane Company, 1916), 489. The stile was probably located at Fourth Street and Indiana Avenue.

[17]490.

family in 1894, it was a handsome and richly ornamented Richardsonian Romanesque interpretation of collegiate Gothic.[18] Designed to hold the library, with its collections still being reconstructed after the 1883 fire, as well as the president's office and some classrooms, the hall became a template for future buildings in its use of limestone for its exterior. Bloomington's location within an extensive belt of high-quality limestone was a boon for the growing campus, providing an ideal building material that could be shaped for academic halls with Gothic features. The library interior featured richly textured native hardwoods fashioned into doors and window frames, stairs and balustrades, and partitions. "About the only natural resource that traveled any distance was sunlight, which illuminated the interiors through skylights, transoms, and tall windows. The grounding presence of nature permeated the campus."[19] Shortly after Maxwell Hall opened, janitor Stuart received a raise and a budget to hire assistants as needed.[20] Student enrollment continued to grow, and by the fall of 1894, it stood at 748.

The next limestone hall, named after Daniel Kirkwood and designed by Parker & Jeckel, an Anderson, Indiana, firm, was finished that fall. It stood next to Wylie Hall, lined up precisely in a so-called Yale Row, pioneered by Yale University, where the early buildings were arrayed in a line facing the town of New Haven's common green. At the dedication in January 1895, professor of philosophy William Bryan spoke: "This is Dedication Day and also Foundation Day. We cannot dedicate and forget the founders.... More directly we are indebted to our own people, to those who cut away these

[18]Both David H. Maxwell and son James Darwin Maxwell were IU trustees in the nineteenth century. For the naming of Maxwell Hall, see Indiana University Board of Trustees, "Minutes of the Board of Trustees of Indiana University, 20 March 1894–23 March 1894" (Bloomington: Indiana University Archives & Indiana University Libraries Digital Collections Services, March 22, 1894), https://purl.dlib.indiana.edu/iudl/archives/iubot/1894-03-20.

[19]Tom Roznowski, "The Trees Grew First: IU's Woodland Campus," *The Ryder*, April 2017, 24–25.

[20]Indiana University Board of Trustees, "Minutes of the Board of Trustees of Indiana University, 11 June 1891–17 June 1891" (Bloomington: Indiana University Archives & Indiana University Libraries Digital Collections Services, June 16, 1891), https://purl.dlib.indiana.edu/iudl/archives/iubot/1891-06-11. By 1898, the budget for Stuart and staff was $2,000. For comparison, the president, Joseph Swain, was receiving $5,000 and full professors' salaries ranged between $2,000 and $2,500; see Indiana University Board of Trustees, "Minutes of the Board of Trustees of Indiana University, 16 November 1898–18 November 1898" (Bloomington: Indiana University Archives & Indiana University Libraries Digital Collections Services, November 18, 1898), https://purl.dlib.indiana.edu/iudl/archives/iubot/1898-11-16.

woods and built a schoolhouse almost as soon as they had built a cabin."[21]

The campus, now consisting of five academic halls, was taking shape, oriented toward the seasonal green of the woods like an oversize Gothic quadrangle. But instead of four buildings enclosing a common lawn in the medieval design, IU was generating a picture frame of buildings around an expanse of forest. A consensus to conserve the woodland was already emerging in the academic community as the first corner of the building design was established.[22] Ubiquitous in southern Indiana, trees were becoming valued for their aesthetic qualities in addition to their myriad practical uses. The Dunn's Woods campus took shape as a ceaseless conversation between limestone architecture and the woodland landscape.

History was part of the conversation as well, both in discourse and in physical artifacts. The university started celebrating Foundation Day in 1889 at the suggestion of President Jordan. David Banta gave annual addresses from 1889 to 1894 on the history of Indiana University. In 1896, eleven years after the move to Dunn's Woods, the old sundial from the Seminary Square campus was moved to the southwest corner of Maxwell Hall. Installed in 1868 near the main entrance on College Avenue and Second Street, the venerable timepiece was "a point of central interest" on the old campus. The move was prompted by a suggestion from the Physics Department to better regulate the electric bells marking the beginning and ending of classes.[23] The sundial came attached to an apocryphal story about President Cyrus Nutt (1860–75) consulting it at night by striking a match to see the time. During daylight, it served as a practical timepiece, although other means of time-telling gradually relegated it to the status of an heirloom souvenir of the old campus. That same year, a pair of gingko trees was planted along the walkway between Owen Hall and Maxwell Hall.[24]

[21]Woodburn, *History of Indiana University*, 1940, 431–32.

[22]Much later enshrined as the Old Crescent, after 1980. See Chapter 6.

[23]Clapacs, *Indiana University Bloomington*, 324; "'Local' column," *Indiana Student*, May 26, 1896, 29.

[24]Edith Hennel Ellis, "The Trees on the I.U. Campus," *Indiana University Alumni Quarterly* 16, no. 3 (1929): 328–31.

4.2 Campustry: Romance in the Woods

The environment for learning was enhanced by the new buildings and surrounding landscape of Dunn's Woods. The woodland was also conducive to extracurricular activities—including one that did not receive official sanction but was common throughout the student body and even faculty members upon occasion. Called "campustry," it was a discipline that most were eager to learn. It meant courting out-of-doors, romance under the trees, building personal relationships in the pastoral setting of the campus.

Campustry at IU began as soon as students encountered each other in the fall of 1885, and written descriptions started appearing in the 1890s. The combination of beautiful surroundings and increasing numbers of students provided a basis for its emergence. Not surprisingly, students wrote about it in the *Arbutus* yearbooks and in the pages of the campus newspaper, the *Indiana Student*, which offered "Information for New Students" as a guide:

> Campustry and chemistry are not the same science. Both offer chances of working, the law of affinity applies to both, both are experimental sciences, both include processes with varying results, in both many fragile articles are broken, but the first science is always more pleasant than the second, and is always more popular with the girls. A class in campustry consists of no more than two members, needs no oversight from the faculty, and recites on the campus. The only requirement for entrance is the prospect of a spring case.[25]

Campustry depended on an appreciation of the scenic value of trees and surrounding vegetation, something southern Indiana was known for. As the former farm woodlot—previously cut for firewood to feed fireplaces and stoves that were still ubiquitous in homes and businesses—was reimagined as a bucolic University Park, students and faculty alike reveled in the natural beauty.

In the 1899 *Arbutus*, a story described campustry as a synergy between human feelings and the natural environment:

[25] *Indiana Student*, April 6, 1901, 12. A "spring case" refers to a springtime infatuation.

> The Indiana University campus is never more attractive than in May. It is then that the leafy, whispering boughs of the maples and sugar trees are most inviting for "campustry," that most fascinating pleasure of college life. The overworked Freshman and the worldly Senior alike finds it refreshing to lounge in the shade at a respectable distance from the recitation rooms in company of a fair maiden. Nothing will more effectively drive away the thoughts of the blunder made last hour or make one forget when the next recitation period begins. The visitor at this time of year will notice "cases of campustry" in all stages of development.[26]

Extravagant practitioners of campustry became the subject of stereotyping and the butt of humor, in similar fashion to college football players, fraternity members, or cheerleaders. An *Indiana Student* writer described some of the qualities of the stereotype, referring to a French nobleman who was in the news in the late 1890s:

> There is one type of undergraduate that is more interesting and more widely known than any other. I refer to that happy-go-lucky individual who parts his hair down the middle and takes a cocktail on the side. He sticks a flower in his buttonhole and a cigarette in his face and imagines himself a superior of Count de Castallane [*sic*] or any other titled foreigner. He is sipping the joys of life and throwing out the dregs. He is a curious combination of saint and sinner, fool and philosopher. He spends fifteen minutes digging on his mathematics and thirty polishing his shoes. You ask him about his work, and he is driven to death. In the forenoon he attends recitations and takes campustry.[27]

Many of these romantic encounters were considered casual and flirtatious, but in some cases, they grew into serious relationships and even marriages. "Instead of frowning on Campustry, the University management and faculty, with the result that for many years one-half of the faculty marriages have been the outgrowth of the 'college case.' " By 1903, the *Daily Student* reported that 68 percent of the IU faculty were married to Indiana girls.[28]

[26]"Balls and Strikes: A Story," *Arbutus*, 1899, 174–79.
[27]*Indiana Student*, April 1, 1898, 53.
[28]"The Decline of Campustry," *Daily Student*, November 11, 1903.

Not all of the IU students at the turn of the century practiced campustry, however. For instance, in 1898–99, Carrie Parker, the university's first African American female student, did not have time to cavort in the woods as she labored for room and board in the house of a professor and his wife. There were also reports of "immoral students" in Dunn's Woods.[29]

Although campustry proved to be a durable tradition for nearly a quarter century, it faded with the advent of collegiate sports, the rise of automobile transportation, and changing student fashion. Even the word *campustry* atrophied through disuse and eventually disappeared from collective memory.

4.3 Campus Planning and Design

In early 1896, David Mottier, a professor of botany on leave in Europe, wrote to his department colleague, Joseph Pierce, to discuss how the department might use a greenhouse for teaching and research, but he thought there was no need for an extensive botanical garden because of the natural setting of the campus. He added:

> It is a pity, too, that the Trustees do not make an effort to annex the portion of woods just east of the campus. That would be a good place to transplant and prevent from becoming extinct many of the wild plants which must soon pass into history with the present destruction of the forests and their conversion in sheep pasture etc.... That the acquisition of the woods on the east to the campus as a part of this garden is a necessity and likewise their duty. I think that plot of ground with its matchless forest trees could be made the most beautiful campus in the country.[30]

Mottier, once he returned to campus, became an ardent proponent for the preservation of native plants for both their scientific value and their inherent beauty.

[29]David Mottier to President Bryan in 1911, reported in Thomas D. Clark, *Indiana University: Midwestern Pioneer: Volume II: In Mid-Passage*, 4 vols. (Bloomington: Indiana University Press, 1973), p. 14.

[30]David Mottier, "Letter to Joseph Pierce" (Indiana University Archives C174/B31/F Mottier, David, February 13, 1896).

In the same year, President Joseph Swain hired Olmsted, Olmsted, and Eliot to get advice on further campus improvements. The firm, headed by the two sons of Frederick Law Olmsted, the designer of New York's Central Park, and the son of Charles W. Eliot, the president of Harvard, was the most distinguished landscape architect partnership in America.[31] Their twenty-three-page report started with five pages arguing that the university should purchase additional land for the campus now in preparation for growth. "In other words it is better that the University should control more land than it actually needs at the time," they wrote, "rather than be crippled afterwards for lack of room, or rather than that it should be compelled to pay exorbitant prices for land when actually needed."[32]

The report did not include a topographical map or architectural plans for specific buildings but presented a general overview of planning considerations for campus design. The recommendations included having one dominant building material, placing the administration building at the main campus entrance, lecture halls and laboratory buildings divided by function, a library that would have room to grow, specialized discipline collections rather than a general museum, conveniently located gymnasium and athletic fields, a botanical greenhouse and garden ("not less than two or three acres and better ten or twenty acres"), and steam heating with central boilers and conveyed through dry tunnels. The report commented: "It has not been the custom of our State Universities to furnish dormitories, but there seems to be no good reason why they should not be provided." They recommended, if built, the dormitories should not be over three stories tall and have a "domestic aspect" somewhere between "a city hotel and a suburban villa."[33]

Under the heading "Water Supply," the report stated, "We understand that the present city supply is at times inadequate and not always attractive in appearance, if altogether wholesome." They suggested drilling an artesian well supply to be pumped to a water tower, "all under the direct control by the University," and touted

[31]For a history of the firm, see Olmsted Firm.

[32]Olmsted, Olmsted, and Eliot, "Letter to Joseph Swain" (Indiana University Archives C174/B32/F Olmsted, Olmsted, and Eliot—Campus Plan 1896, December 8, 1896).

[33]Olmsted, Olmsted, and Eliot.

its value in case of fire. Care must be taken, they cautioned, to locate the tower away from campus.[34]

As far as vegetation, "the general landscape character of the university should be that of a shady grove with the ground covered with turf only," which would include shrubbery around building foundations. Concerned with the thinning of the forest by natural causes over the following ten to twenty years, they recommended planting replacement trees. Native trees were preferable for two reasons: "they are better adapted to the climate and soil, and also because they look more appropriate."[35]

The trustees received the report and took the advice to buy more land to heart. The next year, they purchased another thirty acres of the old Dunn farm, surrounding Dunn's Woods on all but the south boundary of Third Street. The campus now extended to Indiana Avenue, Seventh Street, and what is now Hawthorne Avenue. The additional land extended Dunn's Woods to the west, brought additional woodlands to the east, and included a creek—Spanker's Branch—and a meadow to the north. The purchase included a growing giant burr oak and a large beech tree on opposite sides of the creek.[36]

By the end of 1897, the size of the campus had increased 150 percent, to fifty acres, leaving ample room to grow the 600-student university.[37] Money to pay for new buildings would have to wait a few years, but tree planting and other landscaping efforts could be started immediately. And now the athletics teams had a convenient field, named Jordan Field in honor of the former president, to play sports rather than trekking to the athletics field on the old campus.[38]

Within this purchase area, the Dunn Cemetery, on the south bank of Spanker's Branch, was excluded. Deeded for perpetual use as a family burial ground in 1855, the land was originally acquired by Samuel Dunn Jr. as part of a 160-acre homestead. The remains of three Revolutionary War heroines were buried here—Ellenor

[34]Olmsted, Olmsted, and Eliot.

[35]Olmsted, Olmsted, and Eliot.

[36]The bur oak, located at the north entrance to the Indiana Memorial Union commons, is still alive; the beech tree was removed when the Tudor Room was built in 1957.

[37]Myers, *History of Indiana University*, 1952, 755.

[38]Clapacs, *Indiana University Bloomington*, 384–87.

(Brewster) Dunn, who was Samuel Dunn Jr.'s mother, and her sisters, Agnes (Brewster) Alexander and Jennet (Brewster) Irwin. Old gravestones, grass, and a few trees gave the space, popularly known as "God's Little Acre," the peace it deserved as the campus developed around it.[39]

With the increase in land area, janitor Stuart's title was changed to superintendent of buildings and grounds.[40] After a decade and a half of working, Stuart resigned in the spring of 1899, and the president and the trustees conveyed "their appreciation of his long and faithful service" to the campus.[41] That spring, William R. Ogg was among the workers hired to help with the physical plant.[42] Ogg was the brother of Robert A. Ogg, who was serving as an alumni trustee.[43] Like Stuart, he managed both buildings and grounds. Ogg performed all of the outside work by himself "with only the aid of a wheelbarrow."[44]

In May 1899, President Swain received a letter from Rudolph Ulrich, a landscape architect who was making his name working on gardens for national expositions around the country, offering his services.[45]

---

[39]Clapacs, 320–21.

[40]Indiana University Board of Trustees, "Minutes of the Board of Trustees of Indiana University, 04 November 1897–06 November 1897" (Bloomington: Indiana University Archives & Indiana University Libraries Digital Collections Services, November 5, 1897), https://purl.dlib.indiana.edu/iudl/archives/iubot/1897-11-04.

[41]Indiana University Board of Trustees, "Minutes of the Board of Trustees of Indiana University, 23 March 1899–25 March 18997" (Bloomington: Indiana University Archives & Indiana University Libraries Digital Collections Services, March 25, 1899), https://purl.dlib.indiana.edu/iudl/archives/iubot/1899-03-23.

[42]Indiana University Board of Trustees.

[43]Robert Ogg served as a trustee from 1896 to 1902. When Ogg's brother Robert died in 1936, President Bryan remembered the brothers: "Robert A. Ogg and William R. Ogg—they were brothers on a farm more than eighty years ago. It was decided within the family that one of the brothers could go to college. Many a time, often through storms and over roads when the mud was bottomless, the brother who was to stay on the farm brought to Bloomington the brother who was to have the great prize of a college education. Graduation day of 1872 came bringing glory to Robert and unselfish happiness to William and to all of the family." Bryan quoted in "In Memoriam: William A. Rawles, '84, Robert A. Ogg, '72, William T. Patten, '93; and Necrology List," *Indiana University Alumni Quarterly* 23, no. 3 (1936): 303–13, pp. 309–310.

[44]"Football Men Wore Mustaches When He Came to University," *Indiana Daily Student* 50, no. 56 (December 3, 1921): 2.

[45]Ulrich (1840–1906), a German-born landscape architect, worked with Frederick Law Olmsted laying out the grounds of Chicago's 1893 World Columbian

With the recent increase in campus size from twenty to fifty acres, the trustees hired Ulrich. He visited the campus and eventually produced a highly detailed sketch of his suggested building sites, roads and pathways, and other facilities. The campus site was square shaped, bounded by Indiana Avenue on the west; Third and Seventh Streets on the south and north, respectively; and Forest Avenue (now Hawthorne Avenue) on the east. The plan, produced in 1902, showed several sites for buildings that were eventually constructed around the edges of the quadrangle (Student, Science, Biology, Commerce and Finance) as well as two sites within the woods that were not used.[46]

The construction of the campus observatory in 1900, named for Daniel Kirkwood, within Dunn's Woods indicated the administration's priorities about land use. The woods at the heart of the campus, beautiful as they were, could be built on if necessary. Landscape designers such as Ulrich were employed to give ideas about future development. IU did not have the financial resources to implement many of the suggestions immediately, but it was helpful to know the latest thinking of landscape professionals. Ulrich's concept for the recently acquired Dunn Meadow included an "Arboretum with Experimental Garden" and a string of three small lakes fed by Spanker's Branch, which never went beyond the planning map. Having experience working with local government authorities, he offered to meet with City of Bloomington officials in the hopes of awakening "their interest in the improvements, which if completed, at least to a certain extent, could be used as a Public Park [and] be a great adornment to the University & City."[47]

Professor Mottier wrote to his old colleague psychologist William Bryan, who had just been named the new president of IU in November 1902, and followed up on some of Ulrich's recommendations, including his support of a botanical area along the meadow near Seventh Street. Mottier reported that "a number of trees," mostly hard maple, had been transplanted on the campus over the previous few years. "These young maple trees together with the older ones

Exposition. Rudolph Ulrich, "Letter to Joseph Swain" (Indiana University Archives C174/B44, May 1899).

[46]See "R. Ulrich plan of campus with proposed locations of future buildings, walkways, etc." The current names are: Student = Frances Morgan Swain Student Building; Science = Ernest H. Lindley Hall; Biology = Joseph Swain Hall East; and Commerce and Finance = William A. Rawles Hall.

[47]See "R. Ulrich plan of campus with proposed locations of future buildings, walkways, etc."

will preserve the original character of the primitive forest," he stated. But he worried about the cost of fulfilling Ulrich's excellent planting scheme. Instead, Mottier suggested that trees be obtained from the surrounding countryside at little to no cost and that groundskeeper Ogg and his assistants continue to transplant them. Mottier praised Ogg on his diligence: "With constant care and vigilance he had kept alive under adverse conditions transplanted trees that with ordinary care would have perished."[48]

Another element of stone was added to the campus landscape in 1902—a low wall of limestone along the Third Street south campus boundary. Inspired by a limestone wall of the residence of Joseph Swain, the outgoing president, the trustees arranged to have a similar one constructed.[49]

After five years of dependable service, in 1904 William Ogg's title was changed to keeper of the grounds.[50] Ogg developed an effective partnership with Mottier to preserve and enhance the campus landscape. The student newspaper wrote about Mottier's efforts as head of the university's campus committee to make the grounds the "most beautiful in the country." The article noted that several hundred native trees had been planted over the previous two years.[51]

Over time, generations of students and faculty interacted with the modest gardener Ogg as he went about his daily work, and he became a beloved figure of the campus community. In addition to planting flowers and trees that "brightened the lives of those who

---

[48]David Mottier, "Letter to William Bryan" (Indiana University Archives C174/B31/F Mottier, David, November 5, 1902).

[49]Indiana University Board of Trustees, "Minutes of the Board of Trustees of Indiana University, 24 March 1902–25 March 1902" (Bloomington: Indiana University Archives & Indiana University Libraries Digital Collections Services, March 25, 1902), https://purl.dlib.indiana.edu/iudl/archives/iubot/1902-03-24; Indiana University Board of Trustees, "Minutes of the Board of Trustees of Indiana University, 03 September 1902–15 September 1902" (Bloomington: Indiana University Archives & Indiana University Libraries Digital Collections Services, September 6, 1902), https://purl.dlib.indiana.edu/iudl/archives/iubot/1902-09-03.

[50]Indiana University Board of Trustees, "Minutes of the Board of Trustees of Indiana University, 16 June 1904–22 June 1904" (Bloomington: Indiana University Archives & Indiana University Libraries Digital Collections Services, June 22, 1904), https://purl.dlib.indiana.edu/iudl/archives/iubot/1904-06-16.

[51]"Campus Improvements Due to Prof. Mottier," *Indiana Daily Student*, February 5, 1904, 1.

took the campus paths," he was approachable as he performed his duties. "Many a one has gone out of his way a little just to have a chat with Mr. Ogg, their friend," with his steady and accepting demeanor, talking "with people in his calm, pleasant and manly way."[52]

In 1904, Eugene "Dick" Kerr was appointed superintendent of buildings and grounds at the university, following a career as a Bloomington police officer and service as the city's fire department chief. As the campus expanded, he oversaw all phases of construction and maintenance of the physical plant and became a stalwart adviser to President Bryan and the board of trustees.[53]

4.4 New Buildings for Science and for Students

Rising enrollments led to the construction of a new building on the eastern line of halls (Wylie and Kirkwood) dedicated to education and research in science. Mitchell Hall, the 1885 frame building, was moved a couple of hundred feet east to make room for Science Hall. In January 1903 during Foundation Day activities, President William Bryan, an experimental psychologist who had just been elected president of the American Psychological Association, delivered his inaugural address and the building's dedication. The limestone building, with specialized laboratories for research and instruction, was finished in rough-faced ashlar in regular courses. With its many windows and symmetrical design, it presented an austerely modern appearance.[54]

The Swain presidential administration also planned a women's building. With the rise of female enrollment to nearly a third

[52]Indiana University Board of Trustees, "Minutes of the Board of Trustees of Indiana University, 01 October 1948–02 October 1948" (Bloomington: Indiana University Archives & Indiana University Libraries Digital Collections Services, October 1, 1948), https://purl.dlib.indiana.edu/iudl/archives/iubot/1948-10-01.

[53]"No man within my knowledge has given a more honest, skillful, successful and devoted service to Indiana University than Eugene Kerr. He knew what to do. He knew how. He knew how to make men work hard and like the work and like him. He was every inch a man," William Lowe Bryan's tribute to Kerr at his death.

[54]Clapacs, *Indiana University Bloomington*, 38–41.

of the student body by the turn of the century, President and Mrs. Swain advocated for space to serve the needs of women students: a gymnasium, an auditorium, meeting rooms, and lounges. The planned building was not a candidate for state funding, however, so a student-centered capital campaign was started, and $50,000 was raised, from 2,000 donors. President Swain solicited funds from John D. Rockefeller Jr., who agreed to give an additional $50,000 provided that a wing for male students be included.[55]

Some writers have rightfully stressed its importance as an intentional space for women students and the role of private philanthropy in funding the building, albeit with a change in conception to serve the entire student body. Fewer have noted its salutary effect on the campus environment. The building became a signature structure not only for its striking design and its red-tiled roof but also for its monolithic clock tower and sonorous chimes. The bells transformed the soundscape of the quadrangle, adding a new element that supplemented the auditory environment emanating from the campus. The typical sounds of the campus—wind whistling through trees, birds singing, the crack of thunder, the patter of rain, students talking, the hush of snowfall, squirrels chattering—was augmented at regular intervals by pealing bells.

The bronze bells, funded by a campaign jointly mounted by the classes of 1899, 1900, 1901, and 1902, numbered eleven, the largest of them four feet in diameter. After installation, the bells were struck every quarter hour, playing the traditional "Westminster Quarters" melody, followed by strikes for the number of the hour. In 1906, President Bryan requested that IU's alma mater be played every day at six o'clock. Bells added something special to the campus experience, as one student from the class of 1909 recalled: "I wondered if there really was such a thing as college spirit, and whether it would ever descend on me. Suddenly, the chimes pealed forth in the old college tune. My heart leaped up and as the tone of the last verse died away in the distance, I almost shouted, 'Dear old Indiana!' "[56]

The Student Building tower harkened back to medieval times when sound was used to mark the hours, and clockfaces were added later for visual reference. The large four-sided Seth Thomas clock,

[55]Clapacs, 42–45.

[56]Myers, *History of Indiana University*, 1952, 38–44; Clapacs, *Indiana University Bloomington*, 42–45.

illuminated at night like a full moon, was a boon for students who did not carry pocket watches. And everybody in earshot received a message, often subliminal, about the passage of time—and the reminder that time was passing as well.

As the campus matured, attentive students took notice of its design integrity and natural beauty. In the 1906 *Arbutus* yearbook, one finds an articulation of IU's spirit of place by an anonymous student author:

> "Indiana has the most beautiful campus in the West;" these are the words that visitors are so often heard to remark. The great wooded slope, crowned with the six large halls situated in the form of an "L," never fails in its first impression. If seen in the summer the foliage is dense, and through it and in contrast with it appear the gray limestone buildings. In winter the view is often more beautiful than that in summer. Just after a heavy fall of snow the ice-laden trees are brilliant in the sunshine. In autumn the grounds are one mass of crimson and yellow leaves from the beeches and maples.
>
> This campus which impresses the visitor when he looks upon it, completely wins the heart of the student who spends four years here. Each has his favorite nook to which he likes to retire in spring and autumn. Perhaps the most secluded of these retreats is the little plot of ground know as God's Acre. It is situated in a clump of trees on the Jordan River. Around the plot runs a stone fence. Inside are a score or so of graves, covered by trailing vines....
>
> Everything about the University has a distinctive appearance. It is "Indiana-like." Once impressed upon the student it does not leave him. What we learn here may pass from our minds, even the images of familiar faces may grow dim, but the Indiana Campus, with its natural scenery, its loved retreats, and its well-remembered trysting places will not be forgotten.[57]

In two decades of occupancy under four presidents, the campus, using locally sourced materials in a classic design, had developed into a pleasing and harmonious whole.

[57] *Arbutus*, June 1906, 388–90.

Alumna author Edith Hennel Ellis, a member of the class of 1911, expressed her appreciation of the campus landscape, especially the many trees. She reiterated the common feeling that "its natural charm was the chief asset of the campus" and collectively thanked the individuals who were responsible for preserving that beauty. A sharp observer, she talked about campus design considerations with respect to department faculty who directly shaped planting regimes—and often supplied the physical labor. Ellis singled out botany professor Mottier, "who has real genius in landscaping," for special treatment. He and his colleagues "have actually raised and with their own hands transplanted to the campus hundreds of trees necessary in the process of reforestation."[58]

Ellis noted that native plants were preferred, but the occasional imports, like the ginkgo trees between Owen Hall and Maxwell Hall, planted in 1896, provided welcome variety. "The campus is virtually a catalogue of trees native to this region," she wrote. "One can find beechnuts, hazelnuts, walnuts, chestnuts, hickory nuts, butternuts, haws, locust, black currants, service berries—practically every tree and shrub used by the Indians and early settler for nuts and fruits."[59] She paid homage to groundskeeper Ogg and his associates: "The men who have worked with nature to preserve the beauty of the campus may well glory in their work. Like the saints of old, their shadow has blessed all on whom it has fallen."[60]

4.5 Enfolding the Woods

In addition to the sundial that was moved in 1896, other souvenirs of the old campus were incorporated into the Dunn's Woods campus. In 1907, trustee Theodore F. Rose volunteered to pay for a decorative well house to be constructed over the campus cistern between Maxwell Hall and the woods. Equipped with a hand pump and a tin cup, it provided drinking water to the campus community. Previously, the cistern played a role in fighting a major fire in 1900 that destroyed the tower of Wylie Hall. The *Daily Student* newspaper enthused about the plan: "Among all the buildings which will ultimately adorn the University, there will be none so suggestive of sacreder [*sic*] reminiscences to the old student and so pregnant

[58]Ellis, "The Trees on the I.U. Campus," 329.
[59]Ellis, 329.
[60]Ellis, 331.

of possibility for the new as the beautiful new well-house which the trustees will erect on the site of the present cistern pump."[61]

Professor of physics Arthur Foley, who consulted on campus building plans and engineering improvements, executed an eclectic design for the Well House, incorporating the 1855 limestone portals from the College Building, the oldest survivor from the early days of the university, still in use as the Bloomington High School.

Although it had a utilitarian use, the Well House harkened back to eighteenth-century English estate garden follies—fanciful structures devised as ornaments to the grounds. The trustees were interested in the plan to reuse the old portals, and Rose offered to pay the entire cost and dedicate it on behalf of the alumni.[62] Rose, who graduated in 1875, was a member of an early IU fraternity, Beta Theta Pi, and the footprint of the structure was an elongated octagon, mirroring the shape of the fraternity pin.

Once constructed, the Well House was a magnet for student activities that had little to do with classwork. Placed next to the woods on a main path, it welcomed the entire campus community to slake their thirst. It also served as a social center and meeting place for undergraduates. In 1912, a fictional story—"Drinking Fountain at I.U."—was published in the *Indiana Student* featuring a first-year coed searching for a drink of water after studying in the library. The water in the library lavatory seemed unpotable, so she went, in turn, to the Student Building, Maxwell Hall, and Kirkwood Hall, to no avail. Spotting men students loafing and smoking around the Well House, she decided not to go there. She found an old water pump near Maxwell Hall, got over her fear of germs, and used a rusty tin cup and "quaffed a deep, satisfying draught of the cool, crystal water." "How foolish of me," she said. "It is I who am not up to date. Indiana is following the style of preserving 'old things.' Before long we will have a real, old-fashioned old-oaken-bucket well."[63]

---

[61]"Well-House Innovation," *Daily Student*, October 15, 1907, 1, 6.

[62]Mrs. Rose was the granddaughter of President Andrew Wylie. Indiana University Board of Trustees, "Minutes of the Board of Trustees of Indiana University, 19 June 1908–23 June 1908" (Bloomington: Indiana University Archives & Indiana University Libraries Digital Collections Services, June 22, 1908), https://purl.dlib.indiana.edu/iudl/archives/iubot/1908-06-19.

[63]"Drinking Fountain at I.U." *Indiana Daily Student*, March 9, 1912. The football tradition to award the "Old Oaken Bucket" to the winner of the IU vs. Purdue game was begun in 1925.

The best-known student tradition associated with the Well House was kissing. Built as an open-air pavilion with a roof, the structure provided a refuge that afforded some privacy on campus and a protected lookout. There is ample evidence that it was soon the site of dates, the exchange of fraternity pins, and, as social mores allowed, hugging and kissing. In a review of campus traditions, student Marvin Shamon noted that first-year students learned about the Well House kissing tradition. Undergraduate women were not considered as true coeds until they kissed at "this famous campus shrine for the full twelve strokes of midnight...it has been observed that the chimes of the Student Building clock seem to have a more mellow and full ring to them at midnight than at any other time."[64]

In addition to the Well House, another building was being constructed at the same time—a new library. The library, located in Maxwell Hall since 1890, had run out of space, and burgeoning enrollments made this project imperative.[65] The university drew up plans for a building twice the size of Maxwell Hall and requested $250,000 from the state legislature for construction costs. The legislature appropriated $100,000. Librarian William Jenkins made a fact-finding tour of the best libraries in the country and consulted with President Bryan to plan a building to which additions could be made over time. Patton and Miller, a Chicago architecture firm that had built more than one hundred Carnegie community libraries, oversaw construction.

Located west of the Student Building, on the corner of Indiana and Kirkwood Avenues, near the main entrance to campus, the library completed the north row of buildings framing the quadrangle. The sizable reading room presented design challenges:

> Construction of the University Library was delayed when the contractor and then also the architects stated that they did not know how to make the ceiling of the large reading room of one concrete slab in such a manner that the structure would be safe. A Chicago engineer called in consultation was likewise unable to give satisfactory

[64]Marvin Shamon, "The Traditions of Indiana University" (Indiana University Archives/Reference file: Buildings—Bloomington Campus Well House, Rose., c1935?).

[65]From 1884–85, when attendance was 157, to twenty-five years later, in 1909–10, when 2,562 students were in attendance. Myers, *History of Indiana University*, 1952, p. 85.

> advice. We then asked three of our professors—Lyons (Chemistry), Foley (Physics), Miller (Analytic Mechanics)—to consider the problem. They made the necessary chemical and mathematical studies and submitted plans and specifications for a safe construction. These were adopted and building proceeded accordingly.[66]

When the building was completed in December 1907, the books were moved during winter break. In March 1908, President Bryan noted approvingly that the use of the library had jumped at least 25 percent. He boasted that the 200-seat reading room had been filled to capacity already, and "the great reading room is the lightest and quietest reading room of the size I know of and compares favorably in attractiveness of any similar room in the country."[67]

The University Library was the biggest building on campus, and its distinctive English Gothic style mixed with Jacobean features in native limestone supplied an anchoring presence. Its red-tiled roof provided visual continuity to the neighboring Student Building. The university seal was carved high in the south-facing gable, "announcing the motto *Lux et Veritas*—light and truth—to all who pass."[68]

In 1909, another science building, dedicated to biology, was among the priorities of the university's budget request to the state legislature. The general assembly granted $80,000, about a third of the amount requested. A decision was made to place the building near Third Street, southwest of Science Hall, to start another side of the frame of buildings enclosing Dunn's Woods. The primary entrance faced the woods to the north; the south entrance was on Third Street. This would be the eighth academic hall constructed in the quadrangle since the campus was opened a quarter-century earlier. Robert Frost Daggett was the architect. With simple but effective symmetry in collegiate Gothic design executed in limestone, the building was the first on the south campus boundary. A faculty space committee decided that the Department of Botany would occupy the first floor and the Department of Zoology the third floor, with the Department of English on the second. Because of a

[66]Robert E. Lyons, Arthur L. Foley, John A. Miller. Myers, pp. 34–35.
[67]Myers, 47.
[68]Clapacs, *Indiana University Bloomington*, 50.

continuing campus space shortage, Biology Hall was populated in the middle of the 1910 fall semester.[69]

In April 1910, a 200-year-old tree was destroyed to make way for the heating plant tunnel, and the editor of the *Indiana Daily Student* was incensed. "None of the natural growth of trees," he fulminated, "are less than 125 years old. Storms and decay are destroying the magnificent trees at a rate of six a year."[70] Apparently, student reporters were not aware of the continuing efforts of Ogg and Mottier to replant native trees.

4.6 University Lake

When the campus moved from Seminary Square to Dunn's Woods, cisterns and wells supplied water, but as the institution grew, it came to depend on Bloomington's water utility. The city was between two forks of the White River rather than on a lake or river. Beginning in the mid-1890s, a series of dams was created to form artificial lakes on the town's southwestern outskirts. But the limestone bedrock was full of sinkholes and underground streams, so the lakes were leaky, and the water plants proved inadequate.[71] By the 1903–04 academic year, the trustees were in meetings with the city administration, and they decided to have two additional wells dug on campus. By 1908, the situation had escalated. "What had long been an inconvenience and annoyance now had become a great menace," wrote Burton Myers, dean of IU Bloomington School of Medicine, as the administration began to take steps to provide the university with its own independent water supply.[72]

In 1909, the Indiana legislature appropriated $20,000 for a university water supply. IU geology professors advised looking at the northeastern outskirts of Bloomington, where limestone karst gave way to sandstone formations that were less permeable. Test wells

[69] Myers, *History of Indiana University*, 1952, 149–53; Clapacs, *Indiana University Bloomington*, 58–61.

[70] Much later, Thomas Clark took issue with that estimate, stating that Mottier and Ogg had been planting native trees from the university's nursery for the last decade. "This gave the appearance that the trees had sprouted from seed where they stood," (*Indiana University*, 1973), p. 14.

[71] Stephen S. Visher, "Water Supply Problems of Bloomington, Indiana," *Proceedings of the Indiana Academy of Science* 66 (1956): 188–91.

[72] *History of Indiana University*, 1952, 270–71.

were dug in the Griffy Creek valley, but they proved inadequate, so a narrow gorge farther up the valley was dammed. Additional funds were appropriated in the following years to raise the height of the dam and to purchase the 250 acres of land surrounding the impoundment.[73]

After the dam was completed in 1914, a coal-powered waterworks plant was built, and pipes were laid to campus a mile away. The sixteen-acre reservoir, dubbed University Lake, supplied the needs of IU's physical plant, but water shortages still affected students and staff because their residences were served by the inadequate Bloomington water utility. Governor Samuel Ralston grew irritated at the city's failure and threatened removal of the university: "The water situation in Bloomington is very serious. I have about made up my mind as Governor to ask the legislature to take account of the situation and, if necessary, to remove the University from its present site."[74]

Public opinion was galvanized, and the Bloomington water utility constructed a reservoir downstream of University Lake, damming the main channel of Griffy Creek. The resulting Lake Griffy was completed in the mid-1920s and solved the community's chronic water shortage.[75] For a time, University Lake was popular among students as a hiking destination and for picnics.[76] Although it was institutional property and it served the university infrastructure, it was not considered part of the campus proper.

4.7 Three Decades in the Woods

In November 1913, botanist David Mottier teamed with Ulysses Hanna, a mathematics professor, to submit a report to the IU Board of Trustees, "Suggestions on the Improvement of the East Campus." Referring to a twenty-one-acre plot east of the quadrangle purchased a few months before, the faculty members' recommendation was for a forest landscape like the original University Quadrangle. They

[73]For a description of the dam, see E. R. Cumings, "The Geological Conditions of Municipal Water Supply in the Driftless Area of Southern Indiana," *Proceedings of the Indiana Academy of Science* 21 (1911): 124–29, https://journals.indianapolis.iu.edu/index.php/ias/article/view/14025.

[74]Myers, *History of Indiana University*, 1952, 273.

[75]Myers, 270–90.

[76]Myers, 270–90; Clark, *Indiana University*, 1973, 32–38.

envisioned a second quadrangle of buildings, a garden, and an athletic field, with the possibility of a small lake from the damming of a tributary of Spanker's Branch.[77] No action was taken on the report, and the purchase of another twenty-six acres in the vicinity the next year prompted a search for a landscape architect.

With rising enrollment as well as the growing popularity of college athletics, campus sentiment was in favor of a new gymnasium. The existing gym, built in 1896, was already too small. A wooden structure, it was located awkwardly east of Owen Hall, right outside of the quadrangle.

In December 1914, the trustees prepared a report to the governor and the visiting committee about this urgent priority. Reflecting conventional wisdom about the foundational role of physical education, the report stated, "It is needed by all the men of the University; not only by those who take part in athletics, but still more by the hundreds and thousands who do not take part in athletics."[78] In addition to a new gymnasium, several other construction needs were mentioned, including an education building, an administration building, an auditorium, a library addition, and a dormitory for women.[79] It would take the next quarter century to accomplish these building projects.

By 1915, the Bryan administration had successfully established the School of Medicine, with its program split between Bloomington and Indianapolis, and dealt with steadily rising enrollments. A fine physical plant had developed over thirty years. It boasted eight substantial academic halls, plus a gymnasium, an observatory, and a well house, arranged in an expansive quadrangle with Dunn's Woods at the center. The aspirational label "University Park" faded quickly, but the conservationist ethos did not. It aligned with the repeated financial exigencies presented by meager state funding as well as the pioneer "make do" attitude. There were still building sites on the great quadrangle that framed Dunn's Woods, plus more undeveloped land, on the 118-acre campus.

[77] David Mottier and Ulysses S. Hanna, "Suggestions on the Improvement of the East Campus" (Indiana University Archives C174/B31/F Mottier, David, November 10, 1913). Report to IU Board of Trustees.

[78] Myers, *History of Indiana University*, 1952, 171.

[79] Myers, 172.

5 Beyond the Quadrangle

Figure 8: Indiana Memorial Union

> The numerous symbolic references that have marked the history of universities are also captured in "placemaking." The arrangements and styles of buildings and spaces on a given territory are cultural glue. They attract and fix student and faculty loyalties. In fractured disciplinary environments, they create a sense of the whole being greater than any of its parts. They provide continuity: emotional and sentimental anchors in a world where experiences are fleeting. They unite the generations, keeping graduates close to the institution.
>
> —Sheldon Rothblatt, "A Note on the 'Integrity' of the University"

Academic rhythms change slowly—the school calendar and class meeting times; commencement and summer school; the progression of freshman, sophomore, junior, senior. The tempo of campus development has a different cadence, however. As new buildings and facilities are planned, constructed, and occupied, the calculus of possibilities is always changing. Likewise, when areas of green nature are marked, modified, preserved, or enhanced, new horizons of potentiality are revealed. Taken together, the man-made (human) and the natural (nonhuman) exist in a dynamic relationship.

As an intentional community of learning, by 1915 IU was settling into the campus it had occupied for a third of its ninety years as an institution. One sign of healthy growth was student enrollment, which in 1915 stood at 1,600—eight times as many as in 1885. Handsome limestone halls were arrayed around the original plot of Dunn's Woods, and the campus footprint had grown to nearly 120 acres—six times larger than the original plot in 1885. The academic program was expanding with the creation of new professional schools and the offering of graduate work.

Concerned about reaching potential students who were not able to come to the Bloomington campus, President William Bryan established the Extension Division in 1914, which offered college courses as well as other educational services to citizens of the state. Aided by the advent of the automobile to augment the excellent intrastate rail services, Bloomington faculty traveled to many Indiana cities and towns to offer classes and programs. The extension programs filled a need, and by the mid-1920s, the number of statewide enrollments exceeded the student body in Bloomington.

The Bryan administration took steps to mobilize the growing number of living alumni. The Society of the Alumni had been formed in 1854 in response to the devastating campus fire that destroyed the main academic hall. Since that time, efforts to rouse this group to provide moral and financial support to the university had been successful but sporadic. Now there were some two thousand alumni, and their ranks swelled by several hundred each year at commencement. Keeping alumni informed about the university as well as their particular graduating class was a key part of the mobilization strategy. In 1914, a new publication was launched—the *Indiana University Alumni Quarterly*—designed to have broad appeal to former students as well as friends of the university. A special section titled "Alumni Notes" in the magazine was dedicated to news of former students, arranged by graduation year.

In 1915, John W. Cravens, university registrar and secretary to the board of trustees, wrote a note in the new *Alumni Quarterly* after the recent purchase of additional land for the campus. He praised the work of botany professor David Mottier and the campus committee, who had been helping to enhance the campus landscape by planting native trees and shrubs for well over a decade. "As a result," Cravens declared, "Indiana University has one of the most beautiful campuses in the country. Its hollows, hills, and level places, primeval forests and recently planted trees, make the campus very attractive. There is a charm about the campus that stays with one through his entire life. When a person has once been on the campus of Indiana University he is forever afterwards enthusiastic about its many entrancing features."[1] Perhaps not surprisingly, an alumnus and employee of Indiana University expressed these sentiments.

Another former student, novelist Theodore Dreiser, who attended during the 1889–90 school year, paid a visit to Bloomington in 1915 and marveled at the changes that had occurred since he last saw the campus twenty-five years before: "After this came the university, wholly changed, but far more attractive than it had been in my day—a really beautiful school. I could find only a few things—Wylie Hall, the brook, a portion of some building which had formerly been our library. It had been so added to that it was

[1] "History of University Land Purchases," *Indiana University Alumni Quarterly* 2, no. 2 (1915): 159; land purchases are summarized in Myers, *History of Indiana University*, 1952, 755.

scarcely recognizable."[2] Many new academic halls and supporting infrastructure served the growing student body, five times the size it was during Dreiser's day, and the campus footprint had expanded nearly sixfold, to 117 acres.

5.1 A New Gymnasium

What had begun with the right-angle placement of Owen Hall and Wylie Hall in 1885 had developed into a large quadrangle, with the center green provided by trees rather than grass. Orderly rows of buildings framing the woods were complete on two sides and had been started on the other two—along Third Street and along Indiana Avenue. The main entrance to campus remained on Kirkwood Avenue, next to the 1908 University Library. With the recent availability of more campus land lying northeast of the quadrangle, including the Dunn family homestead, there was room to grow.

In 1915, the trustees decided that a new gymnasium would be the next building erected on campus, and they selected a site in the old apple orchard adjacent to the Dunn family house. To clear the site, the trustees permitted the students to cut down the trees and create piles of firewood for bonfires. About half of the student body, numbering eight hundred or so, showed up on October 21. The day started at the Student Building with a concert by the university band and a short talk by President Bryan, who then led the procession to the site. Both the president and Mrs. Bryan wielded axes to initiate the cutting. The men students joined in eagerly, chopping trees and piling wood, while women students made and served sandwiches. Enough wood was gathered for three bonfires at pep rallies for football season. IU anatomist and historian Burton Myers, who was there, later reported: "This was a joyous occasion. The students felt that they were helping clear the way for this long-desired structure."[3] In the days following, the news reported that Bedford attorney Moses Dunn, who sold the family

[2] *A Hoosier Holiday*, 503. He was referring to Mitchell Hall as the former library.

[3] Myers, *History of Indiana University*, 1952, 188.

farm that became the core of IU's campus, had died the day of the orchard's destruction.[4]

Representing the leading edge of campus expansion, the site was on Seventh Street, a couple of blocks away from the main part of campus on Kirkwood Avenue. As the first campus building on the north side of the stream known as Spanker's Branch—informally referred to as Jordan River—the gymnasium's imposing Gothic limestone architecture would be magnified by its site atop a terraced hill, commanding a view to the west.

With the prospect of new development on campus, President Bryan and the board of trustees thought it prudent to hire a consultant to prepare a master plan. Well-known for his work in the park system of Indianapolis, George Kessler, a landscape architect who worked around the Midwest, had a thriving business and was engaged in 1915.[5] In November, Kessler shared his general ideas for campus planning with President Bryan and the board of trustees. He thought that "planning should be comprehensive. Even though a grand design could only be realized in bits and pieces, and over a long period of years, still, we should always know where we are going."[6] By the following March, Kessler had reported back to the trustees with some suggestions, including ideas for buildings in the center of the quadrangle.

In May, President Bryan wrote to Kessler, conveying a diplomatic but firm message for the preservation of Dunn's Woods:

> Fully realizing your great ability as an artist, and my own position as a layman, I nevertheless get my courage together to say that I hope it may not be thought necessary to place any buildings in the front quadrangle between the Wylie, Kirkwood, Science line and Indiana Avenue. Whether the present forest can be replaced by another or not, this great space seems to me to have more distinction than any building which could be placed in it. This is the view, I happen to know, of Professor Brooks, Mr. Jenkins, the Trustees, and indeed

[4]Lee Ehman, "The Dunn Name, but Not the Spirit," *Monroe County Historian* 3 (August 2010): 10–11.

[5]Myers, *History of Indiana University*, 1952, 174.

[6]Quoted in Clapacs, *Indiana University Bloomington*, xx, from Theodore A. Brown and Lyle W. Dorsett, *K.C.: A History of Kansas City, Missouri* (Boulder, CO: Pruett, 1978), 163–164.

> of all of us. I am sure you would like to have us give you our view whatever it may be worth.[7]

Bryan, expressing a clear consensus among the IU academic community, took the remaining forest off the table for further development. There was no compelling reason to jettison the existing design of the thirty-year-old quadrangle.

As plans were developed for the new gymnasium, the entire board of trustees, along with architect Robert Frost Daggett, visited the site and the surrounding campus lands. This signaled the aspiration to coordinate the work of building architects with the efforts of landscape planners. The completed building, opened in 1917, was thronged with students at all hours. It served as a lonely architectural sentinel as future facilities were expected in the recent land purchases northwest of the quad. In the same period, replanting of the green space continued. A report indicated that "32,000 trees had been ordered as follows: 25,000 yellow poplar seedlings; 2,000 hard maple; 2,000 red oak; 3,000 pine, spruce, and fir."[8]

The care expended on the physical plant was noticed by a distinguished visitor in 1918. Former US president Theodore Roosevelt visited Bloomington as the June commencement speaker. The ceremony was held in a natural ravine converted into an open-air amphitheater, behind Wylie and Kirkwood Halls. Equipped with a stage and bench seats, the amphitheater was a gift from the classes of 1909 through 1912.[9] The former president began his remarks:

> I want to say at the outset that I don't think I have ever been at a more beautiful university commencement than this. I shall always keep in mind this scene here in the open by the university buildings, a university which...is approaching its centenary, here under these great trees, these maples and beeches, that have survived over from the primeval forest, to see all of you here and the graduating class composed mainly of girls this year—

[7]"Letter to George Kessler" (Indiana University Archives C286/B150/F Kessler, George, May 25, 1916).

[8]Myers, *History of Indiana University*, 1952, 206.

[9]Clapacs, *Indiana University Bloomington*, 166–67.

> it is a sight I shall never forget,—it will always be with me.[10]

President Roosevelt expressed what students, staff, alumni, and other visitors already knew and appreciated about the campus.

In 1922, another distinguished visitor came to campus and stayed awhile. Theodore Clement Steele (T. C. Steele), a well-known painter from the art colony in neighboring Brown County, was appointed honorary professor of painting. He had a long association with the campus, painting portraits of many IU faculty, President Bryan among them, before turning to landscape interpretations. Bryan's idea was that Steele's very presence would help stimulate art appreciation on campus, thus contributing to the moral uplift of the student body. For his part, Steele rendered his mission to the students in a straightforward way: "to see the Beautiful in nature and life."[11]

The university provided studio space in the attic of the main library, above the large reading room. During his residency, Steele and his wife, Selma, spent the winters in Bloomington and the summers in Brown County, at their home near Belmont. The artist was modest and unpretentious about his work, and he welcomed visitors dropping in when the studio was open on Thursday, Friday, and Saturday each week. During clement weather, Steele set up his easel outdoors and painted *en plein air.* The resulting canvases showed different campus buildings, such as the Student Building and Kirkwood Observatory, and landscape features, such as the central woods and the Jordan River. In 1923, the Union Board bought six of Steele's paintings, which provided the nucleus for the art collection of the Indiana Memorial Union. Although his original term as honorary professor was meant to last only a year, he stayed on happily until 1926, the year of his death.[12]

5.2 Campuses, the Old and the New

To mark the centennial of the first buildings on the old campus, in 1922, administrative factotum John Cravens penned a series of three

---

[10] "Straightout Americanism," *Indiana University Alumni Quarterly* 5, no. 3 (July 1918): 295–307.

[11] Capshew, *Herman B Wells*, 27.

[12] Capshew, 27–29. The IMU now owns over seventy paintings of T. C. Steele.

articles for the *Alumni Quarterly.* By that time, the university had been occupying the campus at Dunn's Wood for a third of a century. A former school superintendent and court clerk for Monroe County, Cravens occupied a unique position in the university. Appointed as IU registrar in 1895, he became the secretary to the board of trustees in 1898 concurrently. In 1915, he added another duty—secretary of the university. Thus, Cravens played a key role in gatekeeping for the student body and witnessing trustee decision-making. As the trustee board authorized campus infrastructure driven by the needs of the student body, Cravens had access to relevant records of IU's building program as he wrote "Buildings on the Old and New Campuses of Indiana University."[13]

He started, not surprisingly, with the original Seminary Building on the old campus. Cravens intoned reverently: "What a train of thoughts comes to one when he stands on the very site which marks the beginning of that institution destined to become in law and in fact 'the head of Indiana's public-school system.' One feels that he should stand here with uncovered head. San Salvador, Plymouth Rock, and Jamestown each has its special significance. Each was the beginning of an important movement. The Old Seminary Building is the cradle of higher education in Indiana."[14] He went on to describe the process of choosing the site and the details of construction of the simple two-story brick structure, then launched into a description of the building's uses over time and listed many of the early graduates who had made names for themselves. As the only academic building, it saw constant use from 1824 to 1836. When the larger College Building was finished in 1836, the older building was pressed into service as needs arose. It was torn down in 1858.

Cravens was attempting a word portrait, to fix in the reader's mind the primordial significance of the structure that was the first physical embodiment of the idea of Indiana University. The trouble was, he admitted, "the *exact* location of the Old Seminary Building had passed from the memories of the oldest graduates and citizens of

[13]John W. Cravens, "Buildings on the Old and New Campuses of Indiana University: I. The Old Seminary Building," *Indiana University Alumni Quarterly* 9, no. 1 (1922): 1–11; Cravens, "Buildings on the Old and New Campuses of Indiana University," 1922; John W. Cravens, "Buildings on the Old and New Campuses of Indiana University: III. Buildings on the New Campus and Elsewhere in Monroe County," *Indiana University Alumni Quarterly* 9, no. 3 (1922): 303–20.

[14]Cravens, "Buildings on the Old and New Campuses of Indiana University," 1922, 1.

Bloomington" in the two-thirds of a century since it was demolished. People remembered it was "'on the high ground near the southwest corner of the old campus,' but all outward traces of the building had disappeared."[15] Undeterred, Cravens got permission and a crew of men to excavate for any remains of the original building.

Charles Hays, the assistant superintendent of buildings and grounds, was the foreman.[16] In addition to the university work crew, a group of older residents of Bloomington served as location consultants, including Hays's father-in-law, who pointed to a spot within fifteen feet of where the old building had stood. They discovered the ruins of the Seminary Building, unearthing part of the foundation and entrance steps, and found the base of the College Building, which was constructed in 1836 and destroyed by fire in 1854. They marked the location with a stone and considered the construction of a suitable monument.[17]

In his second article, Cravens covered the remaining six buildings on the original campus—the professor's house (1824–1864), the College Building (1836–1854), the Boarding-House (1838–1864), the Laboratory Building (1840–1858), the second College Building (1855–present), and Science Hall (1873–1883)—with details of construction and use.[18] He delineated the trustee board's debate after the fire that destroyed Science Hall in July 1883, about whether to rebuild on the seminary site. In September 1883, the trustees entertained seven sites, including the existing campus, ranging from ten to fifty acres. After discussion, a test vote was taken, with three favoring the present site, three for the Blair property (located northwest), and one for the Dunn property (located east). After

[15]Cravens, 3. Original emphasis.

[16]Charles H. Hays (1897–1937) was a native of Monroe County and spent a thirty-one-year career at the university. Starting in 1906 as a custodian for Kirkwood Hall, he became assistant superintendent of buildings and grounds in 1917. After being promoted to superintendent at the death of his predecessor, Eugene Kerr, in 1926, he served until his sudden death from a heart attack in 1937. President Bryan noted his artistic interests, which took various forms: scenery manager for student plays, decorator for university events, and campus landscape designer. See "Charles H. Hays," *Indiana University Alumni Quarterly* 24 (1937): 511–12.

[17]"Discover Ruins of Seminary Building," *Indiana Daily Student*, January 18, 1922, 3. See map in Cravens, "Buildings on the Old and New Campuses of Indiana University," 1922, p. 161.

[18]The second College Building, sometimes referred to as the first University Building, was sold to the Bloomington school system in 1897 and served as Bloomington High School until 1965, when a new school was opened at 1965 S. Walnut Street and the former IU building was razed.

further debate, the final vote was taken, with five for Dunn's Woods and three for the existing site. Cravens summarized: "And thus our present magnificent campus, recognized as one of the finest in the United States, was selected."[19]

Cravens then went on to recount the story of the first buildings on the new campus in the third article, starting with Wylie Hall and Owen Hall, that eventually formed "three sides of a quadrangle on the crest of the campus proper."[20] He enumerated in order of construction the seventeen buildings and structures that populated the campus in 1922, nearly thirty-five years after the move to Dunn's Woods. He noted that all except two of the trustees who engineered the relocation were deceased. In each of the capsule histories, Cravens gave a myriad of architectural, construction, and financial details, in addition to the naming of the building, whether functional (Power Plant No. 1 or Student Building) or honorary (Maxwell Hall or Kirkwood Observatory). The result was a trove of rare information, combining data from records but also from campus lore and personal observation. The article ended with the newest building, the Commerce and Finance Building, for the use of the recently founded School of Commerce and Finance, which was still under construction in 1922.[21]

Cravens's series, coming on the heels of IU's centennial in 1920, was a unique compendium of campus architectural and social history. It married the old and new campuses in a straightforward chronicle of institutional progress, in which the devastating fires on the old campus served as an impetus for the relocation and led to brighter prospects for the university. The hidden variable in this focus on the physical plant was an exponential increase in the size of the student body, from less than two hundred at the start of the 1880s to nearly three thousand in 1922, with a concomitant expansion of faculty and staff numbers. The escalating growth of the campus infrastructure was also a result. Not only did Cravens's articles draw attention to this formative period of campus development in its material embodiment, but they were also a refreshing complement to the exclusive focus on educational philosophy, policy, and practice

[19] "Buildings on the Old and New Campuses of Indiana University," 1922, 164.

[20] "Buildings on the Old and New Campuses of Indiana University," 1922.

[21] Cravens, 319–20. The Commerce and Finance Building was renamed William A. Rawles Hall in 1963 by the trustees.

that was found in the *Centennial Memorial Volume* published in 1921.[22]

5.3 Literary Appreciations

As enrollments kept rising through the 1920s, from 2,300 to 3,500 students, a remarkable efflorescence of prose occurred among students that featured the Bloomington campus. Whether addressing their remembered or present experience, student writers described the weather, the trees, and the buildings and pathways, thus evoking the university's unique spirit of place. Some evidenced a deep attachment to place; others used the campus as a setting to describe personal feelings or states of mind.

Ernie Pyle, a columnist and editor for the *Indiana Daily Student*, penned a paean to IU's spirit of place as students were returning to classes for the 1922 fall semester:

> Nearly everyone who has ever attended Indiana University will tell you there is no place in the world like Indiana. They sometimes attempt to explain that statement but they cannot. When they ejaculate that there is no place in all the world like Indiana, they are thinking about something else. They are thinking about spring days when the campus is bursting with fragrance, vivid with color of blossoms and new leaves, and then the moon is bright—it is undeniable that spring is nowhere in the world as it is at Indiana. They are thinking about autumn evenings when dusk has settled.

Moving from the ambiance of nature to the human milieu, Pyle observed the deep interpersonal attachments the college experience fostered, continuing: "They are thinking about hundreds of wholesome, pleasant people, who were their friends. They are thinking something about Indiana which none of them could ever express in words. These persons who make such broad unqualified statements about Indiana say that they have since tried living in many other places but somehow that tang is missing."[23] Trying to grapple with an ineffable spirit of place, Pyle showed glimpses of his gift for

[22] Chamness, *Indiana University, 1820–1920.*

[23] Ernie Pyle, "It's in the Air," *Indiana Daily Student*, September 5, 1922, 4.

description and his penchant to take the ordinary universals of life as his subject.

Another student of the 1920s shaped by his time on the Bloomington campus was Hoagy Carmichael, who wrote about the main student hangout in a memoir. Located across the street from the campus, the Book Nook, a former bookstore turned into a soda fountain, was "the hub of all student activity" in the days before the Indiana Memorial Union.[24] Carmichael later recalled the teeming social life—indelibly associated with the composition of "Stardust"—contained within:

> On Indiana Avenue stood the Book Nook, a randy temple smelling of socks, wet slickers, vanilla flavoring, face powder, and unread books. Its dim lights, its scarred walls, its marked-up booths, unsteady tables, make campus history. It was for us King Arthur's Round Table, a wailing wall, a fortune telling tent. It tried to be a bookstore. It had grown and been added to recklessly until by the time I was a senior in high school it seated a hundred or so Coke-guzzling, book-annoyed, bug-eyed college students. New tunes were heard and praised or thumbed down, lengthy discussions on sex, drama, sport, money, and motor cars were started and never quite finished. The first steps of the toddle, the shimmy, and the strut were taken and fitted to the new rhythms. Dates were made and mad hopes were born.[25]

Carmichael, a Bloomington native, had a special feel for his home in a college town. In his first, impressionistic memoir, published in 1946, he described the campus as he remembered it in the 1920s:

> A low stone wall borders the campus on the south. This is the "spooning wall" and it is usually dotted by quiet indiscernible couples late at night who have stopped there on the way home from the Book Nook or a picture show. To the north of the campus, bounding Dunn Meadows [*sic*] and the old athletic fields, runs the famous Jordan River. Famous because of its high-sounding

[24]Wells, *Being Lucky*, 33.

[25]Hoagy Carmichael and Stephen Longstreet, *Sometimes I Wonder: The Story of Hoagy Carmichael* (New York: Farrer, Straus; Giroux, 1965), pp. 54–55. To sort out the folklore surrounding the composition of "Stardust," see Richard M. Sudhalter, *Stardust Melody: The Life and Music of Hoagy Carmichael* (New York: Oxford University Press, 2002), pp. 103–123.

name and yet its waters—a foot deep in floodtime—barely trickle during the dog days of August.[26]

Tinged with nostalgia about times past, more wistful than sentimental, Carmichael's writing was retrospective as he recalled his Bloomington roots years later.

For the first time, the campus woodland was the setting for a novel. Published in 1925, the novel *Initiation* was written by George J. Shively, a member of the class of 1916 who majored in English.[27] A coming-of-age story, much of the action took place on university grounds under a fictionalized name for the institution. *The Vagabond*, the campus literary magazine, enthused: "For the first time Indiana University lives under its own name and at full length in modern fiction. The veil is frankly not drawn over reality by calling the place Monrovia College and renaming Jordan Field. It deals with Indiana University more openly than does the University catalogue. Any student or alumnus knows where he is.... It is by far the best description of student life so far written about the school."[28]

Following graduation, Shively went to Yale University to pursue literary studies, but after a year, his graduate program was interrupted by the Great War in Europe. He served in the Yale ambulance unit with the French Army during the war, where he was wounded. His first publication, a concise history of his ambulance unit, came out in 1920.[29]

Initiation was his second publication. As described in the novel, his recollections of IU campus life were fresh and vivid, tinged with longing for a more innocent time:

> Upon John grew that affection which no one can escape who walks long under campus trees; that naïve and sentimental fondness at once fatuous and deep, that

---

[26]Hoagy Carmichael, *The Stardust Road* (1946; repr., New York: Greenwood Press, 1969), 34.

[27]George J. Shively (1892–1980) was the son of Benjamin Franklin Shively (1857–1916), a US senator (1909–16) and IU trustee (1893–1916) who served as president of the board from 1906 until his death. He died on March 14, 1916, when his son George was weeks away from IU graduation.

[28]F. C. S[enour], "A Novel of Indiana University," *The Vagabond* 2, no. 3 (March 1925): 51–52.

[29]George J. Shively, ed., *Record of S.S.U. 585* (New Haven: Brick Row Book Shop, 1920).

> clings to a man long afterward, and that has been known, of mention of Alma Mater, to show up soft in gnarled citizens otherwise hard-shelled as the devil himself. To a peculiar degree the Indiana milieu was created to inspire love. It has the unspoiled generosity, the frankness, the toil, the taciturn courage and the exasperating ineptness of natural man himself. One listens to the winds sighing through beeches, or plods through autumnal drizzle with gaze divided between the cracks of the Board Walk and that miraculous personal vision that for no two people is produced alike, whether it be conjured from books, or from inner song, or from liquor, or from a co-ed's smile or from all together. Because of this one berates Indiana and loves her doggedly.[30]

Shively went on to publish one other novel, *Sabbatical Year* (1926), a saga of an upper-class American family, before making a career in the publishing industry as a senior editor at Doubleday & Company in New York.[31]

In 1929, writer and humorist Don Herold penned a remembrance of his student days. Originally from Bloomfield, in a neighboring county, Herold graduated in 1913. He stated:

> It is hard not to get soft about the Indiana campus. I know of none in America which surpasses it in beauty. Indiana buildings, some good, many architecturally atrocious, have been set in a forest of fine old trees, as the real estate agents would say. No adolescent saplings these, but grand old patriarch timber to touch the souls of sensitive boys and girls. I think the really worthwhile college student is a bit sad, and I feel that every campus should offer the comfort of towering trees. I am glad I did not have to go to college in a skyscraper or on a sun-baked subdivision. Romance burns best on a wooded campus. It would take a pretty generous state appropriation to offset the thrill of a stroll on the board walk from Kirkwood Hall to Forest Place.... As I said to myself a lot of times, say I, "I like this campus," and I

[30]George Shively, *Initiation* (New York: Harcourt, Brace; Company, 1925), 122.
[31]See "Mrs. George Shively"

> know every other Indiana undergraduate has had many a similar throb.[32]

Such literary appreciations describe the emotional pull of the campus, heightened by campus society and the developmental challenges of learning and study.

Other students, less self-consciously literary, left their impressions as well. When Eura Ann Sargent, from Indianapolis, came to IU as a first-year student in 1927, the campus was largely as Cravens described it a few years before. The physical plant consisted of about a dozen academic halls arranged around three sides of Dunn's Woods, plus the old Assembly Hall, power plant, and the new Men's Gymnasium. All except the new gymnasium were adjacent to the woods. She remembered:

> The campus was a thing of beauty. All around the Well House to the street was colorful woods. The sun had to force its way through the dense foliage and soft breezes stirred the leaves to make lazy ephemeral shadows on a ground carpeted with some of last year's leaves and dotted with a few wild flowers and other stirring sprouts which dared to live in spite of the shade. Behind most of these ten buildings was picturesque and natural growth. Nature seemed to be pleased to have such latitude and was doing her utmost to make the best of the opportunity.[33]

Sargent joined generations of students who responded to the beauty of the campus and the intermingling of stone buildings and the woodland.

Among those responsible for the physical plant in those times was Charles Hays, then assistant superintendent of building and grounds. He not only supervised the groundskeepers but also tried his hand in landscape design. Because bedrock was located close to the surface in Bloomington, there were small-scale limestone quarries dotting the area. One was on campus near Third Street, west of Memorial Hall, sometimes called Dunn Quarry.

---

[32] Don Herold, *College Humor*, November 1929, 130–31.

[33] Sargent interview, in IU Archives reference file "African Americans at IU. William Smith's Research Files for the 'African American Experience at IU' Project." Sargent was among the tiny minority of African Americans at IU during this period, about 1 percent.

In 1928, Hays designed a rock garden within the old quarry, featuring a pond and attractive landscaping. The Sunken Gardens became "one of the most beautiful spots on campus," and the classes of 1927 and 1928 contributed money for supplies.[34] A local resident vividly remembered playing there as a child:

> It is still a refuge, a playground, a Paradise. Two arches in a low stone wall invite entry to descending flights of rough, shallow steps. These are bordered by trees, ferns and ground cover plants which hold the cool, dark, damp atmosphere born of the wide pond at the foot of steps. Circling the pond, the questing child arrives at her goal—the huge, sloping limestone rock which juts into the water. The rock's surface, about two feet above the water, is superbly placed for watching crawdads and water striders, and is itself studded with fossils. The cool quiet of the Sunken Gardens was then, and is now, that child's safe haven.[35]

Heavily used by sunbathers, swimmers, and artists, it was also favored by college sweethearts, leading to its popular name, the Passion Pit. For over two decades, the gardens provided a tranquil and picturesque setting for communing with nature until they were removed to make way for the construction of Jordan Hall (now Biology Hall) in the early 1950s.[36]

In 1929, alumna Edith Hennel Ellis, a member of the class of 1911, authored an article about the woodland campus for the *Alumni Quarterly*. Simply titled "The Trees on the I.U. Campus," it included poetic descriptions: "Certain scenes stamp themselves indelibly upon the mind: lingering shadows of tall trees creeping across the grass on long summer afternoons; black trunks of trees rising from snow-covered slopes, etched against a leaden winter sky; masses of Forsythia bursting into sudden yellow bloom; and that loveliest of all Indiana springtime pictures, white dogwood and pink redbud blooming against a green background of maples." Ellis asserted: "The Indiana University campus is famous the country over for its natural beauty. It is more than a thing of beauty. Its trees are

[34]Myers, *History of Indiana University*, 1952, 381; "Charles H. Hays," 1937; "Charles H. Hays," *Indiana Alumni Magazine* 19, no. 7 (1957): 1.

[35]Sue Davis Gabbay, "Letter to Brad Cook" (Indiana University Archives/Reference file: B+G Sunken Gardens, March 2013).

[36]See Clapacs, *Indiana University Bloomington*, 181.

sanctuaries under which old men may dream dreams and young men may see visions."[37]

5.4 Campus Development in the 1920s and 1930s

The landscape architectural firm of Olmsted Brothers began consulting with the IU administration in 1929.[38] They prepared site plans for proposed buildings, laid out paths and streets, and advised on landscape design and planting schemes. They also carefully inventoried trees and vegetation in Dunn's Wood, with a blueprint of location, species, and size. Like before, IU officials used the plans as guidelines and suggestions, modifying their implementation according to available finances and current priorities.

After the Men's Gymnasium on Seventh Street opened in 1917, other new buildings sprang up during the 1920s. The first was on the quadrangle: the Commerce Building (now Rawles Hall), completed in 1923, due east of the Biology Hall (now Swain Hall East) on Third Street. To mark a primary entrance to the building, the class of 1926 donated funds for a pair of limestone pillars on the sidewalk adjacent to Third Street. In 1924, a campus home for President Bryan and his wife, Charlotte Lowe Bryan, was constructed. It was east of the quadrangle, along the campus border, on a slight rise between two small creeks. It was known as the President's House (now Bryan House).

It was the last construction project overseen by Superintendent of Buildings and Grounds Eugene Kerr, who died in July. The *Indiana Daily Student* noted Kerr's passing: "For the last twenty years this man has labored earnestly for the good and advancement of the University. He has been instrumental in bringing about many of the needed improvements in buildings and grounds during that time. He took deep pride in keeping the buildings and grounds in the best of condition, and largely through his efforts the campus still ranks as one of the most beautiful of any college or university in

[37]Ellis, "The Trees on the I.U. Campus," 331.

[38]In 1898, John Charles Olmsted (1852–1920) and Frederick Law Olmsted Jr. (1870–1957) formed the Olmsted Brothers partnership, operating under that name until 1961. See Olmstead Firm.

America."[39] After Kerr's death, Charles Hays stepped into the role of superintendent of buildings and grounds and served from 1924 to 1937. A few months later, Kerr was memorialized by a bronze plaque placed in Maxwell Hall.[40]

Also in 1924, the first dormitory for men, South Hall (now Smith Hall), was opened on Tenth Street, colonizing yet another street for the campus building program. It was joined the following year by Memorial Stadium (now Cox Arboretum) to the east. Across campus on Third Street, the first dormitory for women, Memorial Hall, was finished in 1925. It was no accident that living quarters for women and for men were on opposite ends of campus. In 1928, athletic facilities were boosted by the construction of the huge Fieldhouse (now the Garrett Fieldhouse), attached to the Men's Gym, suitable for intercollegiate sports.

Despite the stock market crash in 1929, campus construction continued. That year, the power plant was renovated after a fire and finally made adequate.[41] The class of 1929 funded a set of limestone gates along the campus border on Third Street, between Biology Hall (now Swain East) and Commerce Building (now Rawles Hall).[42]

In 1931, the long-planned Chemistry Building was completed. The large and handsome limestone building, decorated with a bold frieze depicting the elements of the periodic table punctuated with clusters of grapes, occupied a site due east of Wylie and Kirkwood Halls, outside of the quadrangle. The well-used amphitheater, the location of many commencement ceremonies and convocation programs, had to be sacrificed to make room for the new building, although one can still see the remnants of the natural ravine near the north entrance.[43]

---

[39]Quoted in "Death of Eugene Kerr," *Indiana University Alumni Quarterly* 11, no. 4 (1924): 544.

[40]Indiana University Board of Trustees, "Minutes of the Board of Trustees of Indiana University, 13 March 1925–14 March 1925" (Bloomington: Indiana University Archives & Indiana University Libraries Digital Collections Services, March 14, 1925), https://purl.dlib.indiana.edu/iudl/archives/iubot/1925-03-13.

[41]Myers, *History of Indiana University*, 1952, 764.

[42]Indiana University Archives, "Reference File: Class Gifts" (Bloomington: Indiana University; Unpublished archival material, n.d.).

[43]Myers, *History of Indiana University*, 1952, 418–19, 434–35; Robert E. Lyon, "The History of Chemistry at Indiana University, 1829–1931," *Indiana University News-Letter* 19, no. 3 (March 1931).

The last of the facilities financed by the Memorial Fund was the Indiana Memorial Union (IMU). Formally dedicated at commencement in June 1932 with an inaugural dinner in Alumni Hall, the building was located south of Jordan River and north of Maxwell Hall, a few steps away from the quadrangle. Richly ornamented limestone carvings embellished the exterior, and the main Romanesque tower rivaled the tallest building in downtown Bloomington a few blocks away. In the lobby, a bronze tablet in the floor depicted the different branches of the military services of the IU men and women memorialized by the building and the Golden Book listed the names of those who served as well as the contributors who donated to the Memorial Fund drive. (Since 1961, the bronze tablet and the Golden Book have been located in the Memorial Room, an antechamber off the lobby.) The east wing was allocated for the university bookstore, which featured a second-floor balcony and lounge with a fireplace. Taken with the graceful luxuriance of its utilitarian design, President Bryan boasted that it was "the most beautiful college bookstore in America." The bookstore manager, Ward G. Biddle, became the first director of the Indiana Memorial Union. Almost immediately, the union became an essential part of campus life as well as an iconic architectural landmark.[44]

Two months following the IMU dedication, the national economic situation caught up to the Hoosier economy, and the Indiana General Assembly cut Indiana University's budget request by 15 percent. Soon after, the Bryan administration authorized faculty salary reductions ranging from 8 percent to 12.5 percent. President Bryan, who insisted on an even higher cut to his own salary, received expressions of gratitude from the faculty that the reductions were not higher.[45]

It was years before the situation improved. In 1935, the university presented a budget to the state of just under $1.5 million, which was met with success, accompanied by a supplemental request of $335,000 to address deferred needs, which was not. The next year, President Bryan prepared the budget request, noting that salaries had not been restored after the 1932 cut. The state granted $1.9 million in 1937, about 15 percent less than the request, and did not fund the requested $500,000 for capital projects.[46]

[44]Myers, *History of Indiana University*, 1952, pp. 413–417; Clapacs, *Indiana University Bloomington*, pp. 266–271; The Golden Book.

[45]Myers, *History of Indiana University*, 1952, 436–39.

[46]Myers, 504–7.

The federal government, under President Franklin Roosevelt, had several relief agencies operating during the 1930s to assist in providing funds for public works, notably the Public Works Administration (PWA) and the Works Progress Administration (WPA, later Work Projects Administration). Revising previous lists of building needs, in 1935, the trustees sought federal assistance for an extension of the power plant, another women's dormitory, and buildings for the music school, education school, university administration, and one each for the medical school in Bloomington and in Indianapolis. The state government, under Governor Paul McNutt, former dean of the IU School of Law, assisted in obtaining financing.[47]

As the trustees prepared to finance construction of a new administration building in 1935 with the aid of WPA funds, they decided to put it east of Kirkwood Observatory and north of Fourth Street—right in the center of the woods.[48] Students got wind of this plan and expressed their misgivings through the editorial columns of the *Indiana Daily Student* newspaper. There was general concern that it would mar the natural beauty of the campus. Zoology professor Alfred Kinsey sided with the students opposing the plan, but English professor William Jenkins supported placing the building in Dunn's Woods.

The newspaper published each of their statements in full. Jenkins cited the opinions of experts, arguing that "every survey of the campus by qualified landscape architects has put the building on that site." He thought most people could imagine seeing the gray limestone structure half hidden by the trees from Maxwell Hall. Besides, he thought, it was a common error to think that forest trees are desirable near a formal building. "As a matter of fact such a building should have formally treated grounds about it," he concluded. Kinsey, who was an accomplished botanist as well as a zoologist, drew an analogy: "From a landscape standpoint it is better that the center of the campus be kept clear of buildings for the same reason that the center of a lawn should be kept clear of shrubbery and flower beds." He reminded readers that the central quadrangle, under development for a half century, had been framed on two and a half sides with perimeter buildings. "The heart of the

---

[47] Myers, 515–31.

[48] Indiana University Board of Trustees, "Minutes of the Board of Trustees of Indiana University, 04 March 1935" (Bloomington: Indiana University Archives & Indiana University Libraries Digital Collections Services, March 4, 1935), https://purl.dlib.indiana.edu/iudl/archives/iubot/1935-03-04.

picture is the growth of trees which has made our campus famous all over the country." Barring some new comprehensive plan, he argued, "new buildings should be placed to complete three or four sides of the picture without modifying the present center of that picture."[49]

The concerns of students and faculty resonated with the trustees, and they relocated the plans for the administration building to the corner of Indiana and Kirkwood Avenues, due south of the library, making a start on the fourth side of the quadrangle's framing.[50] The administration building, officially named for President William Lowe Bryan in 1936 at the urging of Governor McNutt, was called by its generic name because PWA rules prevented the use of Bryan's name during his lifetime.[51] The class of 1935 provided funds for limestone benches on the first and second floors.[52]

In 1937, three new buildings were completed: a women's dormitory (Goodbody Hall), placed at right angles to Memorial Hall, and the School of Music Building (now Merrill Hall) and the Medical Building (now Myers Hall), both along Third Street. The next year, the Clinical Building of the School of Medicine was completed in Indianapolis, and the School of Education Building, including a laboratory school, University School, was finished, located at the corner of Third Street and Jordan Avenue, anchoring the growing line of university buildings on Third Street stretching westward to Indiana Avenue.[53]

5.5 Beneath the Sundial

Amid this forward-looking expansion, pieces of the campus's past also sprung up. Otto and Mathilda Klopsch were both members of the class of 1896, the year the sundial was relocated from the old campus to Dunn's Woods. They had fond memories of the woodland

[49]"Professors Take Divergent Views on Building Site," *Indiana Daily Student*, March 28, 1935, 1, 3.

[50]Indiana University Board of Trustees, "Minutes of the Board of Trustees of Indiana University, 04 April 1935" (Bloomington: Indiana University Archives & Indiana University Libraries Digital Collections Services, April 4, 1935), https://purl.dlib.indiana.edu/iudl/archives/iubot/1935-04-04.

[51]Myers, *History of Indiana University*, 1952, 523.

[52]Indiana University Archives, "Reference File."

[53]Myers, *History of Indiana University*, 1952, 515–31.

campus and reminisced about their time at IU with their three children. In 1935, after both had died, their son Otto Jr. requested and received permission from President Bryan to scatter their ashes at the base of the sundial. Their children made a wish: "May their spirit rest as peacefully as it lived happily while they studied and loved on these grounds." A bronze plaque at the sundial's base was inscribed:

> Mathilda Zwicker Klopsch / Otto Paul Klopsch / Class of 1896
> They met at this sundial when classmates.
> Their ashes rest here together until eternity.

This memorial joined Dunn Cemetery as a consecrated place of memory on the IU campus.[54]

Keeper of Grounds William Ogg turned eighty in 1931 but continued working throughout the decade. In 1936, President Bryan lauded Ogg as a "master of the fine arts of dealing with all things that grow upon our glorious campus" for the previous thirty-five years: "Dealing rightly with plants is Art."[55] In 1938, Ogg finally got out of the weather and became the "greenhouse man," with his salary line transferred to the Department of Botany.[56] He retired the following year, at eighty-eight. Although Ogg was the senior figure of the groundskeeping staff, many others contributed years of dedicated work in caring for the IU landscape.

5.6 A Vision Realized

President William Lowe Bryan gave notice of his retirement in March 1937, after serving thirty-five years, longer than any of his nine predecessors. His foresight and discernment helped guide the

---

[54]Clapacs, *Indiana University Bloomington*, 324; Gavin Lesnick, "Campus Icon Retains History, Myth from 1868," *Indiana Daily Student*, September 13, 2005, https://www.idsnews.com/article/2005/09/campus-icon-retains-history-myth-from-1868.

[55]Bryan quoted in "In Memoriam: William A. Rawles, '84, Robert A. Ogg, '72, William T. Patten, '93; and Necrology List," 309–10.

[56]Indiana University Board of Trustees, "Minutes of the Board of Trustees of Indiana University, 03 November 1938–04 November 1938" (Bloomington: Indiana University Archives & Indiana University Libraries Digital Collections Services, November 3, 1938), https://purl.dlib.indiana.edu/iudl/archives/iubot/1938-11-03.

university through a time of tremendous growth. The student body increased from 750 in 1902 to 5,000 in 1937. During his administration, the basic structure of graduate and professional education was established, with the organization of the schools of medicine, education, nursing, business, music, and dentistry as well as the graduate school and the extension division.

The physical plant had undergone significant expansion too, as the campus footprint increased from 50 acres in 1902 to almost 140 acres in 1937. The crescent of buildings at the northeast corner of Dunn's Woods in 1902 had, by 1937, developed into a four-sided frame enclosing the woods, reminiscent of an oversize Gothic quadrangle. President Bryan, who had been a student at the Seminary Square campus and started his teaching career during the transition to the Dunn's Woods campus, was a champion of letting the natural beauty of the woodland shine. His vision of the venerable quadrangle as the heart of the campus was realized, even as growth pushed campus boundaries ever farther.

Bryan's successor as president was the dean of the School of Business Administration, Herman B Wells, who was a 1924 IU graduate. His nine-month stint as acting president started in July 1937. By March of the following year, Wells was confirmed as IU's eleventh president, a position he would hold for the next quarter century.

As a student in the early 1920s, Wells participated fully in campus life, both academically and socially, and first knew the campus when it was organized around the Dunn's Woods quadrangle. Wells later recalled his student years as a "time of response, growth, transformation, and inspiration." The natural environment was key: "My senses were so keen that they eagerly absorbed the beauty of the changing seasons in southern Indiana, the pastel colors of spring, the drowsy lushness of summer, the brilliance of the fall foliage, and the still but invigorating atmosphere of winter."[57]

In the early 1930s, he became a junior faculty member and witnessed the growth of the campus beyond the quadrangle. In August 1937, Charles Hays, superintendent of building and grounds, died of a heart attack at only sixty-one years old. He worked for IU for thirty-one years, working his way up from custodian for Kirkwood Hall to the directorship of the physical plant. The *Alumni Quarterly* stated, "Mr. Hays was responsible for much that is pleasing on the campus,

[57]Wells, *Being Lucky*, 42.

and especial mention should be made of the sunken garden near Memorial Hall, made in an old quarry hole. Students will remember his work in arranging stage settings for revues, and in devising decorative effects for social affairs."[58] Both President Emeritus Bryan and Acting President Wells gave brief public statements. Bryan, who had worked with Hays for three decades, summarized, "He was devoted to Indiana University, and never spared himself in its service. I counted him as a true friend and he never failed me." Wells said, "Charlie Hays has a living memorial in the Indiana University campus. For many years he has been quietly at work enhancing its beauty without disturbing its naturalness."[59]

As president, Wells continued to honor the timeworn elements of stone, water, and trees as the foundation of campus design. He was attuned to how the buildings and grounds could enhance learning as the campus was poised for exponential growth in size, programs, and students.[60]

[58] "Charles H. Hays," 1937.

[59] "Charles H. Hays."

[60] James H. Capshew, "The Campus as a Pedagogical Agent: Herman Wells, Cultural Entrepreneurship, and the Benton Murals," *Indiana Magazine of History* 105, no. 2 (2009): 179–97, https://www.jstor.org/stable/27792978.

6 Cultivating New Ground

Figure 9: Herman B Wells Library

> In the United States, the corporate integrity of the university lies in the college idea, as Newman said, which is itself expressed as a territorial entity denominated the "campus." The campus contains the indispensable innumerable symbols and structures: buildings, gardens, bridges, walks, avenues, glades, statues, plazas, fountains, statuary, towers, gateways and also follies, quirky leftover inheritances in the form of inscriptions, unlikely structures and almost unusable ones.
>
> —Sheldon Rothblatt, "A Note on the 'Integrity' of the University"

Between 1938 and 1980, Indiana University grew in size, scope, and stature. The global war that consumed the world from 1939 to 1945 accelerated both the extent and the pace of change, and the postwar campus that emerged was faithful to the unique design tradition that had been growing for sixty years. Under the leadership of President Herman Wells until 1962, the Bloomington campus served a student body that had increased from five thousand to nearly eighteen thousand when Wells stepped down. Growth continued, reaching thirty thousand by 1970 and thirty-five thousand by 1980. To accommodate the growth and diversification of academic programs, new facilities were added. The decision to provide ample housing options for students on campus fueled the construction of an extensive residential life complex, and the expansion of intercollegiate athletics, both regionally and nationally, meant the provision of specialized sports facilities.

At the beginning of this period, the campus comprised 137 acres—about one-fifth of a square mile. By 1968, thirty years later, it had grown exponentially to encompass nearly the entire northeast quadrant of the city of Bloomington—about 1,900 acres, or three-square miles. Since the late 1960s, its size has held steady at 2,000 acres. University planners had gained a large canvas with which to work, but a large and enduring challenge faced them: how to knit together the old intimate precincts surrounding Dunn's Woods with recently acquired ground. As the cosmopolitan research university emerged, the elemental design mainstays of trees, stone, and water were employed on a significantly enlarged campus terrain.

6.1 The Campus as a Pedagogical Agent

At the close of the Bryan administration in 1937, there were several major buildings either planned or under construction that would be finished during the first few years of the Wells regime. They included buildings for education (now Simon Music Library and Recital Center), business and economics (now Woodburn Hall), and the physical sciences (now Swain Hall West). Two dormitories for women, Sycamore Hall and Beech Hall (now Morrison Hall), completed the Memorial Hall quadrangle (now Agnes E. Wells Quadrangle); two for men, West Hall (now Edmondson Hall) and North Hall (now Cravens Hall), completed the Men's Residence Center (now Collins Living-Learning Center), an open quadrangle.[1] Finished in collegiate Gothic style, all were substantial limestone buildings that fit into established campus districts. The last building constructed and dedicated before the attack on Pearl Harbor and the entrance of the United States into the Second World War was the Hall of Music, more commonly known as the Auditorium.

Within six months of losing his "acting" title in 1938, President Wells recommended to the board of trustees that the architectural firm of Eggers & Higgins, from New York City, in collaboration with A. M. Strauss, a Hoosier architect based in Fort Wayne, be responsible for the design of a campus auditorium—the Hall of Music—located at the eastern end of Seventh Street beyond the Men's Gym. Wells was determined to make his mark on the physical campus by hewing to the established architectural tradition in the first building planned during his administration.[2]

Excavation began in 1939, but the contractors ran into limestone bedrock that necessitated additional work. Great shelves of rock and immense boulders were unearthed. Rather than carry them away for disposal, they were set aside to create a rock garden immediately north of the building. This scheme not only saved the cost of disposal but also enhanced the campus landscape with an artful mimicking of a natural limestone outcrop. The rock garden, eventually endowed by philanthropist Elsie Sweeney, joined the Sunken Gardens as another place of beauty featuring limestone in its natural state.

[1] Clapacs, *Indiana University Bloomington*, 68–70, 126–31, 172–75, 204–14.
[2] Wells, *Being Lucky*, 198; Capshew, *Herman B Wells*, 123–25.

Pleased with Eggers & Higgins' work on the Auditorium, in 1940, IU hired the firm to prepare a feasibility study to add a bowling alley to the Indiana Memorial Union.[3] Soon the firm was preparing a site development plan for the entire campus. "It was our plan," Wells later wrote, "to try to preserve the traditional style of architecture on the old campus with as little modification as possible but, as we moved outward, to allow the buildings to conform with architectural styles then in vogue."[4] That meant, in practice, some limited stylistic experimentation with collegiate Gothic as well as a few signature buildings in contemporary modern styles.

Wells lavished care on the planning of a venue that would provide a superior performance space, whether for musical and dramatic productions or lectures and convocations. The Auditorium did double duty as the new permanent gallery for the dramatic murals of Thomas Hart Benton that were exhibited at the 1933 World's Fair in Chicago.[5] The monumental building made possible a new design element previously unseen at the Bloomington campus. Facing west, it was located at the end of Seventh Street atop a small rise and provided an east-west axis along the street. Starting at Dunn Meadow, traveling east, on the right was the IMU and on the left the Men's Gymnasium, and farther, on the right, was the new Business and Economics Building, with the Auditorium anchoring one end of the axis. At the request of Wells, Eggers & Higgins sketched a plan for an open quadrangle of buildings next to the Auditorium. They produced a scheme for a building for the fine arts on the north and an open-air amphitheater on the south slope, near the Jordan River.

In addition, the Wells administration began a relationship with landscape architect Frits Loonsten in 1940. Based in Indianapolis, the Dutch-trained Loonsten had a "great feeling for the natural" and was able to figure out ways to seamlessly combine new landscaping with the old.[6] As the campus grew, additional green areas were set aside in keeping with the woodland theme established in the late nineteenth century.

---

[3]Indiana University Board of Trustees, "Minutes of the Board of Trustees of Indiana University, 25 March 1940–26 March 1940" (Bloomington: Indiana University Archives & Indiana University Libraries Digital Collections Services, March 25, 1940), https://purl.dlib.indiana.edu/iudl/archives/iubot/1940-03-25.

[4]Wells, *Being Lucky*, 198.

[5]Capshew, "The Campus as a Pedagogical Agent."

[6]Wells, *Being Lucky*, 199.

Although classes continued to meet during the war years, mobilization caused significant changes. Several armed forces training programs used the campus buildings and grounds, and the academic calendar was accelerated, with classes year-round and three annual commencements. Students in military uniforms mingled with civilian undergraduates, sharing an earnest spirit. Each class from 1940 to 1945 revived the tradition of funding limestone gates to pierce the low stone walls along campus boundaries on Third Street and on Indiana Avenue.[7]

As the Second World War was ending, Wells prepared for the predicted wave of increased enrollments, which would mean increased pressure on the campus physical plant and facilities. With a banker's foresight, he directed the treasurer's office to buy contiguous tracts of land from willing sellers. Between 1944 and 1955, the campus added nearly 1,000 acres to the 140 acres extant at the start of the Wells administration. Expanding in a northeastward direction, IU now occupied a whole quadrant of Bloomington, a town of less than thirty thousand.[8] Sitting on this land-bank, the university had plenty of room to grow.

6.2 Postwar Growth

The board of trustees had a nostalgic impulse in 1947 when they communicated birthday wishes to William Ogg, who had turned ninety-six on September 12. Every one of the trustees knew Ogg, the former keeper of grounds from 1899 to 1938, who "exalted this humble position to make it one of great importance and inspiration in their lives and in the lives of countless students and faculty members." The board resolved: "Through fidelity to the task which he loved, through kindness, friendliness and virtue of his noble life, he enriched the lives of all of us. He gave flowers for all and their message of beauty and peace went into the lives of all who trod this campus. He gave us trees, and many of the oaks planted by his hands stand today straight and strong to shelter and guide all who

---

[7] From the corner of Third and Indiana, going east along Third Street: 1942, 1941, 1929, 1926, 1943, 1940; and going north: 1944, 1945.

[8] US Census counts for Bloomington were 20,870 in 1940, 28,163 in 1950, and 31,357 in 1960.

come this way. They all symbolized the full life of this kind and faithful gentleman who served his fellow man in full measure."[9]

The unassuming gardener died a year later, a week after his ninety-seventh birthday. The trustees prepared a memorial resolution, similar in substance to the birthday wishes given the year before. In addition to his planting work "that brightened the lives of those who took the campus paths, the measure of which service will never be known," Ogg provided a sympathetic ear. As he was working outside, "he talked with people in his calm, pleasant and manly way, and many a one has gone out of his way just to have a chat with Mr. Ogg, their friend."[10]

The postwar world's shape, with its contradictions and opportunities, was still emerging, but it was already clear it would be different than the prewar situation. On campus, enrollment doubled in 1946, from 5,000 to 10,000, and a great building program was soon underway. No longer would the campus revolve around the historic core of Dunn's Woods as more precincts were developed and activity shifted to new locations. New academic structures and residence halls and dining facilities claimed attention among the campus community. The old quadrangle surrounding Dunn's Woods would remain, still in daily use, but gradually metamorphizing into a historic landmark.

Student housing was the direst need, and temporary quarters in military surplus barracks and house trailers were obtained and pressed into service. For instance, in 1945 a trailer park with three hundred units was set up on Woodlawn Field, across from the Men's Residence Center, named Woodlawn Courts. Meanwhile, plans to construct and build a system of dormitories to the east of the Auditorium were pursued. The first, Rogers II (now the Ashton Center), was opened in 1945, followed by several apartment complexes and the Men's Quadrangle (now Wright Quadrangle) in 1949. They were followed by Smithwood Hall (1955, now Read Hall), Tower Quadrangle (1959, now Teter Quadrangle), Campus View Apartments (1962), Foster Quadrangle (1963), McNutt Quadrangle

[9]Indiana University Board of Trustees, "Minutes of the Board of Trustees of Indiana University, 12 September 1947–13 September 1947" (Bloomington: Indiana University Archives & Indiana University Libraries Digital Collections Services, September 12, 1947), https://purl.dlib.indiana.edu/iudl/archives/iubot/1947-09-12.

[10]Indiana University Board of Trustees, "Minutes of the Board of Trustees of Indiana University, 01 October 1948–02 October 1948."

(1964), Tulip Tree Apartments (1965), Wilkie Residence Center (1965), Forest Quadrangle (1966), and Eigenmann Hall (1968).[11]

Military surplus Quonset huts sprang up everywhere, even near the old quadrangle, to provide needed space for overflowing academic programs. In 1947, to provide practice and performance space for the School of Music, the university obtained a surplus airplane hangar from an Illinois airport and designated East Hall, which included a one-thousand-seat auditorium, the first home for the opera program.[12] During the postwar building boom, President Wells "made a regular tour of construction sites. He talked with contractors, foremen, workmen, and university personnel. He climbed through partially constructed buildings, inquired about schedules, and prayed for good weather, good labor relations, and speed."[13]

Among the new postwar programs, one depended on campus soil. In 1948, Assistant Professor of Botany Barbara Shalucha, with the support of her department and President Wells, started a youth gardening program on undeveloped campus land on East Tenth Street. Modeled after the Brooklyn Botanical Garden's program, where Shalucha was previously employed, it was designed to teach basic horticultural techniques and environmental science. IU cooperated with the City of Bloomington's Parks and Recreation Department and the Bloomington Garden Club to provide a practical outdoor laboratory for area youth.[14]

In 1961, newly installed lighting in the Well House threatened the kissing tradition, the *Indiana Daily Student* reported. At midnight, it seemed as though couples were "giggling and talking to each other" instead of kissing "in keeping with tradition." The reporter noted, "The founding fathers located the building away from campus lights and the beaten path for a purpose.... If the lights remain, the Well House seems doomed to become nothing more than an open-air Commons. Coke and candy machines will probably be installed. This is carrying student enlightenment too far. It is

[11]Clapacs, *Indiana University Bloomington*, pp. 216–248. See Thomas D. Clark, *Indiana University: Midwestern Pioneer: Volume III: Years of Fulfillment*, 4 vols. (Bloomington: Indiana University Press, 1977), p. 197-225

[12]Clapacs, *Indiana University Bloomington*, 72–75; Clark, *Indiana University*, 1977, 485, 498.

[13]Clark, *Indiana University*, 1977, 212.

[14]JoAnn C. Bunnage, "Barbara Shalucha and the Development of Hilltop Garden and Nature Center: The Cultivation of a Community Treasure" (1999).

a glaring error."[15] This lighthearted story proved campus usage patterns were changing as the student body grew and the physical plant increased. Dunn's Woods lost its centrality after the Second World War as other nodes of campus activity came into existence serving the needs of an increasingly cosmopolitan institution.

Another example of the turn away from the old quadrangle occurred in the early 1960s. The campus, in a vigorous postwar building program, also looked to existing buildings to address the perennial problem of creating academic space. But older facilities sometimes suffered under the bias toward the new. In 1963, Lindley Hall (formerly Science Hall), built sixty years earlier as the fifth academic hall on the old quadrangle, was worn and verging on decrepit. The president and the trustees identified Lindley Hall as a possible candidate for replacement in a structural review.[16] The review indicated that the building was not so severely dilapidated that it would make sense to tear it down, so some modest repairs and improvements were approved. Looking back, this decision upheld the design integrity of the original quadrangle, thus "avoiding the mistake of many other universities that destroyed their architectural legacies."[17]

6.3 Tying the Present to the Past

Amid the postwar transformation of the campus to serve a great expansion of IU's mission of education, research, and service, a faculty member reflected on the role of trees in shaping the design of the physical plant. In 1960, botany professor emeritus Paul Weatherwax published a short article, "Familiar Trees Greet Returning Alumni," in *The Review*, a publication for arts and sciences alumni. A specialist on the evolution of the corn plant, Weatherwax received both his undergraduate and graduate degrees from IU and started teaching

[15]Ralph Hunt, "Enlightening Situation? Well House Wattage Encourages Conversation Rather Than Action," *Indiana Daily Student*, November 1, 1961.

[16]Indiana University Board of Trustees, "Minutes of the Board of Trustees of Indiana University, 31 May 1963–03 June 1963" (Bloomington: Indiana University Archives & Indiana University Libraries Digital Collections Services, May 31, 1963), https://purl.dlib.indiana.edu/iudl/archives/iubot/1963-05-31.

[17]Clapacs, *Indiana University Bloomington*, 40.

in 1918. Well acquainted with fellow botany professor David Mottier, he shared an appreciation for the southern Indiana landscape. His article empathizes with returning alumni: "New buildings everywhere, old buildings with new names, new walks and drives, and memories of old thoroughfares which can no longer be found, all add up to a bewildering picture of growth and change." But campus trees "turn out to be faithful old landmarks"—"something to tie the present to the past."

The article went on to briefly recount the history of campus design, focusing on the role and care of trees, including tree surgery. Naturally, the botanist included some comments on tree identification. Countering the common misperception that every kind of tree that grew in Indiana was to be found on the campus and that there were hundreds and hundreds of them, Weatherwax stated that there were fewer than 150 species across the Hoosier state and perhaps fewer than seventy to be found on the campus. He went on a verbal tour around campus, pointing out a dozen or so species, including beech, sugar maple, oak, sycamore, tulip poplar, tamarack, bald cypress, ginkgo, and pine. He gently exhorted, "To live among the trees without knowing anything about them is much like living in a foreign country among people whose names you do not know and whose language you do not understand.... The time and effort invested in learning something about the trees and other natural things in our environment will yield generous dividends for a lifetime."[18] Weatherwax's article caught the eye of President Wells, a fellow tree-lover.

In 1961, in his last year as president, Wells wrote a two-page letter to Weatherwax urging him to expand the article into a pamphlet "to enlighten incoming freshmen about the design history of their campus and to promote this legacy to visitors and alumni." He went into some detail, eleven points in all, about the proposed content. Wells thought it would be "a very great contribution to the building of affection for our Alma Mater." Ending the letter with "one final thought—put in a ringing warning against any plan to put buildings in the wooded areas," Wells reaffirmed yet again the administrative commitment to preserve and protect the trees.[19]

---

[18]Paul Weatherwax, "Familiar Trees Greet Returning Alumni," *The Review*, May 1960, 12–18.

[19]Herman B. Wells, "Letter to Paul Weatherwax" (Lilly institution/LMC 2283/B4/F Wells, Herman B., August 22, 1961).

Weatherwax took Wells's suggestion and revised the text into a booklet, *The Woodland Campus of Indiana University*, first published in 1966. More than a guide for tree identification, it was a testimonial to the campus design path that the university had taken over the previous seventy-five years and was designed to inspire pride in the aesthetic qualities of the contemporary campus. Enlivened with anecdotes and historical tidbits, about half the content concerned tree identification, aided by a map for a self-guided tour of the sylvan beauty of the campus.

Wells, the university chancellor since 1962, provided an introduction in the form of a letter "to the students of Indiana University." Proclaiming "we share a priceless heritage," he wrote, "Our campus is unique and beautiful. It is unique because it preserves areas of forest, maintained in as near natural state as daily use by thousands of us will permit." Wells wrote of the beauty revealed through each season and the need for "breathing space" in the face of increasing urbanization. Paying tribute to earlier conservationists, he stated, "To cut a tree unnecessarily has long been an act of treason against our heritage and the loyalty, love, and effort of our predecessors who have preserved it for us." After a paragraph explaining the mission of the IU Foundation, he suggests: "Our forest trees are your link to the past. The Indiana University Foundation is your link to the future." Wells, paraphrasing an earlier speech, hoped, "May you find on the campus, especially the old quadrangle, the beauty and sanctuary which will inspire you to dream long dreams of future usefulness to society."[20]

In the main text, Weatherwax invited the reader "to pause occasionally and appreciate this unusual beauty which has been enjoyed for many generations which of those who have preceded you," adding the hope that support to "preserve this heritage" will result. After a brief discussion of the old seminary campus and the move to Dunn's Woods, Weatherwax highlighted various groundskeepers, including William Ogg, along with faculty members David Mottier and J. Van Hook, as key figures in the creation of the woodland campus. Weatherwax dryly noted that the "removal of a tree for any reason has always been a fighting matter, with emotion often pitted against sound judgement." He explained, "In spite of misguided protests,

[20]Paul Weatherwax, *The Woodland Campus of Indiana University* (Bloomington: Indiana University, 1966), 2–3.

better judgement generally prevailed, and the campus developed by a series of compromises."[21]

Moving to open space planning, Weatherwax talked about the lands east of Jordan Avenue, where residential halls were being constructed amid wartime surplus buildings serving as temporary dormitories. The makeshift structures, each named after a native tree (e.g., Pine Hall) and known collectively as Trees Center, were to be removed, and afterward, "it is hoped that it will revert to the original forested state." Despite strong pressures to further develop open land for practical uses in the future, "these spots of natural beauty on the campus, our most stable link with our pioneer past, must be preserved for future generation," Weatherwax maintained.[22]

Turning from politics to botany, Weatherwax admitted that "trees on a college campus have, at best, a hard time of it," as they face a host of environmental challenges caused by the man-made hardscape even though they receive dedicated care. "Effort is made to steer a sensible course between what is best for the trees and what use is to be made of the campus." The basic biology of trees and their life cycles were presented, and the roles of native wildflowers and animals were also mentioned. A list of nearly one hundred "trees you may wish to recognize" was followed by a map of the older parts of campus that noted the locations of sixty species. About half of the booklet was devoted to the campus tree guide, describing both common and unusual species found on the campus.[23]

With its pedagogic aims of environmental education coupled with an appreciation of the natural landscape, the booklet had wide appeal and addressed many interests—historical, artistic, ecological, philanthropic, recreational, as well as educational. Waxing poetic, Weatherwax summed up the main point: "There are few places in the world where great laboratories, classrooms, libraries, and other centers of intellectual and artistic activity are located in an environment which retains its primeval character—few places where one may so quickly go to shed the tensions and anxieties of this complex modern world in quiet meditation."

He added a challenge: "Are we so poor that we cannot afford to preserve this precious heritage? Indeed, are we so rich that we can

[21]Weatherwax, 5–7.
[22]Weatherwax, 12.
[23]Weatherwax, 13–28.

afford to lose it?"[24] The pamphlet went through several revisions and republications in the years following.

The Woodland Campus of Indiana University considered the campus worthy of consideration, over and apart from its daily functioning, for a myriad of educational activities. Campus design was explicitly connected to pedagogical purposes, and knowing the history of a basic natural feature—trees—was deemed valuable. Among the important messages conveyed by this publication was that students learn from the environment surrounding them, both indoors and outside.

The booklet was published when the presidential administration of Elvis J. Stahr was well underway. His administration, lasting from 1962 to 1968, saw the conclusion of a major building program at the Bloomington campus that stretched back to the 1930s. As the rate of enrollment increase began to slow, the commitment to house a sizable portion of students on campus neared completion. The main campus reached nearly 2,000 acres—its present size. Of the dozen major buildings and facilities completed during his tenure, seven were housing for students and three were for academic departments.[25]

Beyond Bloomington, there was a surge of construction at the IU Extension Centers located around the state, as the university underlined its educational commitment to regional hubs through bricks or limestone and mortar. In 1968, the centers gained more autonomy and were designated regional campuses.[26]

---

[24] Weatherwax, 17.

[25] Student housing: Foster, McNutt, Briscoe, Tulip Tree, Willkie, Forest, and Eigenmann; academic structures for psychology, radio and television, and business. See Clapacs, *Indiana University Bloomington*, p. 470. In 1966, a faculty Committee on Natural Areas proposed a preliminary plan for University Woods, encompassing the shore of Griffy Reservoir and the University Lake area, for further development of research and teaching. See J. A. Franklin, "Letter to Thomas D. Brock" (Indiana University Archives/C268/B13/F Committee, Natural Areas, July 21, 1966).

[26] For basic information on the history of the regional campuses, see IU History: Campuses & Context

6.4 Earth Day 1970

The startling view of "Earthrise" taken from the Apollo 8 mission to the moon on December 24, 1968, was breathtaking. It offered a new perspective of our planetary home as a beautiful gem in the vastness of space. The idea of "Spaceship Earth," given concrete form by the Apollo photographs, presaged the awakening provided by Earth Day in 1970.

As the 1960s wore on, groups of people in various parts of the country focused on problems of pollution of the environment. Toxic emissions from industries and automobiles befouling the air, poisonous waste dumped in rivers and lakes, landfills leaching chemicals into the water table, dangerous insecticides and herbicides, oil spills along the coast, and the "tragedy of the commons" were debated. The words *ecology* and *environment* started to pepper public discourse. Among the national voices were several IU faculty, Elinor Ostrom, Vincent Ostrom, and Lynton Caldwell among them.

Wisconsin senator Gaylord Nelson, aware of these emerging issues, devised a way to increase public consciousness about the fraying of the nation's ecological fabric: a civic demonstration expressing care of the Earth, first thought of as an environmental "teach-in" and then as an "environmental action day." The senator wisely let planning staff groups from universities, colleges, cities, and towns across the United States plan locally relevant programs. At Indiana University, an organization emerged with the name Crisis Biology to serve as a clearinghouse for Earth Day and related plans. Associate Professor of Botany Donald Whitehead served as chair of the steering committee for Environmental Action Day.[27]

The schedule of activities for the first Earth Day on April 22, 1970, was impressively extensive. Dunn Meadow, the site of numerous music concerts and protest demonstrations in the past, was chosen as the site. Bob Scott, a junior, summed up the attraction in the student newspaper; "The Revolution Is Here, Escape in Dunn Meadow" was the headline:

> It is the communal ground and ancestral home for the young. It is I.U.'s continuing Woodstock. In Dunn Meadow, people run wild and go crazy in the spring, in

[27]Harold Schlechtweg, "Environmental Day Activities Listed," *Indiana Daily Student*, April 20, 1970.

> all of the good weather and some of the bad. In Dunn Meadow there is no saturating up-tightness, only the warmth that comes from the closeness of the earth, the blueness of the sky, and the oneness of people being happy. We all want to escape to a Dunn Meadow of the mind.... Dunn Meadow is the spirit of freedom.[28]

The meadow, acting as the expansive side yard of the Indiana Memorial Union, could handle the large crowd expected.

The organizers scored a coup in attracting Senator Nelson to open the festivities with an address. It was the start of a long two days for him, with speaking engagements in Madison, Milwaukee, Boston, Atlanta, Denver, and Berkeley as well. Bloomington was the smallest metro area on his itinerary.[29] Around 2,000 people attended Nelson's 9:30 a.m. address. Righteous cries of "Right on!" punctuated the air. Pollution, he declared, was the most important issue facing humanity. Briefly interrupting Nelson's speech, about ten women dressed as witches performed some guerrilla theater, dancing in a circle and chanting, "Save our bodies, save ourselves," demonstrating for the free use of contraceptive devices and against abortion laws. Returning to his remarks, Nelson said the problem of pollution had two aspects, the philosophical and the physical. To counteract the ideology that humans are "over, above, and separate from the rest of nature," he called for changes in "philosophical beliefs, feelings, and attitudes toward nature." On the physical side, Nelson wanted remedial actions to take place on the national level in addition to state and local efforts.

On the podium with Nelson was Robert Menke, an IU trustee. He reminded the crowd that "the concern of past leaders of the environment" was demonstrated by IU's beautiful campus. "I have faith in the future," Menke declared, "because I have faith in the young people of America."[30]

After the speeches by Nelson and Menke, the Environmental Fair opened. People were free to visit tables and booths set up in Dunn Meadow where groups with connections to the environment

---

[28] Bob Scott, "The Revolution Is Here, Escape in Dunn Meadow," *Indiana Daily Student*, April 20, 1970.

[29] Sue Bischoff, "Nelson Pleased by Turnout, Originality," *Indiana Daily Student*, n.d.

[30] Harold Schlechtweg, "Nelson Outlines Proposals to End National Pollution," *Indiana Daily Student*, April 23, 1970.

had displays and information. "Their subject matter ranged from Planned Parenthood to organic food; from non-detergent soap to a soft drink company's use of reusable bottles," *Indiana Daily Student* reporters observed, adding, "The sophistication of the exhibits ran the gamut from grade school level crayon posters to a scale model farm pond—complete with fish and frog."[31] Rock music accompanied the Environmental Fair all day, with local favorite bands the Screaming Gypsies, Pure Funk, and others providing the soundtrack. Adults and young people, parents and children all intermingled—wandering, dancing, playing Frisbee, wading in the Jordan River ("one of the campus' primary pollution symbols," the reporter noted). Random guerrilla theater continued. Booth workers engaged people in conversation and passed out information. Some, like IU sophomore Steve Gudeman, worried about the intent of the buoyant crowd: "I'm afraid they really aren't serious. I'm interested in seeing how much work is done by the committees after this." The *IDS* summarized the action at the Environmental Fair: "Beneath a sky that never quite had the heart to rain, I.U. played out its bit of Earth Day. The 'ceremonies' were a stew of Indiana '4-H' with a strong dash of Woodstock thrown in for flavor."[32] Echoing recent protests against the Vietnam War and massive tuition increases, Dunn Meadow was the setting for a new type of demonstration on behalf of the environment.

In keeping with the eclectic and polycentric day, there was a wealth of other activities. There were "pollution tours" of Bloomington by bus. There was an all-day Environmental Film Program, sponsored by the IU Audio-Visual Center, in Whittenberger Auditorium. Environmental justice themes were the focus of film and discussion: "The Environment and the Poor: Someone Pays the Price." A multidisciplinary mini-symposium with IU professors explored "Alternatives to Present Urban Trends."[33] The Interfraternity Council organized the SMUT (Students March Upon Trash) campaign as a campus cleanup. Residence halls and Greek houses, twenty-five in all, had multiple speakers on environmental topics. At night, WTIU broadcast a televised panel discussion (with a simultaneous radio broadcast on WFIU), "Environmental Action Day: A Beginning,"

[31] Ken Ferries and Linda Herman, "Woodstock, 4-H Flavor I.U. Environmental Fair," *Indiana Daily Student*, April 23, 1970.

[32] Ferries and Herman.

[33] The speakers were professors Frederick Churchill, Lloyd Orr, George Smerk, and Al Ruesink.

with local and state government officials and interested citizens to assess existing problems and prospects for the future.[34]

Featuring other national figures, an evening symposium in the IU Auditorium closed Earth Day. Entitled "Environmental Action: It's Up to Us," the symposium was moderated by botany professor and chair of the Earth Day committee Donald Whitehead. The speakers included Leon Billings, chief of staff to Senator Edmund Muskie and staff director of the US Senate Subcommittee on Air and Water Pollution, and US Representative Lee Hamilton, representing the ninth congressional district since 1965.[35] Back on campus was former IU president Elvis Stahr, two years after he stepped down and assumed the presidency of the National Audubon Society, revitalizing the venerable bird-watching organization into an activist environmental watchdog.[36]

Representative Hamilton began, "With astounding alacrity, we have all become environmentalists," adding, "The environment is a politician's delight" because "everyone is for clean air, clear water, and tall forests." But he injected a note of caution: "In spite of all the protests, meetings, commissions, speeches, legislation, organizations, in spite even of the enormous political popularity of the issue, I am not fully persuaded that we have begun to grasp the dimensions of the environmental task." Hamilton went on to say that we must clearly see the complexities of the task of cleaning up the environment and warned about the dangers of single-minded thinking and of assigning blame to others. "The fact is," he declared, "that all of us are polluters and all living Americans are big polluters." He spoke of power politics and the voices of industry and business and the trade-offs that are involved: "Pollution control may mean short term competitive disadvantage." In his view, management of the environment is above all a political issue, and "politics, not science, is the key to whether or not we succeed."

Hamilton saw problems in the proliferation of governmental groups dealing with the environment—"11 federal departments, 16 indepen-

[34]"Environmental Action Day April 22 Schedule of Activities," *Indiana Daily Student*, April 22, 1970.

[35]Billings was a major architect of the Clean Air Act, signed by President Nixon on December 31, 1970. See also Sam Roberts, "Leon G. Billings, Architect of Clean Air and Clean Water Acts, Dies at 78," *New York Times*, November 17, 2016.

[36]Schlechtweg, "Environmental Day Activities Listed."

dent agencies, 13 congressional committees, 90 federal programs, 26 quasi-governmental bodies, and 14 interagency committees"—with hope that the planned establishment of the Environmental Protection Agency would begin to rationalize the system of federal oversight. Moving to individual lifestyle choices, he suggested giving up so-called "luxury" if that means "squandering and spoiling resources." Hamilton reviewed pending federal legislation concerning the environment and some state initiatives, noting that Indiana would spend 1.9¢ per person in the biennium for air pollution control, in contrast to Kentucky, where 10.4¢ would be expended. He concluded his speech with a lengthy list of steps for everyone to take, dealing with community engagement on a variety of environmental issues. "When the hoopla and the shouting die, the flags no longer wave, and Earth Day has come and gone, our task will be to persevere. So join the fray—if you don't, who will?"[37]

Earth Day was a symptom of a rising tide of environmental consciousness that was sweeping the nation. Congress had just passed the National Environmental Policy Act in 1969 to "create and maintain conditions under which man and nature can exist in productive harmony" and to "assure for all Americans safe, healthful, productive, esthetically and culturally pleasing surroundings."[38] It contained an innovative tool of analysis of likely consequences—the "Environmental Impact Statement"—that all federal projects were required to submit. A new federal institution, the Environmental Protection Agency, was formed in 1970, cobbled together from existing departments and bureaus and designed to rationalize pollution control and establish environmental baselines.

At Indiana University, faculty members were contributing to the national discussion as well as creating new academic frameworks to sustain research, teaching, and service in this arena. Lynton Caldwell, a political science professor, was credited with drafting the text of the 1969 National Environmental Policy Act in collaboration with Senator Henry Jackson's office. Earlier, in 1963, Caldwell wrote a groundbreaking article, "Environment: A New Focus for Public Policy?" that helped launch a new subfield.[39] On the IU

[37]Lee Hamilton, "The Popularity of the Environmental Issue" (Indiana University Archives/Lee H. Hamilton Congressional Papers, 1965–1998/MPP2B142/Folder 18, Speech Book 16, Q., April 22, 1970).

[38]"The Guardian: Origins of the EPA," *EPA Historical Publication-1*, Spring 1992.

[39]Lynton K. Caldwell, "Environment: A New Focus for Public Policy?" *Public Administration Review* 23 (1963): 132–39.

campus, Caldwell and others advocated for the formation of a new school—School of Public and Environmental Affairs—which was created in 1972. Known by its acronym, SPEA was an unusual hybrid, with public policy studies coexisting alongside environmental science programs, with aspirations of cross-fertilization. With the concentration on national and international issues, there was less focus on local environmental issues, although that would slowly change. SPEA, a robust response to emerging issues of concern in modern life, was the first new professional school established at IU in decades. Much of the organizational framework for professional schools had been put in place in the 1920s and had served well since then.

A new presidential administration began in 1971, when the vice president for regional campuses, John W. Ryan, was selected by the board of trustees to serve. An IU Ph.D. alumnus in political science, Ryan was in office for sixteen years, until 1987. His administration supervised the construction of several landmark structures that rounded out the physical plant. In 1971, the Musical Arts Center, perhaps the finest opera house on a college campus in the nation, was completed, as was Assembly Hall (now Simon Skjodt Assembly Hall) to provide a venue to showcase IU basketball. Ten years later, the IU Art Museum (now the Eskenazi Museum of Art), with a "starchitect" building by I. M. Pei, complemented the Fine Arts Plaza, and the new Bill Armstrong Stadium provided a field for the IU soccer teams as well as a track for Little 500 cycling races.

In 1980, the original campus at Dunn's Woods, including nine historic buildings on the old quadrangle and the remnant woodland, was listed on the National Register of Historic Places. The listing was a local outgrowth of historic preservation awareness and initiatives that stemmed from the 1976 national bicentennial. The nomination packet of text and pictures referred to these historic buildings collectively as the "Old Crescent," certainly an evocative appellation, albeit completely new. This coinage rounded off the corners of the old quadrangle, bundled the buildings together, and inscribed a venerable label for a historic precinct. "Old Crescent" caught on quickly, unlike "University Park" nearly a century earlier.[40]

[40]I have not found any references to "Old Crescent" relating to the IUB campus until after the NRHP designation. The nomination form was prepared by Daniel F. Harrington, c/o Indiana Geological Survey, on behalf of the Indiana University Heritage Committee. The "Name" box had "historic

and/or common"; "The Old Crescent" was listed as the common name. "The Old Crescent" (NRHP Inventory-Nomination Form; United States Department of the Interior: Heritage Conservation and Recreation Service, 1980).

7 Landscapes of Learning

Figure 10: IU Bloomington Campus

> We know that the campus itself must be the teacher, a place that gives vitality, meaning, and memory to the learning experience, not just within the confines of the institution but in the times and places beyond. I have argued that those are the fundamental attributes of the place-based institution—its soul, if you please—that have enabled it to persevere throughout our restless history, to continuously transform itself as it has tackled the ever-changing needs of American society.
>
> —M. Perry Chapman, *American Places: In Search of the Twenty-First Century Campus*

The flagship Indiana University campus one sees today is but the latest culmination of a partnership between humans and nonhuman nature that began in 1885. The environmental history of the IU Bloomington (IUB) campus between 1980 and 2020 was shaped by a shared understanding of the importance of the woodland theme in campus design that emerged in the 1880s and its successful adaptation to post–World War II circumstances. Presidents John Ryan (1971–87), Tom Ehrlich (1987–94), Myles Brand (1994–2002), Adam Herbert (2003–07), and Michael McRobbie (2007–21) continued this remarkable continuity of vision and practice while their administrations served as stewards of the campus design ethos. But leadership was only one part of the equation. Faculty, staff, students, alumni, and Bloomington townspeople shaped the campus with their actions and care, as did architects, contractors, and gardeners who brought plans and blueprints to life.

Relabeling the Dunn's Woods quadrangle of buildings as the Old Crescent in 1980 served to differentiate the historic core from newer areas on the sprawling campus. But the challenges to integrating academics, residential life, and athletics within the physical plant continued. Construction persisted, with a mix of new buildings, renovations of older structures, and, occasionally, wholesale redevelopment. In this period, university officials occasionally faced organized local public opposition to proposed land use decisions and facility planning, sometimes leading to the modification or abandonment of design schemes.

7.1 Law School Addition

The School of Law building, located at Indiana Avenue and Third Street since 1957, anchored the southwest corner of the historic campus quadrangle. Concern over maintaining accreditation standards led to plans to expand and renovate the law library, and the Ryan administration negotiated with the Phi Gamma Delta (Fijis) fraternity next door to buy their property. After talks collapsed in the fall of 1981, the board of trustees approved the construction of an addition on the back of the existing law building.[1] Soon after, Professor David Parkhurst, in the School of Public and Environmental Affairs, noticed the survey stakes encroaching into Dunn's Woods and raised concern, writing in mid-January 1982 to Bloomington Chancellor Ken Gros Louis as well as the *Indiana Daily Student.*[2]

[1]An addition had been discussed for years, and the trustees had hired architects in 1980 to prepare plans. IU had sought bonding authority for the $11 million project, but the state budget bill reduced the amount to $5 million in spring 1981. Indiana University Board of Trustees, "Minutes of the Board of Trustees of Indiana University, 02 February 1980" (Bloomington: Indiana University Archives & Indiana University Libraries Digital Collections Services, February 2, 1980), https://purl.dlib.indiana.edu/iudl/archives/iubot/1980-02-02; Indiana University Board of Trustees, "Minutes of the Board of Trustees of Indiana University, 09 May 1980" (Bloomington: Indiana University Archives & Indiana University Libraries Digital Collections Services, May 9, 1980), https://purl.dlib.indiana.edu/iudl/archives/iubot/1980-05-09; Indiana University Board of Trustees, "Minutes of the Board of Trustees of Indiana University, 03 March 1981" (Bloomington: Indiana University Archives & Indiana University Libraries Digital Collections Services, March 7, 1980), https://purl.dlib.indiana.edu/iudl/archives/iubot/1981-03-07; Indiana University Board of Trustees, "Minutes of the Board of Trustees of Indiana University, 05 December 1981" (Bloomington: Indiana University Archives & Indiana University Libraries Digital Collections Services, December 5, 1980), https://purl.dlib.indiana.edu/iudl/archives/iubot/1981-12-05; and John Fancher, "IU Trustees OK Law School Addition," *Herald-Telephone* 15, no. 15 (December 6, 1981): 1, 8.

[2]David Parkhurst, personal communication to author, March 11, 2019. ("Letter to Kenneth Gros Louis," January 18, 1982. David F. Parkhurst files). At the Bloomington Faculty Council meeting on February 2, Gros Louis addressed the questions, hewing to the trustees' public position; Indiana University Bloomington Faculty Council, "Indiana University Bloomington Faculty Council Minutes, 02 February 1982" (Bloomington: Indiana University Archives & Indiana University Libraries Digital Collections Services, February 2, 1982), https://purl.dlib.indiana.edu/iudl/archives/bfc/1982-02-02.

The *IDS* broke the story about the plan for the 57,000-square-foot addition, which would require the removal of twenty-two trees. Parkhurst stated, "I want nothing less than total preservation of the woods, so I object to this very strongly. I thought those woods were sacrosanct." University Physical Facilities Director Terry Clapacs said that steps would be taken to minimize impact on the woods. When Parkhurst charged that the plan lacked public discussion, Clapacs and assistant dean of the law school Arthur Lotz disagreed: "We talked to central administration, President Ryan, Chancellor Wells, the vice presidents, Board of Trustees and the Higher Education Committee [*sic*]." The article reported that drawings posted in the law school lobby showed a cleared area three times the size of the addition, but Clapacs maintained that only the perimeter of the building was finalized.[3]

Public debate was thus begun. The Department of Astronomy, incensed that they were not consulted, complained that the addition would "ruin the [Kirkwood] observatory."[4] On February 1, law school dean Sheldon Plager, a former environmental attorney, circulated a memo, "The Woods and the Law School Library Addition," attempting to address concerns about the brewing controversy. Taking a balanced tone, he expressed concern for the woods but also the academic programs. He went through the failed negotiation with the Phi Gamma Delta fraternity to purchase the adjoining property and the lengthy design review, which involved seven alternative plans. From the beginning of the planning, the law school wanted to take advantage of its proximity to the woods and reorient the backside of the building. Plager minimized the concerns about the Kirkwood Observatory expressed by the astronomy department.[5]

A couple of days later, a public meeting was held in computer science professor Douglas Hofstadter's Lindley Hall office to organize a group to "stop this ugly threat" to the woods. Called "Save the Woods," the group circulated an open letter, citing the one-hundred-year history of Dunn's Woods, noting that it had been placed on the National Register of Historic Places just a year before. "If you resent the expedient disregard of the Trustees and the

[3]Christopher Cokinos, "Law Addition Sparks Dispute over Woods," *Indiana Daily Student*, January 19, 1982.

[4]Christopher Cokinos, "Law School Expansion May Incapacitate Observatory," *Indiana Daily Student*, January 21, 1982, 1.

[5]"The Woods and the Law School Institution Addition," February 1, 1982. Memo to Law School Student Body and Staff. David F. Parkhurst files, University Archives, Indiana University.

present I.U. officers for one of I.U.'s biggest drawing cards and the surest symbol of the University's traditions, you should be heard"—the open letter urged individuals to write to the trustees and the president.[6] Save the Woods announced a plan to sponsor a ribbon-tying ceremony that Friday, where they "will tie green ribbons around trees earmarked for removal, and, if enough ribbon is available, also around the observatory."[7] Meanwhile, in that same week, the student Environmental Law Society hosted a forum in the law school about the addition. Faculty member Craig Bradley announced that the plans would be resubmitted to keep it outside the Old Crescent boundary.[8]

Save the Woods started a petition to the IU trustees, and soon over two thousand signatures had been gathered, as well as several organizational endorsements.[9] Parkhurst reached out to a visiting professor of music, Leonard Bernstein, in early February, hoping to garner support from the famous composer. Bernstein's note was published in the *IDS*: "I should like to go on record as opposing strongly the violation of the so-called Old Crescent woods in favor of extended building facilities. In my short stay here I have been deeply impressed by the care taken to preserve the natural beauties of the campus, and it would be sad indeed to see this long-standing tradition broken."[10]

---

[6]Save the Woods, "Save the IU Crescent Forest," *Real Times* 6, no. 6 (February 19, 1982): 2. Originally circulated as "An Open Letter to Indiana University Alumni," February 11, 1982. David F. Parkhurst files, University Archives, Indiana University.

[7]Christopher Cokinos, "Save the Woods Group Organizing to Protect Old Crescent," *Indiana Daily Student*, February 10, 1982, 3. The *Herald-Times* published a photo of Tom Zeller and Donald Hutter tying ribbons, February 13, 1982.

[8]Christopher Cokinos, "Law School Addition Plans to Be Resubmitted," *Indiana Daily Student*, 1982-02-11. The Indianapolis Star covered the controversy, noting the main issues were the intrusion into the woodland preserve and the interference with Kirkwood Observatory, which recently had a $200,000 renovation. Barb Albert, "I.U. Group Launches Battle to Rescue Beloved Woods," *Indianapolis Star*, February 12, 1982, 22.

[9]Lisa Hooker, "RHA Votes to Ask the Trustees to 'Save the Trees'," *Indiana Daily Student*, February 18, 1982.

[10]"Letter to Leonard Bernstein," February 7, 1982. David F. Parkhurst files.; Leonard Bernstein, "Letter to David F. Parkhurst," February 13, 1982. David F. Parkhurst files; David Parkhurst to James Capshew, personal communication, March 11, 2019; Christopher Cokinos, "Bernstein Note Indicates Support for 'Save the Woods'," *Indiana Daily Student*, February 19, 1982.

In mid-February, *IDS* student columnist Dan Brogan admitted confusion: "How do you justify something for one academic unit that will harm so many other aspects of the campus and community?" He added, "Compromise would seem to be the answer." Brogan wondered why "law school officials seem oblivious to any needs but their own."[11]

President Ryan met with law school officials and supporters, as well as people who opposed the plans. He explicitly stated he would seek alternatives and "oppose removal of trees" from the Old Crescent. To prevent future problems, Ryan supported developing a clear policy for the woods and other natural areas on campus.[12]

The Environmental Law Society weighed in and released a statement. The students were opposed because university officials "have failed to consider both state environmental policies and the views of those persons affected by the proposed addition." The group found no evidence of an environmental assessment as plans were developed and noted the failure to share information with the academic community and the public. They supported the expansion of the law school but not at the cost of "the natural and historic environment."[13]

Before the trustees' meeting in early March, letters to the editor of Bloomington's *Herald-Telephone* proliferated. One was penned by law professor emeritus Ralph Fuchs, who recalled a magnificent beech tree standing where the Tudor Room in the Memorial Union was then located. He cautioned against one-sided policies that either favored institutional needs or focused on the natural environment exclusively. "In respect to the law school addition, the question is whether the educational needs of the school prevail over the preservation of the particular trees involved. The value of the trees depends upon their location and quality, their role in the surrounding ecology, and any applicable considerations of law or stated public policy," Fuchs summarized. About the beech tree that was sacrificed to make way for the union's expansion in 1958: no

[11]"Plager's Contempt on Compromise Out of Character for Law Profession," *Indiana Daily Student*, February 19, 1982.

[12]Christopher Cokinos, "Ryan Requests Look at Options for Law School," *Indiana Daily Student*, February 25, 1982.

[13]"Position Statement on the Proposed Law School Addition," February 24, 1982. David F. Parkhurst files.

one raised objections, "yet many doubtless mourned its loss, as I still do."[14]

On March 6, opponents of the addition had their first chance to air their views directly to the board of trustees at meetings of their architectural, faculty relations, and student affairs committees. Addressing the architectural committee, Professor Hofstadter said that on his first visit to the Bloomington campus in 1967, he was "particularly struck by the beauty of the woods" and urged the trustees to affirm it as "a protected entity." Professor of Astronomy Martin Burkhead asserted that "heat and light from the addition would make Kirkwood Observatory useless." At the faculty relations committee, Professor and Chair of Astronomy Hollis Johnson noted that the observatory had recently been renovated to accommodate a new solar telescope, making it "one of the best telescope facilities in the Midwest." At the student affairs committee meeting, senior Mark Kruzan, President of the IU Student Association, read a unanimous association resolution in "opposition to any plan that infringes on the wooded area."[15]

Responding to the public outcry, the trustees took another look at the plan after their March meeting. Privately, trustee Harry Gonso, an Indianapolis attorney, complained to the other members of the board about the misinformation that had been spread across the state, such as rumors that the entire forest would be removed and the Rose Well House razed. President Ryan commiserated and reminded the board that all plans must spare any intrusion into the woods.[16]

In its reporting, the *Herald-Telephone* attempted to quell some of the rumors, such as bulldozers would down trees in the Old Crescent

---

[14] "Letter to the Editor," *Herald-Telephone*, March 2, 1982, 8.

[15] Christopher Cokinos and Barbara Toman, "Trustees to Hear Law Expansion Opposition," *Indiana Daily Student*, March 5, 1982; Barbara Toman and Christopher Cokinos, "Trustees Will Re-Evaluate Plan," *Indiana Daily Student*, March 8, 1982, 1, 5; Christopher Cokinos, "State to Determine If Law Applies to IU Expansion," *Indiana Daily Student*, March 12, 1982; John Fancher, "Law School Addition Still Up in the Air," *Herald-Telephone*, March 6, 1982, 1.

[16] Indiana University Board of Trustees, "Minutes of the Board of Trustees of Indiana University, 06 March 1982" (Bloomington: Indiana University Archives & Indiana University Libraries Digital Collections Services, March 6, 1982), https://purl.dlib.indiana.edu/iudl/archives/iubot/1982-03-06; Toman and Cokinos, "Trustees Will Re-Evaluate Plan."

and that the Well House would be torn down.[17] Although glad that Ryan asked for other options to be explored, the *IDS* Opinion Board was skeptical about officials' concern about minimizing impact on Dunn's Woods. They applauded the efforts of Save the Woods: "Had the group never been formed, the University may have forged ahead with the plan and actually broken ground."[18]

The architects went back to the drawing board and submitted a revised plan within a month. The new plan was farther away from the observatory and pulled back the twenty-four-feet intrusion into Dunn's Woods. Among the design changes were blinds on the windows facing the observatory and white marble chips on the roof to limit possible image distortion. The board of trustees approved the changed plan on April 2.[19] Relieved that the law school needs would still be met, Dean Plager quipped: "It gets us out of the woods—literally and figuratively." Some astronomers remained skeptical, however. The Save the Woods group would be disbanded shortly, their mission accomplished.[20] After a few days, the *IDS* Opinion Board editorial headline read: "How the Trees Were Saved, Law Addition Flap Is Finally Over."[21]

Board of Trustees President Richard Stoner issued a form letter to all who wrote to the board, seeking to smooth ruffled feathers: "I regret the misunderstandings generated by the original announcement. Please rest assured that the Trustees, all alumni, share your deep concerns for the landmarks and traditions of our University." Stoner, in practicing damage control, concluded that "it was heartwarming

---

[17]John Fancher, "IU Law School Addition Will Not Harm Trees," *Herald-Telephone*, March 7, 1982, 1.

[18]Jenny Ferguson, "Working to Save the Woods, Ryan Makes His Feeling Heard," *Indiana Daily Student*, March 1, 1982. For the Opinion Board.

[19]Christopher Cokinos, "New Addition Plan Would Save Woods," *Indiana Daily Student*, April 2, 1982. Thus, the legal status of the plan was rendered moot. See Cokinos, "State to Determine If Law Applies to IU Expansion", p. 2; Christopher Cokinos, "Law School Expansion Inquiry Buried," *Indiana Daily Student*, March 31, 1982.

[20]Barbara Toman and Christopher Cokinos, "Trustees Approve Addition Plan," *Indiana Daily Student*, April 5, 1982; John Fancher, "Law School Addition OK'd," *Herald-Telephone*, April 4, 1982; John Fancher, "Law School Plan That Saves Woods Moves Ahead," *Herald-Telephone*, April 3, 1982; Sheldon J. Plager, "Letter to Alumni and Friends of the University and the Law School Community," April 8, 1982.

[21]Michelle Slatalla, "How the Trees Were Saved, Law Addition Flap Is Finally Over," *Indiana Daily Student*, April 8, 1982. For the Opinion Board.

to me to see so many loyal alumni 'rise to the cause' when they felt something might happen to change the campus they love."[22]

President Ryan also sent personal notes to the main participants, including Professor Parkhurst, thanking him for "expressing your thoughts, and for your loyalty."[23] The board of trustees requested that the University Heritage Committee recommend "policy regarding definition of areas, as well as factors to consider in determining their protection and use."[24]

In the light of history, this episode revealed the emergence of a new force to affect campus planning: a coalition of interested local citizens, many who had ties to the university. The ad hoc group sprung up in response to a threat to natural areas on campus, demonstrating the wide concern about environmental and historic values that was shared among students, faculty, staff, alumni, and townspeople. Tending to buildings and landscapes on campus was within the proper purview of the IU administration, but public sentiment provided needed checks and balances in a university whose aim was to serve the public.

7.2 "University Woods" near Griffy

The University Heritage Committee, chaired by Chancellor Wells, held a hearing on campus green areas on April 29, 1982. Among the sites mentioned were Dunn's Woods, the grove between Myers Hall and the Chemistry Building, the old stadium area, East Seventh Street between Jordan and Union, the Bryan House area, and University Woods near Griffy Lake. A separate committee, the Natural Areas Committee, concerned with teaching and research, was remobilized to provide input to the Heritage Committee.[25] Wells said that the university "can't cut off future development of the campus, but it can try to anticipate problems."[26]

---

[22] "Form Letter," April 26, 1982. David F. Parkhurst files.

[23] "Letter to David F. Parkhurst," April 30, 1982. David F. Parkhurst files.

[24] "Minutes of the Board of Trustees of Indiana University, 03 April 1982" (Bloomington: Indiana University Archives & Indiana University Libraries Digital Collections Services, April 3, 1982), https://purl.dlib.indiana.edu/iudl/archives/iubot/1982-04-03.

[25] John B. Patton, "Location to the Natural Areas Committee," June 30, 1982. David F. Parkhurst files, University Archives, Indiana University.

[26] Christopher Cokinos, "Wells: University to Develop Campus Natural-Areas Policy," *Indiana Daily Student*, April 30, 1982, 2.

John Ross, professor of recreation and park administration, wrote to Chancellor Wells about the green areas on campus, suggesting that campus walkways be enhanced by small gathering places "to watch one another, to engage in conversation with friend and faculty, to dream a little, to argue and debate, and to perceive life and the surroundings." He suggested endorsing his colleague James Peterson's proposal for a "blue ribbon planning effort" in the University Woods–Griffy green area. "The Griffy site is said to be the largest 'natural area' in close proximity to central city of any city of this size in the country. The proposal for a 'nature center' is further enhanced by potential users from nearby Meadowood." Ross said that the idea had been around since before 1960 and had been analyzed by planning classes.[27]

7.3 "A Stadium of Green"

President Ryan, newly sensitized to issues concerning the natural areas of campus, agreed with a plan suggested by Bloomington Chancellor Gros Louis about what to do with the site of the Tenth Street Stadium (the former Memorial Stadium), built in 1925. IU football moved in 1960 to the new Memorial Stadium, in the athletics complex on Seventeenth Street. The Little 500 men's cycling race had been held at the old stadium since the beginning of competition in 1951, and the old stadium provided a major site of filmmaking for the feature film *Breaking Away*, released in 1979. After more than fifty years of service, the old stadium was deteriorating beyond repair, and it was to be razed in 1982.[28]

Located due west of the library building, the seven-acre site was close to several academic buildings lining Tenth Street, so supplemental parking became a popular suggestion. Others thought the space

---

[27]"Although not a new idea (first proposed by Rey Carlson's outdoor education classes before 1960), its [*sic*] been the subject of many planning efforts (including a preliminary master plan by a student in my R-530 planning class in 1971)." John M. Ross, "Letter to Herman B Wells," April 27, 1982. David F. Parkhurst files.

[28]Built in 1925, it was called Memorial Stadium and was constructed with funds from the Memorial Fund drive. In 1960, a new stadium was built on Seventeenth Street. Confusion about the old and new Memorial Stadiums was addressed by the board of trustees in 1968, 1970, and 1971, with the newer one designated Memorial Stadium and the older one Tenth Street Stadium.

should be reserved for future buildings. Instead, Ryan, with the aid of Gros Louis, hatched a plan to convert the area back into green space. Doing so would provide several benefits to this campus precinct: visual relief from the streetscape, a striking backdrop to the massive bulk of the Main Library (now Wells Library), and a pleasant place to walk or wander. Their idea was to symbolically "give" the embryonic arboretum as a gift from the president to the graduating class, thus short-circuiting lobbying efforts from interested parties for alternate uses. Gros Louis, a fine wordsmith, hit upon an apt phrase: "a stadium of green." The two men rewrote Ryan's commencement speech, weaving in descriptions of the trees, flowers, colors, and scents that would grace the emerging "stadium of green."[29]

At commencement, President Ryan unveiled the plans to "create and nurture a place of woodland beauty—a Hoosier Arboretum" on the site of the old stadium. With plantings of trees and shrubs from Indiana and every other state, as well as specimens from around the globe, he continued, "Just as you have come here from throughout the world, so let this new 'stadium,' a stadium of green and growing things, represent you in its diversity. Let it represent you in the Class of '82 in the seasons which stretch out before you, grow in character, in splendor of achievement, in grace and presence; so also the Arboretum will grow in scope and breadth."[30]

Steeped in the culture of the Bloomington campus, Ryan and Gros Louis conceptualized a striking redevelopment of a significant area of campus, recognizing the opportunity to de-urbanize several acres. As the center of campus moved northeastward, toward Tenth Street and Jordan Avenue, an arboretum would connect the main library and Woodlawn Field, providing an unbroken green expanse along several blocks of Tenth Street.

As demolition of the stadium proceeded, several structures were preserved, including ticket booths, flagpoles, and the wrought-iron fence along the west perimeter. Soil was brought in and sculpted into gentle hills, and a small pond was excavated in the center.[31] Reviewing the arboretum through a historical lens, landscape his-

[29] Capshew, *Herman B Wells*, 343.

[30] "Charge to the Class," May 8, 1982. Indiana University commencement location, Indiana University Archives/C45/John Ryan Speeches.

[31] Clapacs, *Indiana University Bloomington*, 354–59.

torian Anita Bracalente suggested that it represented a delayed fulfillment of the 1896 Olmsted, Olmsted, and Eliot plan.[32]

7.4 Courtyards, Gates, and Campus Appreciation

In October 1985, a century after the university relocated to Dunn's Woods, Owen and Wylie Halls were rededicated in a ceremony that included both a tree planting and the conferral of an honorary Doctor of Laws degree on David S. Broder, the distinguished journalist. The Student Building bells played Hoagy Carmichael's "Chimes of Indiana" as President Ryan presided over the occasion. A "Tree Planting Litany" was organized as a call-and-response exercise, with representatives from the university community:

> **Faculty & Administration Representative**: "Trees symbolize growth and continuity."
> **Audience**: "Even as the light of the sun nurtures these trees, the light of knowledge nurtures our minds."
>
> **Student Representative**: "They are sentinels that have grown with the University since Owen and Wylie halls were built."
> **Audience**: "Even as their leaves fall, they remind us of the seasons of our lives."
>
> **Faculty & Administration Representative**: "We plant these trees to remember the founders of this University and the creative leaders who came after them."
> **Audience**: "As they grow, may they bring added beauty to the campus and enrich the lives of those who frequent this place."
>
> **Alumni Representative**: "We plant these trees for those who will follow us and to commemorate this centennial occasion, committing ourselves anew to the mission of Indiana University."

[32]"Indiana University's Woodland Campus," *View* 12 (2012): 25–27.

Audience: "Even as they mature, may we grow in understanding and deepen our commitment."[33]

Nearing the close of his administration in 1987, President Ryan pursued a pet project: a verbal depiction of the design of the Bloomington campus, organized around the trope of courtyards. The template harkened to the English medieval tradition found at Oxford and Cambridge universities in which four buildings, constructed at right angles to each other, enclosed a common lawn or green space. Juliet Frey, the president's speech writer and editor, composed a first draft of twenty-five pages, started a list of quotations, and assembled a bibliography. Ryan edited the draft extensively, rewriting the prose and reorganizing the text, and crafted a lyrical homage to his beloved campus called *Islands of Green and Serenity: The Courtyards of Indiana University.* Illustrated by beautiful paintings and inspiring quotations, the main thrust of the narrative was to illuminate how the campus was designed so that "everywhere the eye rests, it should see something of beauty." Meditative and uplifting, this publication focused on the campus as a cultural landscape that constituted a work of art.[34]

For decades, university administrators aspired to install ceremonial gates at the main campus entrance at Kirkwood and Indiana Avenues, and the university archives accumulated numerous unbuilt plans. In 1987, this long-held vision was realized through a gift from IU financial aid director Edson Sample, made in honor of his parents. Constructed of limestone, the Gothic-style gateway features twin towers connected by short walls with open arches. At the dedication in June, President Ryan mused that the campus grounds were hallowed "by an echo of the footsteps of thousands of members of the Indiana University community who came here throughout 102 years, in their search for greater knowledge and understanding."[35] Vice President and Bloomington Chancellor Ken Gros Louis spoke of the gates as entrances, to the university looking east as well as to the greater world looking west. "The Sample Gates," he continued, "both into the campus and from the campus

[33]"Program for the Rededication Ceremony for Indiana University's Owen Hall and Wylie Hall, October 18, 1985" (Bloomington: University Printing Services, 1985).

[34]Juliet Frey, ed., "Islands of Green and Serenity: The Courtyards of Indiana University" (Bloomington: Indiana University Publications, 1987).

[35]"Remarks at the Sample Gates and Plaza Dedication" (June 13, 1987). John Ryan Speeches, Indiana University Archives/C45.

into the community, hopefully, ideally, and I believe realistically, are not two paths, but one, with access, vision, understanding, ideas going easily and equally in both directions."[36] Afterward, the gates blended so well with the historic precinct that they became iconic, framing the Student Building bell tower in countless photographs.

In 1991, an outside authority affirmed what IU aficionados long believed: the Bloomington campus design was exceptional. Landscape architect Thomas Gaines published *The Campus as a Work of Art*, a comparative study of American campuses. Pressing the claim that the physical college campus in its totality was a legitimate art form, the book attempted to define aesthetic criteria of the ideal campus and analyzed two hundred examples from the United States. The narrative featured comments on the IU campus as well as quotes from longtime university architect Raymond Casati.[37]

As the IU campus grew, "university president after university president refused to cave into the pressures for routine development and determinedly preserved its campus in the woods," Gaines noted approvingly.[38] "Education is an endeavor that is most sensitive to ambience; students respond all their lives to memories of the place that nourished their intellectual growth," suggested Gaines, citing empirical evidence that a campus's visual environment is an important factor in college choice. IU architect Casati pointed out that design standards set by the IU campus could set the bar when students encounter other environments: "In other words, you won't settle for anything less than you've had here."[39]

Gaines commented on the interaction between collegiate Gothic architecture and natural landscaping. The campus was visually coherent, with limestone providing the dominant building material. Any minor variations in the overall architectural pattern, ranging from Romanesque to Art Deco, provided pleasant accents. That meant that unusual buildings, a few built by "starchitects," could be fit into the campus fabric to provide contrast and excitement. Gaines cited two examples. The main library, opened in 1969, was "a strong cubistic statement of stone," designed by the Eggers & Higgins firm and dubbed "The Towers of Silence." It was placed near

[36] "Remarks at the Sample Gates and Plaza Dedication" (Indiana University Archives, June 13, 1987). John Ryan Speeches, Indiana University Archives/C45.

[37] *The Campus as a Work of Art.*

[38] 101.

[39] Gaines, 11.

the residential zone rather than at the center of the classroom area, which was out of the ordinary, and "its long approach relieves the enormity of the building," he explained, "thus avoiding an otherwise overbearing presence."[40] Despite some controversy over a modern building set within the traditional collegiate Gothic environs, Gaines appreciated how the concrete and glass I. M. Pei art museum (since renamed the Sidney and Lois Eskenazi Museum of Art) fitted into the Beaux Arts–inspired Fine Arts Plaza in 1982, noting "its scale, siting, materials, and design excellence do no harm to the fine aesthetic tradition of the campus."[41]

In his summary, Gaines noted that Indiana "never lost that sense of being a university in the woods," understanding that it was a matter of "aggressive cultivation" of the woodland leitmotif. He singled out the lengthy career of groundskeeper William Ogg and his ongoing efforts to replace campus trees by transplanting trees obtained from surrounding forests. "Medieval masterpieces such as turreted Maxwell Hall and rusticated Kirkwood" adorn the still-intact Old Crescent, and the campus added "interesting and related urban spaces" as it grew, staying true to its design goals. He mentions the Union, the buildings and fountain that make up the Fine Arts Plaza, and the art museum. Walking past "the huge and characterless classroom building Ballantine Hall" to another forested area, he quipped, "Little Red Riding Hood would have felt at home on this campus." Gaines concluded,

> Indiana University is exciting. You never know what is coming up next. You must walk through hilly gardens and woods to get to classes, to dorms, to the library, to the union. Surprise is surely a worthy goal of design. It is more difficult, I believe, to develop an interestingly cohesive campus without the traditional axes or quads on which planners hang their hats. And it is more dangerous to try. Indiana succeeds, because its visual quality is largely based on the unexpected.[42]

The IU campus was listed as number five on Gaines's list of the top fifty campuses, within the top-ranked group of thirteen. The

---

[40] 101.
[41] 41.
[42] 134–35.

campuses were rated on four criteria: urban space, architectural quality, landscape, and overall appeal.[43]

A year after the Gaines study was published, the IU arts and sciences alumni publication, *The College*, featured an article about the design history of the Bloomington campus. Dottie Collins, the research associate for Chancellor Wells, spoke about a mulberry tree growing close to the front entrance to Owen Hall, where Wells's office was. It produced abundant sweet fruit, much of it ending up on the sidewalk and stairs and then getting tracked inside. Wells resisted repeated calls to cut the tree down and instead had his assistants gather mulberries for his consumption. The article cited Wells as a campus guardian: "Sixty-one [*sic*] years after he arrived on campus as an undergraduate, he remains the living link with its woodland beginnings." He was taught respect for the woodland campus by the likes of President Bryan and groundskeepers William Ogg and Milburn Beck.[44] After he became president in 1938, he "has been teaching the lessons of preservation to his successors" with the aid of advisers such as landscape consultant Frits Loonsten.[45]

Charles Hagen, professor of plant sciences, was interviewed. When asked about the difference between an urban campus and a pastoral one, he paraphrased university architect Ray Casati: "In an urban campus you have jewel-like green areas in a sea of buildings. In a pastoral campus you try to build jewel-like buildings in a sea of green." Pointing out the "swamp" along the Jordan River north of the Musical Arts Center, Hagen mentioned bald cypress trees,

[43]The top group of thirteen, which all received nineteen out of twenty points, all received the maximum five points for urban space and overall appeal. They differed by one point on either architectural quality or landscape. Indiana received a five on landscape and four on architectural quality. The first four places were: Stanford, Princeton, Wellesley (four on landscape), and Colorado (four on architectural quality). (*The Campus as a Work of Art*), pp. 155-156.

[44]George Milburn Beck (1895–1981), a Bloomington native, began working at IU's physical plant in 1910, first as a janitor and then as a gardener, becoming campus foreman in the 1930s. After the war, he was supervisor of grounds, retiring in 1960 with fifty years of service. Indiana University Board of Trustees, "Minutes of the Board of Trustees of Indiana University, 14 July 1961–15 July 1961" (Bloomington: Indiana University Archives & Indiana University Libraries Digital Collections Services, July 14, 1961), https://purl.dlib.indiana.edu/iudl/archives/iubot/1961-07-14.

[45]Wells began his undergraduate career in 1921, seventy-one years before the article was written. "Conversations about the Bloomington Campus: It Isn't Easy Being Green (But Planning Ahead Helps)," *The College* 16, no. 2 (1992): 8–11, p. 8.

skunk cabbage, white dogtooth violets, and bluebells growing there. "It may be an eyesore for some people," he said, "but I like it."[46]

Students are attracted by the beauty of the campus, stated Michael Crowe, assistant director for campus maintenance and university horticulturalist. "That confirms our idea of why we're here. We're a business, trying to attract customers, and we treat the people we deal with on campus as customers." David Smith, university landscape architect, spoke about the unexpected consequences when Mitchell Hall was removed from the Old Crescent. It allowed new perspectives for other buildings: "It actually gave them a backyard. Those are very beautiful buildings, from whatever side you're looking at them. So the decision was made to continue with the philosophy of the woodland campus and to maintain that backyard as an open green space."

Citing Robert Frost's poem "Stopping by Woods on a Snowy Evening," Terry Clapacs, the director of the physical plant, suggested: "Our hope is that as you cross campus, you find many places where you stop and you look and it's beautiful, and you take that experience away with you."[47]

7.5 Bloomington Campus Land Use Task Force

In 1995, Edgar Williams, vice president emeritus for administration, was appointed chair of the Bloomington Campus Land Use Task Force, initiated by President Myles Brand in the first year of his administration. At first, lands beyond the bypass were the subject of review, but it grew to include all property related to the campus.

---

[46] Charles W. Hagen Jr. (1918–1996) earned his Ph.D. in botany from IU in 1944 and spent his entire career there, retiring in 1983, as both a professor and an administrator. He was chair of the Arboretum Planning Committee. "Conversations about the Bloomington Campus", p. 9–10.

[47] "Conversations about the Bloomington Campus", pp. 10–11. Michael J. Crowe (1955–2010) was instrumental in the development of IU's nursery and flower production programs. He was serving as director of facilities at the time of his death. Mitchell Hall, a wood frame building constructed at the same time as Wylie and Owen Halls in 1884, had seen hard use, many additions, and renovations to the point that little of the original fabric was left. There was controversy over its demolition. See Lahrman and Miller, *The History of Mitchell Hall, 1885–1986.*

With a fifty-year planning horizon, the goal was to provide a basis for policy to govern both long-term and short-term land use.

The following year, in November 1996, the task force reported its findings and recommendations to the board of trustees. Chair Williams said that the university did not have formal procedures to decide on land use; the task force recommended the establishment of a university-wide permanent land use committee. The idea of designating a land bank, with "various parcels of land [that] may be dedicated for periods of time for certain usage, keeping the highest priority for both academic and academic support services," was also suggested. Three areas were identified: the land between Indiana and Woodlawn Avenues from Seventh to Tenth Streets, the land across Seventeenth Street from the athletic complex and west and south of the alumni center, and the land north and east of the State Road 46 Bypass.

The task force went on to recommend that "one of the best uses at this time for some of the land north and east of the SR 46 Bypass is for golf courses," with the suggestion that the land would be designated for a "specified time period [of] 20–25 years" to accommodate any private investments. They asked the Department of Intercollegiate Athletics to prepare a plan "involving the use of private funds only of the enhancement and development of golfing facilities that will better serve the rapidly increasing user rate." They cited as evidence the 43,000 rounds played on the IU course the previous year. "It is almost impossible to maintain that course," Williams stated, "and to meet the increasing demand."

Addressing other uses of the lands beyond the bypass, the task force recommended that the skeet and trap range and the police firing range be relocated and the lease agreement with the Sycamore Valley Gun Club be terminated. Using that ground for shooting sports and training for a third of a century with no accidents, the club had "certainly been a good neighbor," but increasing residential development in the area beyond the campus necessitated a change.[48] The next June, Athletic Director Clarence Doninger mentioned the golf course in his report to the trustees. Still under study was

[48]Indiana University Board of Trustees, "Minutes of the Board of Trustees of Indiana University, 01 November 1996" (Bloomington: Indiana University Archives & Indiana University Libraries Digital Collections Services, November 1, 1996), https://purl.dlib.indiana.edu/iudl/archives/iubot/1996-11-01.

whether to add nine or eighteen holes to the course, with future fundraising a given.[49]

7.6 Council for Environmental Stewardship

In the fall of 1996, Paul Schneller, coordinator of professional development for the physical plant, met with the IUB Professional Staff Council to float the idea of implementing a campus environmental stewardship program. The council created an ad hoc "Green Committee" consisting of staff members from a variety of areas to explore the idea.[50] Staff council president Tim Rice, with the purchasing department, received the endorsement of IU President Myles Brand in January 1997 for an environmentally friendly campus, with the recommendation that the committee work with Vice President for Administration J. Terry Clapacs and his staff. With administrative and financial support from Ken Gros Louis, vice president for academic affairs and Bloomington chancellor, a half-time position of environmental stewardship coordinator was created in August to assist with the initiative.

In January 1998, Gros Louis hosted a meeting with vice presidents, deans, and other campus leaders to launch the environmental stewardship initiative. Featured speakers were Oberlin professor David Orr, a leader in campus ecology efforts, and Ball State University representatives who discussed their campus "greening" program and the biennial national conferences on "greening the campus."

Working with both the academic structure and the operational departments of IU, the Council for Environmental Stewardship (CFES) was formed soon after and had its first meeting in March. Members—around forty to start—represented a variety of offices, departments, schools, and organizations. The mission was "to engage students, faculty and staff in academic programs and administrative efforts that enhance our campus environment and contribute to a

[49]Indiana University Board of Trustees, "Minutes of the Board of Trustees of Indiana University, 27 June 1997" (Bloomington: Indiana University Archives & Indiana University Libraries Digital Collections Services, July 27, 1997), https://purl.dlib.indiana.edu/iudl/archives/iubot/1997-06-27.

[50]Members were, in addition to Schneller: Jeff Kaden and Jeff Owens (physical plant), Ron Jensen (optometry), Bob Ensman (chemistry), Ted Alexander (environmental health and safety), and Mark Lame (SPEA). Council for Environmental Stewardship, "Annual Report," 1998–1999, p. 2.

healthy and sustainable world."[51] The council, growing out of a national movement for campus ecology, harnessed disparate efforts by individuals and small groups to make positive changes in the campus environment by developing formal communication channels between the university's campus operations and its varied academic programs of research and teaching.

7.7 Staying the Course

At the end of August 1999, IU officials revealed plans to negotiate with a private developer to build and operate a Jack Nicklaus–designed championship golf course and associated facilities on the IU campus. The proposed location was Sycamore Valley, where until recently the gun range had been located, and adjacent to the existing golf course, which was showing its age and lack of professional design. The project fulfilled hopes that had been nurtured for years by the athletic department and their supporters.

Reaction soon followed. A letter to the *Herald-Times* editor was titled "IU Country Club?" and urged public discussion on the project. The *Herald-Times* published a staff editorial, "Nicklaus Course Raises Questions." Acknowledging that a Jack Nicklaus Signature Championship Golf Course operated by Arnold Palmer Golf Management "must sound like a dream come true for area golfers," the editorial wondered whether the proposed facility "would be accessible to Hank and Helen Hacker." It was clear that the proposal was for a private club; it was unclear how public use might be managed. The piece also raised questions about the financial arrangements between IU and the developer and the potential environmental impact of the course.[52] Soon IU environmental scientists—plant scientist Keith Clay, water specialist Bill Jones, ecologist Dan Willard—sent a letter to the university administration outlining environmental concerns and recommendations.

In mid-October, the IU Student Association, at the urging of the Student Environmental Action Coalition, sponsored a forum to discuss the golf course project. Held in the law school, the forum

[51] Council for Environmental Stewardship, 2.

[52] James H. Capshew, "IU Country Club?" *Herald-Times*, September 4, 1999; James H. Capshew, "Nicklaus Course Raises Questions," editorial, *Herald-Times*, September 8, 1999.

featured speakers Professor Clay, Bloomington Parks and Recreation Natural Resources Director Steve Cotter, and IU Assistant Vice President for Real Estate Lynn Coyne. "The informational forum turned into a grilling as opponents to the proposal, making up the majority of the 170 people packing the room, lambasted Coyne with tough questions concerning the proposal," a student eyewitness reported.[53] Answering questions for two hours, Coyne maintained, "The goal is to integrate the design with environmental sensitivity," with any environmental concerns, such as soil erosion, water quality, and wildlife habitat, to be addressed adequately. But most of the audience remained skeptical.[54] For those folks, the forum also turned out to be an occasion to make connections with others of like mind.

Soon after the forum, about two dozen students and townspeople, with a sprinkling of faculty, formed an ad hoc group opposed to the new golf course. Open to all, it took the name of Protect Griffy Alliance. Its abbreviation—PGA—was an ironic play on the better-known shorthand for the Professional Golfers' Association. Griffy Lake, which had served as Bloomington's source of drinking water from 1925 to 1955, and its surrounding wooded watershed were the focus of concern, but the deeper issue was the propriety of private land use concessions within a public university. The existence of the Protect Griffy Alliance organization was spread by word of mouth, letters to the editor of the local newspaper, and frequent public meetings of the group. The group's members had no common ideology save a concern for the natural environment represented by the Griffy watershed. Griffy Lake was fed by Griffy Creek, which flowed through Sycamore Valley.[55]

Questions about public access were outlined in November when Vice President Clapacs and Assistant Vice President Coyne briefed the University Faculty Council. IU students, faculty, and staff would have limited access to the private club if they did not purchase a membership, which would include initiation fees ranging from $1,000 to $10,000 with monthly fees ranging from $75 to $200. Coyne said the public-private partnership with the Indiana Club

[53]Jonah M. Busch, "The Protect Griffy Alliance and the Golf War: Collective Action at Its Finest" (April 28, 2000). Seminar Paper, Indiana University.

[54]Mike Wright, "Issues Raised about Golf Course's Impact," *Herald-Times*, October 13, 1999.

[55]For example, Jerry Merriman, "How Should We Grow?" *Herald-Times*, November 10, 1999. Letter to the Editor.

LLC development group was a way to add more golf holes on campus, a long-term goal of the athletic department. Trying to allay ecological concerns, Coyne said, "Each hole will be custom fit to its environment." Summarizing the negotiations, Clapacs observed, "There is a line you can cross by making something too private," adding, "The negotiations are difficult but cordial."[56]

On November 12, the Protect Griffy Alliance staged a protest, dubbed the Rally for Lake Griffy, at the Sample Gates, the main campus entrance on Kirkwood Avenue, attracting a large crowd. In a skit, PGA members, dressed up in costume as birds, trees, and fish, gave objections to the course plans and potential environmental harms. The other PGA members, dressed as golfers, pretended to beat them back with golf clubs. In the newspaper coverage of the protest, Christopher Simpson, IU's vice president for public affairs and government relations, claimed that the university administration shared concerns over the environment, noting that the Nicklaus group had constructed golf courses on environmentally sensitive land, adding, "They have a track record of preserving, and even improving, the environment." Kara Reagan, a student member of PGA, disputed that assessment, stating, "There is no such thing as an ecologically sensitive golf course."[57]

The board of trustees scheduled a public forum the week after Thanksgiving, two days before they were to meet to consider leasing campus lands for the new course. The other issue needing trustee approval was the operating agreement between the developer and the university, tentatively scheduled for a January meeting. Further details about the leasing and operating arrangements between IU and the developer were released. The lease, comprising 311 acres, would be for fifty years initially, based on the land's appraised value of $1.18 million. All state permits, including erosion control, would be obtained.[58]

On the eve of the trustees' forum, the Bloomington *Herald-Times* filled in background information of the development company, Indiana Club LLC, which had been legally incorporated only in October. The three principals—Bob Whitacre, Tom Rush, and

---

[56]Mike Wright, "IU Students, Staff to Have Golf Access," *Herald-Times*, November 10, 1999.

[57]Mike Wright, "Golf Course Opponents Dress Like Fish, Trees," *Herald-Times*, 1999-11-13; *Indiana Daily Student*, November 15, 1999.

[58]Mike Wright, "Trustees Want Public Input on Golf Course," *Herald-Times*, 1999-11-24.

Mark Hesemann—were IU alumni, and their company also was connected to University Clubs of America, "an organization that creates, develops and manages golf resort facilities around the country for colleges and universities." Hesemann, an executive with Golden Bear International, the firm headed by Jack Nicklaus, who achieved fame as a golfer before turning to the development of golfing facilities, had seen the Pete Dye–designed Purdue course and thought it would be "a coup" to bring something similar to IU. He was also on the advisory board of the IU Kelley School's Sports and Entertainment Academy. Hesemann connected with Whitacre and Rush and produced a plan for a private golf resort at no cost to the university except exclusive use of a substantial chunk of campus land.[59]

The morning of the trustees' forum, professor of geological sciences Michael Hamburger wrote a *Herald-Times* editorial, asking an obvious question: "Why is it that this plan was undertaken with virtually no involvement of IU geologists, biologists, and environmental scientists with expertise in the areas of soil erosion, groundwater contamination, ecology, limnology, and wildlife biology?"[60]

Chaired by trustee Fred Eichhorn, the forum took place in the Frangipani Room of the Indiana Memorial Union. Eighty-five people signed up to speak; sixty-one were opposed to the project, five were neutral, and nineteen were in favor. (Due to time constraints, sixty-seven individuals actually spoke.) After two hours, the forum moved to the Whittenberger Auditorium for three more hours. Proponents were mostly connected already to the project or were members of the men's IU golf team, with some economic development and tourism officials. Many more opposed the plan. "These citizens ranged from an angry ex-librarian to the venerable George Taliaferro, who stated, 'We don't need another golf course. And the university doesn't need to further isolate itself from the city and the county.' "[61] Professor Hamburger presented a petition with 300 faculty signatures in opposition; Protect Griffy Alliance had one with 2,000 community signatories. The near-unanimous public outcry, "including numerous little old ladies in tennis shoes saying

[59]Mike Wright, "Group Behind New IU Golf Course Includes Alumni, Development Firm," *Herald-Times*, November 30, 1999.

[60]Michael Hamburger, "Editorial," *Herald-Times*, November 30, 1999.

[61]Mike Wright, "Critics Flock to Golf Forum," *Herald-Times*, December 1, 1999; Busch, "The Protect Griffy Alliance and the Golf War," 4–5. Seminar Paper, Indiana University.

'we'll lie down in front of your bulldozers,' " might have given the trustees pause. And pause they did. The next day, John Walda, president of the board of trustees, announced the postponement of a decision on the land lease to Indiana Club LLC until January 21 as well as the creation of an ad hoc committee of students, faculty, and administration to study the issues raised by the proposed course.[62] In an editorial, the *Indiana Daily Student* wondered whether the delay was "to give the trustees time to think, or to give opponents time to forget."[63]

The Protect Griffy Alliance kept up the pressure, with phone calls, flyers, yard signs, newspaper editorials, and interviews on radio and TV, through the university's winter break. On January 13, a group of faculty members submitted an alternative proposal for the Griffy land for a teaching and research preserve in the natural sciences. One of the proposal's developers, biology professor Clay, noted that there had been no response to a previous letter recommending amendments to the golf course plan to mitigate possible environmental impacts. He said that a potential compromise might emerge, "but so far the administration hasn't given us any compromise positions."[64]

The trustees and President Brand received an unusual letter that same week, from music teacher Daisy Garton, an IU alumna and donor, whose family homesteaded in the Griffy watershed about 1814. When Griffy Creek was dammed for the city water reservoir in the 1920s, her grandfather was forced to sell some bottomland, and he bought other land in the vicinity, which she inherited in 1937. In the early 1950s, the IU administration wanted to buy her property, for "educational purposes." Garton resisted but eventually sold part of the farm. When she learned that it was to be used as a golf course, she thought "that was ridiculous." Now, over four decades later, the golf resort plan would affect the remaining lands on Griffy Creek. Incensed, she wrote, "I do not believe this endeavor is consistent with the educational mission of the university, or its public character.... I therefore join with many other citizens

[62]Mike Wright, "IU Delays Action on a New Golf Course," *Herald-Times*, December 2, 1999.

[63]Indiana Daily Student, December 7, 1999, cited in Busch, "The Protect Griffy Alliance and the Golf War." Seminar Paper, Indiana University.

[64]Mike Wright, "Golf Course Alternative Offered," *Herald-Times*, January 14, 2000, A1, A9.

in asking that you preserve this land in its natural state, for the education and enjoyment of all."[65]

In order to finance the fight, the PGA coalition held a benefit "Lake Griffy Concert" in the historic Buskirk-Chumley Theater on January 16, a Sunday evening. It was a showcase of concerned local speakers and performers, some with national reputations, on behalf of a beloved local landmark. Musicians performing included Carrie Newcomer, Malcolm Dalglish, the Dew Daddies, Vida, and the 4th Street Irregulars. Keynote speakers were IU professor of English Scott Russell Sanders and local writer James Alexander Thom. Information was available in the lobby, where two online computer terminals were located so people could email their objections directly to IU officials. The atmosphere was electric in the packed house of seven hundred. The emcee, Professor Hamburger, proclaimed, "Tonight we're here to motivate, stimulate, vibrate, and, if necessary, castigate and repudiate!" The concert was a success, raising $5,000 for PGA.[66]

The day after the concert, the IU trustees' office announced that the private golf resort proposal was canceled. They explained, "The Trustees recognize the potential for the incongruence of mission between a public university and a golf club, which includes private membership." President Brand cited two reasons: a private club within a public university, and the various faculty objections, to which "the trustees listened carefully."[67]

7.8 Environmental Literacy and Sustainability Initiative

After the trustees formally designated some lands for the IU Research and Teaching Preserve in 2001, the Council for Environmental Stewardship continued its work.[68] During the 2001–02 academic

[65] Daisy Garton, "Letter to Trustees of Indiana University, President Myles Brand, and Members of the Higher Education Commission," January 12, 2000.

[66] David Horn, "Golf Course Opponents Jam Benefit Concert," *Herald-Times*, January 17, 2000.

[67] Erin Nave and Kara Saige, "Golf Course Cancelled," *Indiana Daily Student*, January 18, 2000.

[68] Indiana University Board of Trustees, "Minutes of the Board of Trustees of Indiana University, 04 May 2001" (Bloomington: Indiana University

year, its environmental literacy working group decided that basic knowledge of the environment should be a competency of all graduates. To that end, they updated the list of environment-related courses at IU and surveyed other universities to determine whether a basic course in environmental literacy was a curricular requirement. Less than 10 percent of the institutions surveyed required such a course, although many offered similar courses as electives. Working group members developed a detailed proposal for a faculty seminar series to help create a freshman environmental literacy course.[69] The next year, modest funding for the Environmental Literacy seminar was acquired, a wide variety of IU speakers and participants were recruited, and keynoters David Orr from Oberlin College and Christopher Uhl from Pennsylvania State University were confirmed for the fall 2003 event.[70]

The seminar series addressed two key questions: "What should an environmentally literate person actually know?" and "What teaching and learning strategies are most effective in promoting this level of environmental literacy campus-wide?"[71] Weekly speakers and commentators from a variety of disciplines and perspectives approached these fundamental questions. The series was co-coordinated by faculty in biology and anthropology in collaboration with Campus Instructional Consulting, assisted by graduate students in SPEA and biology. Presenters included faculty from anthropology, biology, English, law, physics, religious studies, and SPEA, among others. Faculty and graduate students, as well as several staff members, participated in the lively seminar. Interest in continuing the discussion was so great that the seminar series continued over the spring semester.[72]

In addition to the knowledge shared and discussed, an attempt was made to address the seminar's animating questions in a short position paper. The result, "Environmental Literacy: A Pedagogical Approach to Greening IU," was a précis of orienting philosophy, learning goals, and strategy.[73] Because of the success of the seminar,

Archives & Indiana University Libraries Digital Collections Services, May 4, 2001), https://purl.dlib.indiana.edu/iudl/archives/iubot/2001-05-04.

[69]Council for Environmental Stewardship, "Annual Report," 2001–2002, 2–3.

[70]Council for Environmental Stewardship, "Annual Report," 2002–2003, 3.

[71]An earlier iteration: "What constitutes the basic level of environmental literacy that all citizens should have?"

[72]"ELSI's History," from archived ELSI website.

[73]"Environmental Literacy: A Pedagogical Approach to Greening IU," 2004, from archived ELSI website.

the group spun off and took on a new name—Environmental Literacy and Sustainability Initiative (ELSI)—to continue this work.

In the fall 2004 semester, a second, more informal seminar series was held, focused on the idea of greening IU and planning steps to institutionalize the twin aims of environmental literacy and campus sustainability. By August 2005, a small group of the larger ELSI body developed a proposal, "Environmental Literacy and Sustainability Initiative at Indiana University: Strategy and Institutional Structure," for consideration by the IU administration. The organizational design included a sustainability coordinator (full-time professional staff member reporting to the chancellor or dean of faculties) and joint participation from CFES and ELSI in a campus-wide advisory board. Using temporary working groups to organize projects would be continued. The project's annual budget was nearly $200,000.[74]

In October 2006, many members of ELSI signed a letter to Provost Michael McRobbie urging the appointment of a task force on sustainability. Vice President Terry Clapacs appointed the task force in March 2007. Students, faculty, and staff comprised the sixteen-member group, aided by more than one hundred individuals in various working groups. Their 122-page report, *Campus Sustainability Report*, was issued in January 2008.[75] One of its main recommendations was to create an Office of Sustainability on the Bloomington campus, thereby beginning another chapter of the university's response to living within its environmental means.

7.9 The Journey toward Sustainability

The year 2009 was catalytic for the future of the Bloomington campus. On the organizational front, the IU Office of Sustainability was established in March, with dual reporting lines to campus leadership of academic affairs and facilities administration. Architect and educator William M. "Bill" Brown was selected as the founding director. Before long, students, faculty, and staff were engaged

[74]"Environmental Literacy and Sustainability Initiative at Indiana University: Strategy and Institutional Structure," 2005, from archived ELSI website. The proposal coordinators were Eduardo Brondizio, Victoria Getty, Brianna Gross, Diane Henshel, Catherine Larson, and Heather Reynolds.

[75]IU Task Force on Campus Sustainability, "Campus Sustainability Report" (Bloomington: Indiana University, January 7, 2008).

in a comprehensive program of assessing various aspects of the campus environment with the overall goals of improving resource use coupled with environmental education, and a strong student internship program began.[76]

In April, the field laboratory at the IU Research and Teaching Preserve was completed, providing research and classroom space. Located near University Lake, the lab followed the principles of green construction and was certified at the silver level by LEED (Leadership in Energy and Environmental Design), an international metric. The field lab was the first IU building to be LEED-certified.[77]

In June, the limestone buildings on campus were highlighted by a pocket-size publication, *Follow the Limestone: A Walking Tour of Indiana University.*[78] Brian Keith, a limestone expert employed by the Indiana Geological Survey, wrote the twelve-page guide explaining the architectural features and styles of the university's signature building material.

Six months later, in October 2009, Indiana University was catapulted onto the world stage when political science professor Elinor "Lin" Ostrom was awarded the Nobel Memorial Prize in Economic Sciences for her work on economic governance and the management of common property. Ostrom had worked at IU for forty-five years and co-directed the Workshop in Political Theory and Policy Analysis with her husband, Vincent Ostrom, also a professor of political science. She was the first woman to receive the prize, which had been awarded since 1969. Much of her research focused on how humans devise cooperative strategies outside of markets

---

[76]Nick Cusack, "First IU Sustainability Director Named," *Indiana Daily Student*, February 19, 2009; William M. Brown and Michael W. Hamburger, "Organizing for Sustainability," in *Enhancing Sustainability Campuswide*, ed. Bruce A. Jacobs and Jillian Kinzie, New Directions for Student Services 137 (Wiley, 2012), 83–96. See also Bruce A. Jacobs and Jillian Kinzie, "Editors' Notes," in *Enhancing Sustainability Campuswide*, ed. Bruce A. Jacobs and Jillian Kinzie, New Directions for Student Services 137 (Wiley, 2012), 1–6.

[77]The Field Lab.

[78]Brian D. Keith, "Follow the Limestone: A Walking Tour of Indiana University" (2009; repr., Bloomington: Originally published June 2009 by Indiana Geological Survey; Bloomington/Monroe County Convention; Visitors Bureau; republished July 2013 by Indiana Geological Survey; Visit Bloomington; current edition published July 2018 by Indiana Geological; Water Survey; Visit Bloomington, July 2018). In 2015, a digital version was produced: B. D. Keith, B. T. Hill, and M. R. Johnson, "Indiana University Campus Limestone Tour," Digital Information (Indiana Geological Survey, 2015), https://legacy.igws.indiana.edu/bookstore/details.cfm?Pub_Num=DI02.

or governments to manage natural resources—such as fish stocks, lakes, and groundwater—in sustainable ways, using the tools of social-ecological analysis.[79]

In 2010, continued progress toward campus sustainability was maintained. The 2008 *Campus Sustainability Report* also informed a new planning document for IUB. The IU Campus Master Plan was published by the SmithGroupJJR firm in March 2010 after a three-year period of analysis and refinement. "The most substantial and comprehensive plan of its type ever developed for the campus," President McRobbie declared, adding, "Sensitive to the great traditions of the campus while describing a carefully conceived path to an even more impressive future."[80] Five key themes animated the plan's vision: promotion of unique natural features, preservation and reinvigoration of the core, an embrace of the Jordan River, a commitment to a walkable campus, and the creation of diverse campus neighborhoods. Affirming "the continued relevance of the historic structures and distinguished open spaces," campus development "should emulate the quality and planning principles employed in the historic core."[81]

Early in the 2010 spring semester, the book *Teaching Environmental Literacy: Across Campus and Across the Curriculum* was published. Edited by faculty members Heather Reynolds, Eduardo Brondizio, and Jennifer Robinson, it contained ideas from the Environmental Literacy and Sustainability Initiative faculty seminar a few years earlier.[82] In February, the 147-page *Greening the IMU: Eco-Charrette Report* was released, providing a summary of a charette exercise in December 2009 to explore "ways to make Indiana Memorial Union operations and maintenance more environmentally effective." Seventy-two individuals (professionals, students, faculty, and administrators) participated in the two-day charette, perhaps the first ever held on campus with an explicit sustainability focus.[83]

[79]Elinor Ostrom, *Governing the Commons: The Evolution of Institutions for Collective Action* (New York: Cambridge University Press, 1990); Press release.

[80]SmithGroupJJR, "Indiana University Bloomington Campus Master Plan," March 2010. Michael A. McRobbie wrote the foreword.

[81]SmithGroupJJR, 4.

[82]Heather Reynolds, Eduardo Brondizio, and Jennifer Robinson, eds., *Teaching Environmental Literacy: Across Campus and Across the Curriculum* (Bloomington: Indiana University Press, 2010). In the interest of full disclosure, I authored a chapter in the edited book.

[83]"Greening the IMU: Eco-Charrette Report" (Bloomington: Indiana University, February 23, 2010).

During the 2010 fall semester, the College of Arts and Sciences sponsored a "themester" focused on the environment. Entitled "sustain · ability: Thriving on a Small Planet," specially themed coursework, lectures, art installations, movies, and other programs were abundant. In November, writer and activist Wendell Berry came to campus to deliver the Patten Lectures as part of the themester. Biology professor Heather Reynolds organized an interdisciplinary group of students, staff, and faculty as the Dunn's Woods Project to research, restore, and educate about this iconic woodland. Much of the effort was to mitigate the invasive purple wintercreeper (*Euonymus*) and to reintroduce native plants to restore biodiversity. Two years later, Latimer Woods, part of the City of Bloomington parks and trails system, was added and the name expanded to Bloomington Urban Woodlands Project to pursue community partnerships.[84]

7.10 The Bicentennial Era

Mindful of the university's two hundredth anniversary in 2020, the Office of Sustainability adopted a set of twenty aspirational goals to guide the next decade of work. These goals were organized into categories including leadership; academic programs; energy, atmosphere, and the built environment; transportation; food; environmental quality; and funding.[85] Similar goal-setting and planning efforts occurred within university administration in anticipation of the bicentennial.

In December 2014, the board of trustees approved the Bicentennial Strategic Plan, which was built on ten Principles of Excellence that articulated the aims of the university's mission to provide superior education, research, and health sciences and services. Number eight, Building for Excellence, addressed the physical plant: "Ensure that IU has the new and renovated physical facilities and infrastructure that are essential to achieve the Principles of Excellence, while recognizing the importance of historical stewardship, an environment that reflects IU's values, and the imperative to meet future needs

[84] Promoting healthy forests and reconnecting communities with their woodlands.

[85] IU Office of Sustainability, "Office of Sustainability 2020 Vision," 2010.

in accordance with long-term master plans."[86] Among the action items were the renovation of the Old Crescent area to make it the core of student academic life once again and the validation of all new major buildings with the LEED Green Building Certification System at the gold level or above.[87]

Another university-level initiative was the establishment of the Office of the Bicentennial in 2016 to coordinate historical and commemorative programs and activities across all campuses. Guided by a report from the Bicentennial Steering Committee that articulated goals, principles, and values, the bicentennial office organized its work under two dozen signature projects. Among the major categories were historical markers, archive development, publications and media, oral history, and campus beautification.[88] The first IU historical marker was installed on the IUB campus, honoring Professor Elinor Ostrom, in the fall of 2019, on the south side of Woodburn Hall.[89]

The bicentennial office supported a third wave of marking campus boundaries with gateways as part of the campus beautification project. During the first wave, in the 1920s, tall limestone gates punctuating low limestone walls were installed along Third Street. The second effort occurred in 1987 when the main campus entrance received the Sample Gates. This new effort was to mark different edges of the campus boundaries. "We really didn't have our major gateways identified," said university landscape architect Mia Williams. "It wasn't clear to people where campus proper started and stopped ...it's about a sense of place. We're saying, 'Hey, you're at Indiana University.' "[90] Four new gateways were constructed, along with the relocation of an existing set of gates. The largest was a limestone monolith at Dunn Street and State Road 46 Bypass, consisting of a sixty-one-foot tower reminiscent of the bell tower on the Old Crescent and nine-inch carved letters proclaiming INDIANA UNIVERSITY. Another, smaller set of gates, given to

[86]Indiana University Board of Trustees, "Minutes of the Board of Trustees of Indiana University, 05 December 2014" (Bloomington: Indiana University Archives & Indiana University Libraries Digital Collections Services, December 5, 2014), https://purl.dlib.indiana.edu/iudl/archives/iubot/2014-12-05.

[87]Indiana University Board of Trustees.

[88]The Office of the Bicentennial created a website to document IU bicentennial activities. The author served as the university historian from 2015 to 2023 and was a staff member of the Office of the Bicentennial.

[89]Elinor Ostrom IU Historical Marker Ceremony.

[90]Gates.

the university a half century before by the Chi Omega sorority, was moved to Woodlawn Avenue and the State Road 46 Bypass, in front of the baseball and softball fields. The gate at Third and Union Streets marked the southeast corner of the campus. On the southwest corner, at Third Street and Indiana Avenue, a similar gate was constructed, a legacy gift from law alumnus Lowell E. Baier. The last gate, completed in 2018, was installed at the corner of Seventh Street and Indiana Avenue, at Dunn Meadow.[91] The limestone gateways not only provided helpful landmarks but also tastefully reinforced the signature building material.[92]

In office from 2007 to 2021, the McRobbie administration pursued a vigorous program of facilities development, with new and renovated buildings across the campus, guided by the 2010 master plan. Two signature projects that were completed during the bicentennial year are instructive. One was rebuilding the golf course, dating to 1954, to championship standards—a dream long deferred. Named after a major donor, the Pfau Course at Indiana University was designed to take advantage of the forested setting and to offer golfers a demanding test of skill.[93] The other project was the Arthur Metz Bicentennial Grand Carillon. Fifty years prior, right after IU's sesquicentennial celebration, the original Metz Carillon was dedicated atop a hill on North Jordan Avenue. Played by faculty and staff of the School of Music, it was one of only six hundred carillons worldwide. Decisions were made to relocate the instrument closer to the heart of the campus, in the IU Arboretum (named in honor of Jesse and Beulah Cox), and to increase the number and size of the bells to qualify as a grand carillon—a rare distinction. Rivaling the tallest structures on campus, the cylindrical support holding the chimes, faced in limestone, elevated the bells so the sound carried for nearly two miles. Like the Student Building bell

---

[91]Michael Reschke, "IU Building Wave to Keep Going in 2018," *Herald-Times*, December 25, 2017, https://www.heraldtimesonline.com/story/news/local/2017/12/26/iu-building-wave-to-keep-going-in-2018/117591668/.

[92]The bicentennial era also brought other initiatives that promised changes for IU's flagship campus, including funding for the Prepared for Environmental Change Grand Challenge, including an Environmental Resilience Institute; the establishment of the IU Campus Farm; and the naming gift from Paul H. O'Neill for the School of Public and Environmental Affairs.

[93]Indiana University Board of Trustees, "Minutes of the Board of Trustees of Indiana University, 14 June 2019" (Bloomington: Indiana University Archives & Indiana University Libraries Digital Collections Services, June 14, 2019), https://purl.dlib.indiana.edu/iudl/archives/iubot/2019-06-14.

tower, installed more than a century ago, the new grand carillon promises to add to the remarkable soundscape of the campus.[94]

7.11 A Campus Legacy

In 2017, Indiana University Press published *Indiana University Bloomington: America's Legacy Campus.* Authored by Terry Clapacs, former vice president for university administration and facilities, it was the inaugural volume in the bicentennial Well House Books series.[95] The book contained an encyclopedic survey of the buildings and grounds of the flagship campus. Told from an insider's perspective, the volume's focus was architectural, but stories of campus life enlivened the text. In the introduction, Clapacs gave his considered opinion after his forty-year career in administrative stewardship: "In the midst of the gently rolling hills of southern Indiana is America's most beautiful college campus." Generations of students, staff, and visitors would heartily agree.[96]

The image of IU has been shaped over time by the physical plant, contributing to the university's identity as a place of learning. As Clapacs suggested, "A significant core value and institutional commitment at Indiana University is to provide an environment that is more than pleasant and comfortable—the campus is meant to inspire and to instill the idea that one's surroundings do make a difference."[97] By exploring that development historically, one can better understand the aspirations as well as the challenges of those who went before. There was no predetermined path to today's campus. It was nurtured through the efforts of countless individuals as it grew through more than a century of academic dwelling.

Historically, there was an unswerving fidelity to the landscape of southern Indiana. Limestone, native trees, and running water were

---

[94] Indiana University Board of Trustees, "Minutes of the Board of Trustees of Indiana University, 05 October 2017–06 October 2017" (Bloomington: Indiana University Archives & Indiana University Libraries Digital Collections Services, October 5, 2019), https://purl.dlib.indiana.edu/iudl/archives/iubot/2017-10-05. See also Arthur Metz Bicentennial Grand Carillon.

[95] Clapacs, *Indiana University Bloomington.* IU Press Director Gary Dunham played a major role in guiding this complex coffee-table volume.

[96] Clapacs, xv.

[97] Clapacs, xv.

the hallmarks of the IUB campus and its raw materials as it expanded a hundredfold in size since 1885. Expressing the ideals of higher education, the campus has served as a physical embodiment of the agency and apparatus of learning. Simultaneously, it has supplied an enduring emblem of Indiana University, a richly textured symbolic image, available for immediate apprehension by all. Through the efforts of its academic community, generation after generation, the campus at Dunn's Woods has made a place of learning and culture by remaining rooted to nature.

Part Three: Hidden Histories

Study the historian before you begin to study the facts.
—E.H. Carr, *What is History?*

Figure 11: Poster for the Centennial Pageant in 1920. With the campus bell tower in the background, feminine spirits occupy the foreground, left to right, symbolizing Indiana University, the State of Indiana, and the United States of America.

8 The Keeper of University History

Figure 12: Ivy L. Chamness

> If the history of Indiana University is ever written, much of it must needs be culled from the catalogues, papers, commencement and other programs which have been preserved by individuals as well as by the University. The mind of man runneth not back to the earliest days, and some of the University records were destroyed in the fires of 1854 and 1883. Extant records, moreover, give us only official acts, and it is to periodicals of the times and to programs of "activities" that we must turn for a picture of college life in those far-off days, seemingly so very, very unlike the present.
>
> —Ivy L. Chamness, "Indiana University in Earlier Days: I. As Reflected in Commencement and Exhibition Programs"

The first person to hold the position of editor of publications at Indiana University, Ivy Leone Chamness (1881–1975), is little remembered today. Her career began before the First World War and concluded after the Second, from 1914 to 1952. She made signal contributions to the writing, editing, and production of nearly all IU official communications, chief among them the periodic catalogs, bulletins, and registers. In addition, Chamness became the sole editor of the *Indiana University Alumni Quarterly* soon after it was begun in 1914. She made a special effort to nurture the understanding of the institution by making the *Alumni Quarterly* the journal of record for IU's history. She worked closely with the two preeminent architects of the modern university, William Lowe Bryan (president 1902–37) and Herman B Wells (president 1937–62), to shape its textual image to students, faculty, and staff as well as to attract and foster loyalty among its alumni and friends. When she was called on to assist elderly faculty historians as a developmental editor for long-delayed projects, she did not hesitate to lend her talents and skills. Yet she is barely remembered, remaining in the background as a hidden figure whose editorial and communicative work for the university did much to advance its fortunes during the first half of the twentieth century. In her role as the keeper of campus history, Chamness's efforts to edit, publish, and make known the history and culture of Indiana University are well worth noting.

8.1 From Student to Employee

Chamness was born on December 3, 1881, in Hagerstown, Indiana, near Richmond, the county seat of Wayne County. She graduated from Hagerstown High School in 1900 after suffering a bout of malaria two years before. She and her sister, Gracie May, enrolled at IU in 1902, during the first year of the administration of President William Lowe Bryan, and joined a student body of 750. Ivy graduated in 1906, majoring in English, and read the class poem at Senior Day. In the summer she wrote to the IU registrar, John W. Cravens, for help finding a job teaching English. With no teaching experience, in the fall of 1906, she landed a position at the Carlisle School in Sullivan County near Terre Haute. She contracted a serious case of diphtheria in the winter. During the next few years, Chamness was employed as an English teacher at a couple of schools in her home county, and in 1911, she got a job in Indianapolis at the Bobbs-Merrill Publishing Company, working in the law books division as a junior editor. The next year, she was on a streetcar that wrecked and injured twenty-one people, but she escaped with only bruised arms. After three years at Bobbs-Merrill, she was hired by IU as assistant editor of publications. She was not quite thirty-three years old, becoming "the first full-time appointee in this work."[1]

When Chamness started work at IU in 1914, there was no title of "editor of publications"; the responsibilities had been folded into the duties of John Cravens, university registrar and secretary to the board of trustees, since the turn of the century.[2] He was a trusted member of the small administrative staff and known to nearly all in the university community. In fact, Chamness had written to him several times for job advice after graduation. Cravens was appointed to the additional post of secretary to the university in 1915, soon after Chamness's arrival on staff.

[1]Myers, *History of Indiana University*, 1952, 170.

[2]Cravens served as registrar from 1895 to 1936, secretary to the board of trustees from 1898 to 1936, and secretary to the university from 1915 to 1936.

8.2 Early Years at the *Alumni Quarterly*

Chamness witnessed the infancy of the *Indiana University Alumni Quarterly*, born in 1914. The Alumni Association of Graduates and Former Students of Indiana University, as it was known formally, had tried various ways to communicate with the alumni in the past, and the quarterly was designed to be an expanded channel, with articles of current interest, news of the university, book reviews and literary notes, and class notes arranged by graduation year. The reform of the association also included a full-time executive secretary to oversee strategic plans as well as day-to-day operations.

The *Alumni Quarterly*'s initial editor was Samuel Bannister Harding, a history professor. A prolific author, he had edited the historical sketch *Indiana University, 1820–1904* ten years before.[3] The first issue started with an examination of the institutional beginnings of IU, with an article on "The Seminary Period" by the late David D. Banta. With the printing of all of Banta's Foundation Day addresses for the first time—six in all—in the first six issues of the *Alumni Quarterly*, his historical viewpoint was given fresh life to a new generation, and its publication in an organ of the university gave it an official imprimatur.

In the fourth issue, published in October 1914, Chamness contributed a book review of *Readings in Indiana History*, edited by a committee of the Indiana State Teachers Association and published by IU's new Extension Division. By that time, she was working at IU as assistant editor of publications (her book review was submitted months earlier).

In 1915, Chamness jumped in to help the fledging *Alumni Quarterly* with volume 2 and began to edit the section "Alumni Notes by Classes." The head note for that section contained a recurring plea: "It is urgently requested that each class proceed forthwith to the choice of a permanent class secretary who will undertake news of his class, and transmit it to the Editor." Taking her own advice, Chamness began serving as the class of 1906 secretary.[4]

For the July 1915 issue, history professor James A. Woodburn continued the historical narrative begun by Banta. He published

[3] *Indiana University, 1820–1904*.

[4] "Alumni Notes by Classes," ed. Ivy Leone Chamness, *Indiana University Alumni Quarterly* 2, no. 2 (April 1915): 207.

a total of eight articles over the next two years, dealing with the university's development during the period 1840 to 1860. Thus, by the end of the *Alumni Quarterly*'s first four years, a total of fourteen historical articles were published, starting a lasting trend.[5]

Beginning with volume 3 in 1916, Chamness appeared on the masthead as assistant editor, alongside the alumni secretary, R. V. Sollitt, as managing editor, and Professor Samuel B. Harding as advisory editor. Chamness was lauded by Sollitt for her "fine cooperation...in getting out the Quarterly," with "vigilance and zeal in securing news items of the alumni," which had made her department one of the most important.[6] In addition to her part-time work on the *Alumni Quarterly*, Chamness had been given more responsibility in her main job of editing official IU publications. Because of her proficiency, in 1917, she was made editor of publications for the university. But the recognition of her increasing competency was marred by the behavior of her administrative superiors at the alumni association.

In July 1918, Sollitt took a leave of absence in New York City, and Chamness took on his duties. He was still listed as managing editor, and she assumed that they would communicate regularly while he was away, but he failed to write a single letter. So, she was responsible for the entire operation: "procuring and editing of all signed articles, the writing of all unsigned articles, and the proofreading."[7] After putting up with the silent treatment for nine months, she wrote to the alumni council about the situation, requesting "a change in the statement of editorship" to insert her name as "editor-in-chief" while Sollitt was away.[8] Adding insult to injury, two months later and yet to receive a reply to her request, a different acting editor was named. She complained to President Bryan about her "arduous and gratuitous service" on the quarterly being "repudiated in a sense, that is by the appointment over my head of someone without any experience in the work."[9] Her com-

[5]*History of Indiana University*, 1940, v.

[6]"Work of the Alumni Council," *Indiana University Alumni Quarterly* 3, no. 3 (July 1916): 401.

[7]"Letter to William Lowe Bryan" (Indiana University Archives, May 11, 1920). IUA/C286/B54.

[8]"Letter to Alumni Council" (Indiana University Archives, March 22, 1919). IUA/C286/B54.

[9]"Letter to William Lowe Bryan" (Indiana University Archives, June 18, 1919). IUA/C286/B54.

plaint did bring some extra compensation but no acknowledgment of the legitimacy of her criticism.

Sollitt's leave turned into a separation, and in 1919, the alumni council selected a new secretary—Humphrey Mahan Barbour—who became the *Quarterly*'s managing editor, and Chamness was promoted to associate editor. The council also directed Barbour to send Chamness "a letter of deep appreciation for her great and generous services in acting as the sole editor of the *Quarterly* in the absence of Mr. Sollitt."[10] That was a measure of affirmation of her grievance.

When Sarah Parke Morrison, the first female student and graduate of Indiana University, died in Indianapolis in July 1919, Chamness republished Morrison's reminiscences from the *Indianapolis Star* in the *Alumni Quarterly*. Under the title "Some Sidelights of Fifty Years Ago," Morrison recounted the reasoning that brought her to the university in 1867, noting the fact that her brother Robert entered twenty years before, "though I was two years his senior." Her father, an IU trustee, supported her education, first at home and then at Mount Holyoke, a female seminary at the time, and Vassar College, and finally at IU, graduating in 1869. "But my school days were about over," Morrison wrote. "I could only rejoice at the opening prospect for young women as already exemplified," concluding with a dose of sarcasm, "and sit at home."[11]

8.3 IU Centennial

Indiana University celebrated its centennial birthday on January 20, 1920. IU counted around 7,000 alumni, along with 17,000 former students. Yet, despite a recent membership drive, the alumni association possessed about 2,000 members.

Chamness became even busier with editing and publishing items surrounding the commemoration. When alumni secretary Barbour left in June 1920, she was appointed acting editor of the *Alumni Quarterly*. The following year, the alumni council belatedly acknowledged her value and steady presence within the parade of short-term

[10] "Alumni Council Meetings," *Indiana University Alumni Quarterly* 6, no. 3 (July 1919): 394.

[11] "Some Sidelights of Fifty Years Ago," *Indiana University Alumni Quarterly* 6, no. 3 (July 1919): 530.

managing editors—all men, not coincidentally—and promoted her to the position of editor. Simple, unadorned "editor"—of which she had been doing the work for half a decade already. "Miss Chamness has been actively engaged with the editorial work of the *Quarterly* for a number of years and it is fitting and proper that she should be given the position as editor of the *Quarterly* because of her long and efficient services in connection with it."[12] Moreover, the new alumni secretary said, "Too much cannot be said of the services of Miss Chamness in connection with the *Alumni Quarterly*. For years she has worked on the *Quarterly* under the title of Associate Editor when in fact, for all information I can ascertain, she has practically edited the magazine. The Alumni Council owes Miss Chamness a vote of thanks for her efficient services."[13] Her delayed appreciation fit a common historical pattern of under-recognition and segregated employment endured by women.

Chamness reported on the voluminous activities of the Centennial Commencement in the July 1920 issue of the *Alumni Quarterly*. The festivities lasted for nearly a week, from the baccalaureate address on May 30 to the ninety-first annual commencement on June 4. "The week was crowded full of interesting events" in which a record number of alumni attended. "The campus was lovely, as always, and the weather on most days favorable," and "everyone was happy to be here," she wrote.[14]

The production of *Indiana University, 1820–1920: Centennial Memorial Volume* fell into the capable hands of Chamness (then editor of university publications). Part one reprinted the six articles by Banta on the history of the university from the *Alumni Quarterly*. Part two comprised thirteen addresses presented at the Centennial Educational Conference in early May, on topics ranging from science to spirituality, all relating to education. The final part reprinted Chamness's report on the Centennial Commencement, originally published in the *Alumni Quarterly*.[15] Widely distributed, the book became a lasting memento of the occasion. It revealed the ceremonial use of IU history as a background to current views and contentions of possible futures connected to university life,

[12]The decision was made June 6 to take effect on September 1. "Ivy Chamness to Edit Quarterly," *Indiana University Alumni Quarterly* 8 (1921): 331–32.

[13]"Ivy Chamness to Edit Quarterly," 332.

[14]"The Centennial Commencement," *Indiana University Alumni Quarterly* 7 (1920): 370.

[15]*Indiana University, 1820–1920*.

addressed by a parade of establishment figures. Only in the last section did the commentary turn to more quotidian activities on the local scene.

As the university continued to grow under the Bryan administration, Chamness kept pace with the demands of her position as chief editor of the bulletins, catalogs, and other university publications.

8.4 "Mother of College Presidents"

Less than a year after the IU centennial celebration, Chamness wrote a short article titled "Indiana University—Mother of College Presidents" for the journal *Educational Issues.* "Her graduates," she wrote, "have been called to the presidencies of universities, colleges and normal schools from Maine to California, from Minnesota to Florida."[16] There might be larger universities who have produced more, but, she added, "considering the size and age of the institution, the University has an unusually large proportion of men at the head of institutions of higher learning." The article included a list of twenty-five college and university presidencies held by IU alumni, including state and private universities, normal schools, and denominational colleges.

To explain this trend, Chamness cited a policy credited to David Starr Jordan, IU president from 1885 to 1891. He encouraged promising undergraduate alumni to obtain graduate training, either in the east or Europe, before returning to Bloomington to qualify as members of the faculty. When Jordan left to become the inaugural president of Stanford, he took six faculty members with him, some future presidents among them. Concluding on a bittersweet note, Chamness wrote, "Since that time increasing numbers of faculty members and alumni have left the University and the state to become educational leaders in other fields. Their fellow alumni rejoice in their progress and advancement in the educational world, but feel regret that the University and the state of Indiana must be deprived of their leadership."[17]

---

[16] "Indiana University—Mother of College Presidents," *Educational Issues* 2, no. 8 (1921): 28–29.

[17] 28–29.

The next year, Chamness republished her article in the *Alumni Quarterly*, adding a few more names to the list of presidents.[18] Over time, she would continue to add names, and her assessment that the institution was the "mother of college presidents" became embedded in IU's historical identity.[19]

As a follow-up to the IU centennial, Registrar John Cravens noted the 1922 centennial of the university's first building—the Seminary Building—and published a series of three articles in the *Alumni Quarterly* detailing the architectural history of Indiana University. He was careful to document sources to the written record, but much information depended on the oral tradition as well as his personal experience reaching back to the 1890s.[20]

Five years later, in 1927, Cravens published the results of his study of the IU trustees, which totaled 148 individuals, updating an earlier list found in Wylie's 1890 historical catalog. He noted the silver anniversary of the administration of President Bryan, who had served longer than any other president. In addition to outlining the trustee board's evolving structure, he listed some of the accomplishments and official positions of individual trustees, including service in state and national governments.[21] Both of Cravens's publications were timely contributions to conversations about the past among the IU community as well as valuable additions to the permanent historiography.

In 1928, Chamness completed a master's degree in journalism. Drawing on her daily work, she conducted a thesis titled "A Study of Editorial Matters in the Catalogs of the Members of the National Association of State Universities."[22] The existing literature

---

[18] "Indiana University—Mother of College Presidents," *Indiana University Alumni Quarterly* 9 (1922): 46–49.

[19] For example, ("More College Presidents," *IU Alumni Quarterly* 10 (1923): 334); ("Another College President," *IU Alumni Quarterly* 10 (1923): 512); ("Another College President," *IU Alumni Quarterly* 25 (1938): 59). See also Capshew, "Indiana University as the 'Mother of College Presidents': Herman B Wells as Inheritor, Exemplar, and Agent".

[20] "Buildings on the Old and New Campuses of Indiana University," 1922; "Buildings on the Old and New Campuses of Indiana University," 1922; "Buildings on the Old and New Campuses of Indiana University," 1922.

[21] "The Trustees of Indiana University," *Indiana University Alumni Quarterly* 14 (1927): 465–83.

[22] "A Study of Editorial Matters in the Catalogs of the Members of the National Association of State Universities" (Indiana University, 1928). Master's thesis, Indiana University.

was scant—only three publications—and her approach was strictly empirical.

Based on responses from forty-nine institutions and their catalogs, she compared typography and form, information and its arrangement, and miscellaneous matters. In the last section, Chamness discussed editorship, suggesting, "Editors are usually a modest lot; they almost have to be. They become quite accustomed to doing hard work to which no name or someone else's name is attached. Editors of college catalogs seem to be no exception. Many of these publications give the reader no hint as to who is responsible, and, indeed, if something goes wrong 'twixt manuscript and printing press, the editor may well be content with his anonymity."[23]

Her study revealed a wide array of answers to the question "Who is responsible for editing your catalog?" ranging from administrative staff to members of a committee. About 60 percent of the institutions surveyed had an advisory committee. She noted that "the best practice would call for an advisory committee to discuss and determine matters of policy, which the editor could carry out."[24]

She completed her 150-page thesis with a one-paragraph conclusion suggesting ways to improve the college catalog, focusing on the important role of editor. If the work falls to a committee, "uniformity in details will be well nigh impossible. There are many, many minutiae which must be watched, and patience, endurance, and eternal vigilance are prerequisite to the work of editing a college catalog."[25]

8.5 "In Earlier Days"

In 1929, Chamness launched an article series under her byline in the *Alumni Quarterly* with the general title "Indiana University in Earlier Days." It surveyed the historical documents that Professor Emeritus Woodburn had recently given to the university, consisting of old catalogs and programs, and issues of the *Indiana Student*. Some of the material was collected by his father, James W. Woodburn, who graduated in 1842 and served as a faculty member

[23] 127. Master's thesis, Indiana University.
[24] 130. Master's thesis, Indiana University.
[25] 150. Master's thesis, Indiana University.

before his early death. Other documents were from his own collection, dating back to his student days in the 1870s, augmented by another collection from Professor Frank Andrews. Revealing her penchant for writing and her understanding of the importance of documentary sources, Chamness introduced the series by saying official publications are important, but "extant records, moreover, give us only official acts, and it is to periodicals of the times and to programs of 'activities' that we must turn for a picture of college life in those far-off days, seemingly so very, very unlike the present."[26]

IU's institutional archives, such as student records and board of trustees' minutes, were woefully incomplete due to campus fires in 1854 and 1883 that obliterated the bulk of them. Theophilus Wylie's painstaking work for the 1890 historical catalog, *Indiana University, Its History from 1820, When Founded, to 1890*, partially remedied the damage by compiling lists of students, faculty, and trustees, but records of the early history of student life were gone. Chamness attempted to reconstruct this lost history using the collections of historical materials recently donated to the university. What emerged were fascinating glimpses into nineteenth-century collegiate life in Bloomington.

Chamness described the students of the 1840s to the 1890s by using past commencement programs.[27] Each graduating student had to deliver a public speech—a commencement oration—at the graduation ceremonies. The subjects were varied. Chamness characterized early graduates as being abstract, ambitious, broad, and inquisitive, reminding readers that those students carried the same traits as students of today. Student solidarity and the practice of protesting perceived injustice remained similar, Chamness suggested, "even in those days, for we read that sixty-three fellow-students proposed to go with a student who, it was claimed, was dismissed without investigation."[28] Even past student newspapers, which looked significantly different from the contemporary *Indiana Daily Student*, showcased the similarities between present and past collegiate life.[29] While the *Indiana Student* advertised "activity tickets" for music concerts

[26]"Indiana University in Earlier Days: I. As Reflected in Commencement and Exhibition Programs," *Indiana University Alumni Quarterly* 16, no. 1 (1929): 33.

[27]"Indiana University in Earlier Days," 1929.

[28]"Indiana University in Earlier Days: II. As Reflected in Early Issues of the *Indiana Student*," *Indiana University Alumni Quarterly* 16, no. 2 (1929): 218.

[29]Chamness, 199.

and the Union Series, one of the past newspapers, *The Student*, advertised opportunities to attend lectures, an occasion that provided students with entertainment and the chance to hear renowned speakers.[30] Even with the passage of many years, continuities can be observed in collegiate life.

Despite such similarities, however, Chamness acknowledged that college life had evolved over time and did not mirror the present exactly. The old *Indiana Student* newspaper had a literary cast, with literature, reviews, and letters exchanged among the IU community. In contrast, the contemporary *Indiana Daily Student* emphasized news, sports, and entertainment.[31] Chamness reprinted the 1878 university rules for students. She noted that present-day departments in the university did not have equivalents of two of the original departments: civil engineering and mental, moral, and political philosophy.[32]

The seventh and last article in the "Indiana University in Earlier Days" series appeared in 1934.[33] Chamness produced one hundred pages of material, including programs from commencements, literary societies, and other events; official catalogs; and student newspaper publications from the last quarter of the nineteenth century. Chamness divided the information up into three categories—programs (one article), *Indiana Student* (three articles), official publications (two articles)—plus one miscellaneous article. It truly was a grab bag, but it did contain valuable archival information for future historians. It generated interest among the alumni and, in some cases, stimulated responses that were subsequently published, adding more

[30]Ivy Leone Chamness, "Indiana University in Earlier Days: IV. As Reflected in Issues of the *Indiana Student* in the Nineties," *Indiana University Alumni Quarterly* 18, no. 2 (1931): 170.

[31]Chamness, "Indiana University in Earlier Days," 1929, 202.

[32]Ivy Leone Chamness, "Indiana University in Earlier Days: VII. As Reflected in Official Publications," *Indiana University Alumni Quarterly* 21, no. 2 (1934): 42.

[33]Chamness, "Indiana University in Earlier Days," 1929; Chamness, "Indiana University in Earlier Days," 1929; Ivy Leone Chamness, "Indiana University in Earlier Days: III. As Reflected in the Issues of the *Indiana Student* in the Nineties," *Indiana University Alumni Quarterly* 17, no. 1 (1930): 22–38; Chamness, "Indiana University in Earlier Days," 1931; Ivy Leone Chamness, "Indiana University in Earlier Days: V. As Reflected in Historical Material Recently Given to the Institution," *Indiana University Alumni Quarterly* 18, no. 1 (1931): 16–29; Ivy Leone Chamness, "Indiana University in Earlier Days: VI. As Reflected in Official Publications," *Indiana University Alumni Quarterly* 20, no. 2 (1933): 159–68; Chamness, "Indiana University in Earlier Days," 1934.

texture and context to the documents.[34] Her respect for the documentary record extended to the past, as evidenced by her thorough discussion of historical documents pertaining to the university's past that had survived to the 1920s.

8.6 Woodburn and *History of Indiana University*

By 1933, Chamness had become actively involved in Woodburn's history of Indiana University project. President Bryan asked her to work with Professors Henry H. Carter and Albert L. Kohlmeier to prepare an article on the history of the curriculum post-1904 for the history volume. She also volunteered to prepare an index to the section "News of the University" published in the *Alumni Quarterly* to aid Woodburn's research.[35] Nearly twenty years before, she had worked with Woodburn when he published several articles in the *Alumni Quarterly.* Now, he was in his late seventies, living in retirement in Michigan.

The history project dated to June 1929. Five years after Woodburn retired from the faculty and moved to his wife's hometown of Ann Arbor, President Bryan wrote him a letter, beseeching him to write "some chapters in the History of Indiana University during the period that you have known it." Bryan and Woodburn had known each other since childhood in Bloomington, and both entered IU as students in the 1870s. "Your reminiscences of the faculty and of the whole situation will be very valuable," Bryan wrote, adding, "You could continue your chapters as long as you feel disposed, but I hope that you will not stop until you have wound up with the chapter on your later years at the University." The president appealed to Woodburn's personal and family links to IU history: "You are yourself the link which connects the earliest years of the University by your knowledge of some of the men at that time with the present. It seems to me so wholly desirable from every point

[34]For instance, Goodwin, "The *Indiana Student* and Student Life in the Early Eighties."

[35]Indiana University Archives, "Finding Aid, Collection 286, Box 54" (Bloomington, IN: Indiana University, n.d.). IUA/C286/B54.

of view that you should do this, that I can not bear you not to do it."[36]

Woodburn responded affirmatively to this urgent plea, but the historical project was slow to gain traction, exacerbated by his difficulty in returning to Bloomington for archival research. The correspondence between Woodburn and Bryan quickened again in 1934, with another exchange of letters. Bryan ruefully promised to send a chapter that could not appear in the book, illustrating "the point that much of the most interesting history cannot be written until everybody is dead who had anything to do with it or who cares anything about it." To aid the project, Bryan wrote to the faculty, present and past, asking for biographical details, and announced that Woodburn was editor-in-chief for the history project. Noting that a meeting of the board of trustees was coming up, he asked Woodburn to prepare an outline of the book project for their information.[37]

In 1935, Woodburn obliged by sketching an outline, noting that "the History has been carried to about 1887," the end point of Wylie's 1890 historical catalog. The proposed work would have several authors, mostly faculty and staff, writing about various schools, the athletic program, student life, the library, buildings and grounds, and the trustees. The sketch had sixteen items, with eighteen authors contributing.

In keeping with Woodburn's conception of history as a container of the past, authoritatively authored, he suggested including Judge Banta's historical articles as well as his own—seen as a continuation of a singular historical record. Woodburn set himself the task of covering the period from 1856 (the termination point of his earlier work) up to the turn of the twentieth century and the start of the Bryan administration soon afterward.

In addition to Banta and Woodburn, the outline included sections on: trustees and the physical plant (John Cravens), curriculum (Henry Carter and Albert Kohlmeier), medical school (Burton Myers), law school (unspecified), music (Winfred Merrill and John Stempel), journalism and the *Indiana Student* (Joseph Piercy and Walter French), presidents and faculty (Mrs. John Cravens), university

[36]"Letter to James A. Woodburn" (Indiana University Archives, June 17, 1929). IUA/C83/B3/F Publications, Galleys, & Transcripts.

[37]"Letter to James A. Woodburn" (Indiana University Archives, November 17, 1934). IUA/C83/B3/F Publications, Galleys, & Transcripts.

publications (Ivy Chamness), athletics (Charles Sembower and John Sembower), school of education (Lester Smith), fraternities (Karl Fischer), the library (William Alexander and Estella Wolf), and reminiscences (William L. Bryan). As Woodburn put more time in the project, he came to agree with President Bryan about its priority, admitting in 1935: "I have let this thing drag on without doing much at it, but now I recognize, with you, that it should be pushed forward to completion within the year, if possible."[38]

Editor Chamness, still busy with endless rounds of editing of IU catalogs and bulletins, wrote a note to a faculty wife about some alumni association business in 1935: "I began my work on the *Quarterly* twenty-one years ago next fall with Volume I, No. 4. Surely my long service and my financial support, probably longer than that of any on the Council, deserve some consideration when a matter of this kind comes up. One year I did all the work and ran another name as editor, said editor never contributing one word."[39] She had moved on from the injustice, but she never forgot.

Woodburn did not meet his self-imposed deadline, but in June 1936, he convened a meeting of project authors in the Woodburn Room of the Indiana Memorial Union building. The goal was to have completed manuscripts on September 1, 1936. All of the authors reported that their work was completed or in hand to meet the deadline except for one. Fernandus Payne, dean of the graduate school, suggested that Woodburn, as editor, should be authorized to cut or change any of the reports, which received support.[40] Despite the hopeful rhetoric, Woodburn's project continued to flounder.

8.7 From *Alumni Quarterly* to *Indiana Alumni Magazine*

Having resided at 807 E. Tenth Street since 1933, Chamness lived with her widowed mother. In January 1937, her mother died at age seventy-nine, making Chamness the sole survivor of her immediate

[38] "Letter to William Lowe Bryan" (Indiana University Archives, February 28, 1935). IUA/C83/B3/F Publications, Galleys, & Transcripts.

[39] "Letter to Mrs. C. J. Sembower" (Indiana University Archives, June 3, 1935). IUA/C84/B1/F Edited Manuscripts-Alumni Quarterly.

[40] "Meeting in Woodburn Room, June 4, 1936," June 4, 1936. Folder: Publications, Galleys & Transcripts, IUA/C83/B3/F, Indiana University Archives.

family.[41] Other changes were in store. On March 15, President Bryan, now seventy-six years old and in office for thirty-five years, announced his retirement. Taking the IU trustees by surprise, it set off an extended transition period. In June, the trustees appointed dean of the business school Herman Wells as acting president. The dean was young—he had just turned thirty-five—but his character combined shrewd financial judgment with deep empathy for everyone. The presidential search ended nine months later, when the trustees elevated Wells to become the eleventh president of Indiana University on March 22, 1938.[42]

In May, a new alumni magazine was proposed, touted as a way to get more members. The alumni council sent a query card to 17,200 alumni, but only 759 cards were returned. Over 600 approved of the idea, while 71 disapproved. The recently appointed director of the IU News Bureau, E. Ross Bartley, stated that "the proposed monthly sounded like a very excellent idea, that as good as the *Quarterly* has been, it does not quite fit in with the new spirit that Indiana has or compare to other schools." Chamness, not reacting to the casual slight, stated simply that she "could do the book reviews, class notes, copy editing, and proofreading."[43]

So, after one hundred issues and a quarter century, the *Indiana University Alumni Quarterly* ceased publication with its October 1938 issue. Chamness had been identified with the publication since almost the very beginning, keeping the communication channels between the university and its alumni flourishing. For twenty-five years, it served as the journal of record for university history, filling the thirty-six-year gap between IU history books from 1904 to 1940.[44]

---

[41] "Alumni Notes by Classes: 1906," *Indiana University Alumni Quarterly* 24, no. 1 (1937): 74: "Mrs. Marvin E. Chamness, mother of Ivy L. Chamness, died at her home in Bloomington January 11 following an hour's illness."

[42] See Capshew, *Herman B Wells*, Chapter 5.

[43] "Commencement, 1938," *Indiana University Alumni Quarterly* 25, no. 3 (1938): 298–337, p. 309. Chamness's classmate "Mrs. Mary Hamilton Beck, '06, of Evanston, Ill. moved that a vote of appreciation be given to Miss Chamness for having given us a fine publication in the *Quarterly*. Walter Crim seconded the motion and it was passed," p. 316.

[44] Harding, *Indiana University, 1820–1904* and Woodburn, *History of Indiana University*, 1940.

8.8 Publication of the *History of Indiana University*

Meanwhile, Chamness stepped up her work on Woodburn's history project, as the new Wells administration made it among their priorities. She requested more help in 1938 because of the increased workload. During one of Woodburn's periodic visits, Chamness stated to Wells, "I have spent most of my time for two weeks in going over in a rather tentative way the copy which Dr. Woodburn prepared for his history."[45]

In the interest of not delaying the volume further, it was decided to save the draft sections authored by others and to concentrate on finishing Woodburn's narrative. As the book took its final shape, it became a hybrid. The first six chapters were authored by David Banta, recycled from the early issues of the *Alumni Quarterly*. The next eight chapters were by Woodburn, again republished from the early quarterly. The final eight chapters were new material by Woodburn, covering the period from 1850 to 1902, the start of the Bryan administration. Those chapters were a blend of historical analysis and personal observation; Woodburn's memory encompassed the last quarter of the nineteenth century. He also used primary sources and personal correspondence to round out the narrative, sometimes quoting letters at length. It was a brave performance, given Woodburn's age and declining ability.

For her part, Chamness relished the intellectual and compositional challenge. In a note to Woodburn, she declared, "The work on this book I regard as the most interesting task I have had or hope to have," and added, "I have put forth my supreme effort."[46] Although Chamness was not acknowledged as the book's editor on the title page, her extensive rewriting and editorial work was evident, and Woodburn expressed heartfelt gratitude in the preface.[47]

[45] "Letter to Herman B Wells" (Indiana University Archives, 1938). IUA/C213/B118.

[46] "Letter to James A. Woodburn" (Indiana University Archives, November 30, 1940). IUA/C83/B4/F Testimonial Banquet/Correspondence.

[47] Woodburn, *History of Indiana University*, 1940, p. v. A dozen years later, Chamness received retrospective acknowledgment as the editor of Woodburn's *History of Indiana University*, in the succeeding volume. Myers, *History of Indiana University*, 1952, p. xiv.

In 1940, the book was unveiled during a gala occasion—the Woodburn Testimonial Dinner—held in Alumni Hall on November 30, Woodburn's eighty-fourth birthday. President Wells, who had lived at the Woodburn House for eight years and had warm relations with the emeritus professor, wanted to thank Woodburn publicly for his lifetime of service to the institution, culminating in the publication of the *History of Indiana University*, his last book.[48] Over 300 people attended, and former students and colleagues wrote letters of appreciation for the public presentation.

In his address at the Woodburn Testimonial Dinner, Woodburn recalled his efforts to have David Banta's speeches on the early history of IU published in the first issues of the *Alumni Quarterly* and modestly took credit for their preservation in print. As "the real historian of the University in its beginnings," stated Woodburn, "Judge Banta had an historical sense and an historical scent. He knew evidence. He went to the sources, and he wrote in such a style as to make the facts as interesting as fiction." If Banta's work was the starting point, "at the other end of the enterprise came Miss Chamness, who refuses to speak for herself, a most valuable editor, a fair and generous critic." Woodburn only hinted at her enormous contributions to the book: "She has verified my statements or eliminated them. She has worked with pencil and eraser and has done some of the best work with the eraser. I wish again to acknowledge my obligations to her, which I have done quite imperfectly in the preface."[49] Chamness, who had worked with Woodburn for nearly a quarter century, was gratified by the public praise of her editorial skills. She would soon be involved in the second volume of *History of Indiana University*, assisting another retired faculty member with the challenge of writing about President Bryan's administration.

---

[48]Less than year afterward, in September 1941, Woodburn gave the Woodburn House to IU. Indiana University Board of Trustees, "Minutes of the Board of Trustees of Indiana University, 25 September 1941–27 September 1941" (Bloomington: Indiana University Archives & Indiana University Libraries Digital Collections Services, September 27, 1941), https://purl.dlib.indiana.edu/iudl/archives/iubot/1941-09-25.

[49]James A. Woodburn, "Presentation of the *History of Indiana University*, Volume I at the Woodburn Testimonial Dinner" (Indiana University Archives, n.d.). IUA/C83/B4/F Woodburn, James.

8.9 Myers and *History of Indiana University*

No sooner was the Woodburn manuscript put to bed than Chamness turned her attention to another book project: the history of the Bryan administration. Supervised by retired professor of anatomy and medical school dean Burton Myers, the second volume of *History of Indiana University* would cover the long administration of President Bryan from 1902 to 1937. A trusted member of President Bryan's inner circle, Myers retired in July 1940, at age seventy, and he confidently took up the mantle of amateur historian. Bryan and Myers had helped shape the early IU School of Medicine and maintained a respectful friendship for decades.

Myers had been working on a manuscript dealing with the history of medical education off and on for several years before retirement. Within the year following retirement, he was working on the history of the Bryan administration. In April 1941, Myers and Wells had an exchange about the project. Wells asked, "For pay or labor for love?" Myers replied, stating his book project on medical education was a labor of love, but the history project would be different:

> For this other job I think a pay basis would be fair, tho' the "labor of love" element would not be entirely lacking. It has not been lacking during my years of connection with Indiana University. I have been happy to try to give service worth twice as much as I was paid, which makes it a sort of 50-50 proposition....What the pay basis should be—I will be quite willing to leave to your judgement, and you may reserve judgment, as long as you wish to assure yourself the effort is not a flop.[50]

In the same exchange, Myers revealed a patronizing ambivalence about his coworker: "Miss Chamness as Associate Editor is all right. I have been irritated by her at times, but we have gotten along reasonably well. I realize that she has an experience and judgment that can be very helpful."[51]

Wells took this information in and added it to his elephantine memory. For her part, Chamness approached the collaboration as a professional task. Myers, a longtime administrator used to

[50] "Letter to Herman B Wells" (Indiana University Archives, April 1, 1941). IUA/C213/B404/F Myers, Dean B. D.

[51] IUA/C213/B404/F Myers, Dean B. D.

deference from subordinates, had trouble relating to Chamness as a fellow professional—one who possessed not only editorial dexterity but also a knack for history.

As negotiations on the history project continued, Wells discussed the question of an honorarium for Myers with the board of trustees. They left it to the discretion of their executive committee.[52] In July, Wells wrote to Myers after reading a sample: "This first chapter is commendable in every way. In fact, I am enthusiastic about it."[53] In April 1942, the trustees authorized an advanced payment to Myers of $1,300.[54] Realizing his commitment to the IU history volume, Myers jettisoned another project—the history of medical education in Indiana—and gifted the incomplete manuscript to the university in June 1942. The board of trustees authorized President Wells to offer thanks to Myers as well as to investigate publication possibilities.[55]

As the second volume of the *History of Indiana University* was taking shape, the question arose of what to do with the bits of manuscript that were planned for the first volume but never made it in for one reason or another. As it turned out, many of them were included, which made the editing task that much harder.

8.10 Trustees Volume

The Wells administration inherited an additional history project from the Bryan administration, one focused on the IU trustees. Building on earlier lists compiled by Wylie (1890) and Cravens (1927), in 1939, President Wells asked the university librarian,

---

[52]Indiana University Board of Trustees, "Minutes of the Board of Trustees of Indiana University, 30 May 1941–02 June 1941" (Bloomington: Indiana University Archives & Indiana University Libraries Digital Collections Services, May 31, 1941), https://purl.dlib.indiana.edu/iudl/archives/iubot/1941-05-30.

[53]"Letter to Burton D. Myers" (Indiana University Archives, July 18, 1941). IUA/C213/B404.

[54]Ward G. Riddle, "Letter to Burton D. Myers" (Indiana University Archives, April 21, 1942). IUA/C213/B404.

[55]Indiana University Board of Trustees, "Minutes of the Board of Trustees of Indiana University, 22 June 1942–23 June 1942" (Bloomington: Indiana University Archives & Indiana University Libraries Digital Collections Services, June 23, 1942), https://purl.dlib.indiana.edu/iudl/archives/iubot/1942-06-22.

William Alexander, to continue to accumulate biographical materials on the trustees, including photographs or portraits, with an eye toward eventual publication. Alexander made progress in updating the trustee list to 1940 as well as organizing material for the biographical sketches, but the sketches remained unwritten at his death in July 1943.[56]

Several months later, Wells turned to Myers to take on the uncompleted task in addition to the historical research on the Bryan administration. The trustees received an oral report from Myers on his work in December 1943, during which he pointed out some discrepancies in the various IU histories that had been previously published.[57] For the trustees volume, since the research was well advanced, the trustee board authorized Myers in January 1944 to proceed with the preparation of a book that would contain biographies of each trustee, along with an introduction written by Ora Wildermuth, the board president. "Questions of form, size, and date of publication were postponed" to a future date.[58] So now, in wartime, Myers and Chamness had their hands full of research, writing, and editing as they worked on two important IU history books.

Although the observance of Indiana University's 125th anniversary in 1945 was canceled because of wartime conditions, Chamness managed to produce a four-page timeline of university history for the May 1945 issue of the *Indiana Alumni Magazine*.[59] That month, the war in Europe had concluded with Germany's surrender, followed in August by Japan's capitulation in the Pacific theater, marking the end of the Second World War.

---

[56]Myers, *Trustees and Officers of Indiana University 1820–1950*, 1951.

[57]Indiana University Board of Trustees, "Minutes of the Board of Trustees of Indiana University, 19 December 1943" (Bloomington: Indiana University Archives & Indiana University Libraries Digital Collections Services, December 19, 1943), https://purl.dlib.indiana.edu/iudl/archives/iubot/1943-12-19.

[58]Indiana University Board of Trustees, "Minutes of the Board of Trustees of Indiana University, 28 January 1944–30 January 1944" (Bloomington: Indiana University Archives & Indiana University Libraries Digital Collections Services, January 28, 1944), https://purl.dlib.indiana.edu/iudl/archives/iubot/1944-01-28.

[59]Ivy L. Chamness, "The First 125 Years," *Indiana Alumni Magazine* 7, no. 9 (1945): 11–14.

8.11 Postwar Changes

In the fall of 1945, Chamness would face significant changes in the university's publication profile. Already the Wells administration had modernized the alumni association and its communication channels and created the IU News Bureau to manage the university's public profile. In the postwar years, expansion—of student enrollment, academic programs, and facilities—was a constant preoccupation.

As university publications editor, Chamness was still managing the official bulletins and various research publications under the university's imprimatur. She also had to handle two large and unwieldy history manuscripts written by Myers. First, she would take on another round of editing for the trustees volume, which would take her into 1946. And then she would spend another year wrangling the history book into acceptable form.

Although Myers relied on Chamness's editing skills to render his drafts into presentable form, he was a dogged researcher and placed a high value on getting accurate facts. When Myers took over the trustees' project after librarian Alexander's death, a thorough review of the data that had been gathered revealed significant gaps in some of the biographical materials. Even the list of the trustees had to be reconciled with surviving documentation of those who were elected and served as members of the board. Both Wylie and Cravens counted election as a trustee as the basic criterion. Myers added the criteria of presentation of a certificate of election and the taking of an oath of office, which eliminated 22 individuals, leaving a total of 145 members of the board from 1820 to 1950.[60]

The trustees volume was organized chronologically, divided by changes in the organization of the trustee board, seven sections in all, and then included four sections on the university officers (presidents, vice presidents, secretaries, treasurers). Each board section contained a summary narrative followed by short biographical sketches of the trustees who served during the period. Some of the sketches of early trustees are missing vital information, such as birth or death dates, but most have portraits or photographs to illustrate. An appendix, "Political Affiliations of Trustees of Indiana University, 1885–1945," gives information, at five-year intervals, of the party,

[60]Myers, *Trustees and Officers of Indiana University 1820–1950*, 1951, v–vi.

either Republican or Democratic, of the members of the board. Remarkably, the eight-member board was usually split evenly between the parties, with only two periods of five Republicans and three Democratic members.[61]

In September 1946, with the editing of the trustees volume completed, Chamness moved her focus to the history of the Bryan administration plus the unit manuscripts left over from the earlier Woodburn project. Myers's gargantuan history manuscript was not only unwieldy but also presented problems in continuity and tone. The narrative of the Bryan administration was wooden and plodding, more chronicle than story. The add-ons from the earlier project had various dates of coverage. Some, like the development of the curriculum or the IU library, covered 1824–1937. Others, such as the *Indiana Daily Student* (1867–1937) or the Extension Division (1891–1937), covered starting dates through 1937. Still others, such as athletics and the university bookstore, were integrated into the Bryan administration narrative despite significant coverage devoted to prior years.

In September 1947, the board of trustees received word that Myers had completed drafting the trustees book as well as the second volume of the *History of Indiana University.* Cost estimates, based on one thousand copies, were $5,000 for the former and $9,000 to $12,000 for the latter—considerable sums, especially when previous university histories had had low sales. President Emeritus Bryan, now nearing eighty-seven, urged publication, perhaps not surprisingly. The trustees' minutes stated dryly: "The style does not make it easily read but from an historical standpoint, Dr. Bryan feels it is invaluable." Also noted was that both manuscripts "will require considerable editing before publication." The trustees authorized the editing of the two books, with printing details to be worked out later.[62]

Chamness was faced with one more round of editing in addition to her increased postwar workload of official publications. The trustees book was strictly chronological, and the biographical sketches adhered to a standard template, so the arrangement of content was straightforward. The history volume was anything but. It had

[61] Myers, 533–34.

[62] Indiana University Board of Trustees, "Minutes of the Board of Trustees of Indiana University, 22 September 1947" (Bloomington: Indiana University Archives & Indiana University Libraries Digital Collections Services, September 22, 1947), https://purl.dlib.indiana.edu/iudl/archives/iubot/1947-09-22.

two distinct but related goals: a narrative description of the Bryan administration (1902–37) and a topical survey of institutional units dating as far back as the 1820s. The first narrative was drafted by a medical scientist who was more concerned with factual accuracy than literary style; the second had multiple authors of varying abilities and had been drafted a decade or more earlier. She noted for the file: "This manuscript does not seem to me logically arranged."[63]

To solve this compositional problem, Chamness divided the volume up into two unequal parts: about two-thirds dealt with the history from 1902 to 1937, and the remaining third was arranged by topic. The result was a combination of administrative chronicle and institutional encyclopedia. In the topical part, individual authors are sometimes identified: Velorus Martz on the School of Education, William Alexander on the university libraries, Joseph Piercy on the *Indiana Daily Student*, Fernandus Payne on the graduate school, Cedric Cummins on the Extension Division, and Ivy Chamness on publications. Chamness and Myers did not discuss the leftovers from the Woodburn volume, apparently.[64]

Chamness, the good editor she was, tried mightily to make Myers's prose more readable and engaging, with some success. The beginning of Myers's narrative, chapters 1 and 2 in the published book—"What Was Indiana University Like in 1902?" and "What of the Man, William Lowe Bryan"—were singled out in draft: "The first 23 pp. could be *greatly* and *profitably* condensed."[65] Perhaps Chamness disliked the heroic encomium. Although she respected Bryan, understatement was the institution's default style—and her own as well.

8.12 Publication

In early 1950, the trustees book was finally finished. The trustee board authorized publication, with a print run of 1,000 copies at a cost near $5,000, close to the previous estimate.[66] Unbeknownst to Chamness, there was an administrative reorganization underway

[63]"IUA/C84/B1/f Edited Manuscripts-Myers" (Bloomington, IN: Indiana University Archives, n.d.).
[64]Chamness.
[65]Chamness.
[66]Indiana University Board of Trustees, "Minutes of the Board of Trustees of Indiana University, 17 February 1950" (Bloomington: Indiana University

that would affect the structure of her position as editor of publications. At sixty-eight, she was still vigorous, but retirement would soon be upon her. The Wells administration was aggressively trying to market the university more effectively and determined that an innovative approach to communications was called for, including increased capacity for in-house printing. One possible new hire had surfaced: Robert L. Mossholder, the director of general printing and information at the University of Omaha, who had been "outstanding in getting life and appeal into the publications" as reported in the trustees' confidential discussion. In March, Mossholder accepted the position of director of publications, to start in July.[67]

Editor of Publications Chamness, who was not consulted during the hiring process, wrote a letter to the board of trustees in May 1950, complaining about Mossholder's position title, which implied that he had overall charge of all publications. Her understanding was that he was hired to write promotional materials only, and she would retain control of regular catalog and school bulletins, as well as research publications. The board considered her complaint but ultimately dismissed her concerns. The trustees simply affirmed the appropriateness of Mossholder's title and saw no "serious conflict" between his title and hers.[68]

Trustees and Officers of Indiana University, 1820–1950 came out the first week of February 1951 and went on sale at the IU bookstore.[69] Myers, who had been ill since the fall, died on the last day of February, aged eighty. The dean emeritus had labored for a decade to document the history of IU in two books but only saw one in print. The trustees volume was a foundation stone in IU history

---

Archives & Indiana University Libraries Digital Collections Services, February 17, 1950), https://purl.dlib.indiana.edu/iudl/archives/iubot/1950-02-17.

[67]Indiana University Board of Trustees, "Minutes of the Board of Trustees of Indiana University, 19 January 1950" (Bloomington: Indiana University Archives & Indiana University Libraries Digital Collections Services, January 19, 1950), https://purl.dlib.indiana.edu/iudl/archives/iubot/1950-01-19; Indiana University Board of Trustees, "Minutes of the Board of Trustees of Indiana University, 17 March 1950" (Bloomington: Indiana University Archives & Indiana University Libraries Digital Collections Services, March 17, 1950), https://purl.dlib.indiana.edu/iudl/archives/iubot/1950-03-17.

[68]Indiana University Board of Trustees, "Minutes of the Board of Trustees of Indiana University, 19 May 1950" (Bloomington: Indiana University Archives & Indiana University Libraries Digital Collections Services, May 19, 1950), https://purl.dlib.indiana.edu/iudl/archives/iubot/1950-05-19.

[69]Myers, *Trustees and Officers of Indiana University 1820–1950*, 1951. For date of release, see "Seymour Man Was Trustee of I.U.," *The Tribune* (Seymour, Indiana), February 3, 1951.

and became a ready reference to both current and past institutional leadership.

In June 1952, the second volume of *History of Indiana University* hit the IU Bookstore.[70] With over 800 pages of text and lavishly illustrated with photographs, the bulk of the book dealt with the Bryan years, but it also went back to earlier times to pick up the story of curriculum, athletics, publications, educational extension, and other topics when they started, in keeping with Woodburn's earlier project to survey developments at IU since its founding. Bound in mahogany brown pebble-grained cloth, the large volume contained the title and the author's name embossed in gold on the cover. Campus maps comprised the endpapers; the front depicted 1902, the back 1937. The title page was elaborate—*History of Indiana University. Volume II: 1902–1937, The Bryan Administration*—followed by Burton Dorr Myers, MD, as author. Below that, listed as editors were Ivy L. Chamness and, again, Burton D. Myers. Like the title page of the *Trustees and Officers* volume, it is not clear why Myers's name merited a double listing as editor as well as author.

President Bryan, in his ninety-second year, contributed the foreword. He extolled the virtues of recently deceased Myers and reflected on their long association and friendship. In addition, he singled out the contributions of Chamness: "Among those who have given generous aid to Dr. Myers in his work one has been pre-eminent. This history of Indiana University, like that of Dr. Woodburn, is under great obligation to the expert Editor of University Publications, Miss Ivy Leone Chamness."[71] Myers contributed a brief introduction, explaining the sources and the process of putting the book together. He acknowledged the help of President Emeritus Bryan, who read each chapter as it was written, offering suggestions but cautioned, "But you have to verify it." Bryan, to avoid any appearance of interference, waited until the book was published before reading the entire text. An unsigned one-page "Earlier Histories of Indiana University" recapped the existing historiography with brief descriptions of books of Wylie (1890), Harding (1904), and Woodburn (1940). The paragraph on the last work began: "The James A. Woodburn *History of Indiana University, 1820–1902*, edited by Ivy L. Chamness, was planned as a series of volumes to be completed down through the years....Certain special chapters, those

[70]Myers, *History of Indiana University*, 1952.
[71]Myers, vi.

on athletics, the curriculum, the School of Law, and others were not completed in time for inclusion in Volume I, and are therefore included in this present volume."[72] This passage was a belated public acknowledgment of Chamness's key role as well as a succinct explanation for the hybrid nature of the second volume.

8.13 Retirement and Beyond

In summer 1952, Chamness retired. Her IU career spanned thirty-eight years, bookended by the world wars, and encompassing the two decades between. When she started, the university was a small, intimate institution, with about 1,500 students enrolled. At her retirement, the student body in Bloomington had mushroomed to 10,000, and there were several extension centers around the state. Many professional schools were developed, initiated by the Bryan administration, and nourished by the Wells administration. The alumni association had grown and professionalized, helped along by Chamness's superb efforts with the *Alumni Quarterly.* She had managed all the university's official publications for decades, developing a reputation for accuracy, dignity, and understatement that became an IU hallmark. Chamness was a fanatic about accuracy. She had a standing bet with her readers to pay for any errors discovered; no one ever collected.

Soon after her retirement, the office of university publications was reconfigured under Director of Publications Robert Mossholder, starting a new chapter in the presentation of IU's written word. Her title, editor of publications, disappeared. Her books continued onward, however. The most recent, the second volume of *History of Indiana University*, appeared in June 1952. By the middle of 1953, almost 800 complimentary copies of the initial press run of 1,000 had been distributed, leaving 77 sold and 114 copies on hand.[73] Many IU offices had copies of the *History of Indiana University*, volumes I and II, and the *Trustees and Officers* volume. These publications became part of the permanent record of the institution,

---

[72] Myers, xiv.

[73] Indiana University Board of Trustees, "Minutes of the Board of Trustees of Indiana University, 12 June 1953" (Bloomington, IN: Indiana University Archives; Indiana University Libraries Digital Collections Services, June 12, 1953), https://purl.dlib.indiana.edu/iudl/archives/iubot/1953-06-12.

an interpretation of the events, the people, and the times of the university's life.

Chamness was always ready to lend a hand. In the mid-1950s, campus construction was booming, leading to the creation of an ad hoc committee on names to assist the president and the trustees in finding appropriate names for new buildings. In 1954, President Wells started consulting with Chamness informally, as well as other trusted advisers, including university archivist Mary Craig. When the Names Committee was formalized in 1957, Chamness was a member.[74] Around that time, Chamness found herself editing yet another book authored by Burton Myers, on the history of medical education in Indiana. Even though Myers had passed away in 1951, the university retained possession of his manuscript. Former editor Chamness was persuaded to lift her pen once again to edit the modest manuscript, and the book was published in 1956.[75]

Still living in her house across Tenth Street from the Men's Residence Center, the eighty-five-year-old Chamness received the Distinguished Alumni Service Award in 1966. The citation read:

> Ivy Leone Chamness was a pioneer in the development of an outstanding publications system at Indiana University, and an unquestioned authority on the history of the institution. As a kind, understanding mentor, she guided students in the meaning of both printed and spoken words of the English language; always with discriminating judgement [*sic*], a disciplined intellect, and unswerving determination. A wise counselor possessing many skills, she was blessed with a bright spirit that endeared her to everyone she worked with; devoting her time and energy to the university long beyond retirement.[76]

She had graduated sixty before and spent nearly all her life serving her alma mater.

On May 29, 1975, a brief note in the *Palladium-Item* of Richmond, Indiana, stated, "Ivy Leone Chamness, History Authority, Dies."

[74]"IUA/C239/B3 All-University Committee on Names" (Bloomington, IN: Indiana University Archives, n.d.).

[75]Burton Dorr Myers, *The History of Medical Education in Indiana* (Bloomington: Indiana University Press, 1956).

[76]"About Ivy L. Chamness," n.d., https://honorsandawards.iu.edu/awards/honoree/2297.html.

She died in Bloomington at ninety-three years old. The article called her "a recognized authority on the history of Indiana University."

As editor of publications, Chamness channeled her writerly ambitions into getting the word out about Indiana University. She backed into a concern for history at the start of her work for the *Indiana University Alumni Quarterly.* Demographically, Ivy Chamness was an outlier of persons who wrote extensively about the history of Indiana University. Major published works appeared in 1890 (Wylie), 1904 (Harding), 1921 (Chamness), 1940 (Woodburn), 1952 (Myers), and 1970–77 (Clark), all authored by white persons, the dominant majority in the state and at the university. All were male emeritus faculty members except for Chamness, who was a pioneering female staff member. She made inroads to this male club through her competency, determination, and persistence. She held her own as a writer in this group and kept her focus on the human element, using her unparalleled understanding of alumni experience to craft relatable narratives. Intrinsically modest, she eschewed the limelight, preferring to work behind the scenes, often anonymously, to present accurate information about the university through its official publications. Chamness realized early on that institutional history was a vital part of the university's image and identity. She spent decades as one of its chief promoters and preservers, so much so that she deserves to be known as the keeper of university history.

9 Academic Community and University Necrology

Figure 13: Harry G. Day (top), Elizabeth M. Greene (left), Donald J. Gray (bottom)

> The university traditionally upholds the ideal of human values in society. One would expect that the university, having had the benefit of the services of men and women at their peak, would retain them in their waning years. It is the totality of their service that should determine the reckoning.
>
> —Herman B Wells, *Being Lucky: Reflections and Reminiscences*

Universities, as human institutions, are composed of individuals who occupy a variety of specific roles. Historically, they are composed of three primary groups: students, teachers, and administrators. Each group has characteristic duties, norms, and procedures that interact to structure the institution in relation to its manifest goals of knowledge creation, transfer, and preservation. The heart of the learning process is the relation between teacher and student, with administrators playing supporting roles to organize and facilitate learning.

Universities keep track of the members of their academic community with bureaucratic procedures of admission and hiring, documentation of advancement toward goals, and the commemoration of accomplishment. All these activities produce written records, whether inscribed on paper, photographically, or digitally.

For the past two centuries, Indiana University has retained a record of each matriculated student and their progress toward a diploma.[1] The completion of degree requirements culminates in the graduation ritual known as commencement. Former students, whether they graduate or not, become members of the alumni body, which also maintains records. In a similar fashion, a faculty records office keeps track of the employment history of members of the academic staff. In contrast to the limited time that students are working toward their degrees, the faculty and administrative staff typically spend longer periods at the university—often much longer. When faculty retire, they are usually given the honorary designation "professor emerita" or "professor emeritus" and feted at a ritual reception hosted by the administration and attended by their colleagues.

[1] The IU Office of the Registrar is responsible. During the university's bicentennial, staff members began making some records public. See "The First 200 Degrees" for biographical records of IU's first two hundred graduates.

Keeping such vital information has been a tortuous process, with natural disasters and technological progress punctuating the history of archival preservation as individual records accumulate. Two major fires—in 1854 and 1883—destroyed books and papers at the small campus. Library collections were painstakingly rebuilt each time, but university records and faculty papers were obliterated, leaving large gaps in institutional archives for the nineteenth century.

Biography is essential to the writing of university history and understanding the limitations of as well as opportunities provided by different forms of archival preservation can be illuminating. Luckily, the nineteenth-century institutional record was partially restored by Theophilus Wylie's monumental work, discussed below.[2]

Like many aspects of IU's history, commemorative policy and practice can be traced back to IU's "second beginning" in 1885, when the university abandoned its original site on Seminary Square and moved across town to establish the campus at Dunn's Woods. The proximate cause was an 1883 fire that destroyed Science Hall, one of the two main buildings. The original campus was occupied for sixty years, from 1825 to 1885, and the buildings had generic or functional names, such as the Seminary Building, College Building, and Science Hall. The new campus was a twenty-acre woodlot, purchased from the Dunn family, located on the eastern edge of town. The trustees optimistically christened it University Park.[3] But the new name did not catch on, and reference to the relocated campus at "Dunn's Woods" endured, a harbinger of a shift in IU's naming practices to personal names.

Bloomington, now numbering almost 3,500 residents, was coming into its own as a city. It was featured prominently in an 1884 commercial publication of county history, and IU was mentioned many times:

> A detailed history of this university cannot be given in this volume; neither can suitable or merited personal sketches be written of the many eminent men [*sic*] who have been connected with it, or have gone as students from its halls to honored positions in almost every State

[2]Wylie, *Indiana University, Its History from 1820, When Founded, to 1890, with Biographical Sketches of Its Presidents, Professor and Graduates, and a List of Its Students from 1820 to 1887.* See also Chapter 3.

[3]Indiana University Board of Trustees, "Minutes of the Board of Trustees of Indiana University, 04 June 1884–11 June 1884."

> in the Union. It is appropriate, however, to say that the institution has been the soul of Bloomington. A majority of the older citizens are graduates or undergraduates, and their children and grandchildren are now treading in their footsteps.[4]

The city was being modernized, with new transportation options and more municipal utilities available.

As city leaders of Bloomington heard about the planned relocation of the IU campus to Dunn's Woods, they decided to honor one of the most distinguished members of the faculty. In March 1884, Fifth Street was renamed for Professor Daniel Kirkwood, a theoretical astronomer who calculated regular intervals in the asteroid belt—the eponymous "Kirkwood's gaps"—leading to the sobriquet "the Kepler of America." The *Bloomington Telephone* reported:

> Since the location of the new University buildings have been known, the citizens, and especially those on 5th street, have been talking of naming that thoroughfare Kirkwood Avenue, in honor of our distinguished townsman, Prof. Kirkwood. Last Friday night a petition was properly presented to the Council, and by a vote the name was so changed. The new University buildings now front on Kirkwood Avenue, if you please.[5]

Kirkwood, at the university since 1856, enjoyed an international reputation for his scientific contributions. A popular teacher, he was tolerant and indulgent in the classroom.

A couple of months later, the IU Board of Trustees decided to name the new buildings—two of brick and one of wood—after esteemed university figures. The larger brick edifice was named Wylie Hall, in memory of the first president, Andrew Wylie, and in honor of Professor Theophilus Wylie, who had taught for almost fifty years. The smaller brick structure was named Owen Hall, to honor three distinguished brothers, sons of Robert Owen of New Harmony, Indiana, fame, including retired professor Richard Dale Owen, who had served on the faculty since 1864.[6] The wood frame structure,

[4]Blanchard, *Counties of Morgan, Monroe, and Brown, Indiana*, 479.

[5]. See also Edmondson, "Daniel Kirkwood—'Dean of American Astronomers"', p. 32, who mistakenly dated it as 1885.

[6]Indiana University Board of Trustees, "Minutes of the Board of Trustees of Indiana University, 04 June 1884–11 June 1884."

serving as the campus chapel and providing classrooms, was named after David Maxwell, the first president of the board of trustees.[7] These honorary namings inaugurated a tradition of recognizing leaders—faculty, trustees, administrators—who had shaped the university by inscribing their names on the new campus.

By the summer of 1888, the trustees ordered a roadway to be built connecting the eastern end of Kirkwood Avenue to Wylie Hall, "to be covered with broken stone or broken stone and gravel."[8] Wide enough to allow two horse-drawn teams to pass, the road was near the northern edge of the Dunn's Woods plot, leaving the bulk of the property undeveloped. It also unintentionally confirmed the main entrance to the new campus at Kirkwood and Indiana Avenues.

9.1 Documenting the Academic Community

In 1881, the IU trustees asked Professor Theophilus Wylie to prepare a historical catalog of the institution's history since its beginning in 1820.[9] After the 1883 fire consumed the previous three decades of records, compounding the losses from an earlier fire in 1854, Wylie turned to the living members of the IU community to salvage historical information. He devised a questionnaire and embarked on extensive correspondence by postal service. Painstakingly collating and organizing reams of written responses, Wylie pressed on after his retirement in 1886. The resulting book, published in 1890, was a remarkably complete biographical compendium of names of students, faculty, presidents, and trustees, with some brief interpretive

[7] Indiana University Board of Trustees, "Minutes of the Board of Trustees of Indiana University, 05 November 1885–11 November 1885" (Bloomington, IN: Indiana University Archives; Indiana University Libraries Digital Collections Services, November 11, 1885), https://purl.dlib.indiana.edu/iudl/archives/iubot/1885-11-05.

[8] Indiana University Board of Trustees, "Minutes of the Board of Trustees of Indiana University, 01 June 1888–07 June 1888" (Bloomington, IN: Indiana University Archives; Indiana University Libraries Digital Collections Services, June 2, 1888), https://purl.dlib.indiana.edu/iudl/archives/iubot/1888-06-01.

[9] Wylie was the seventh faculty member hired and had known all but three faculty before him—Baynard Hall, John Harney, and Ebenezer Elliott—who had left before his appointment in 1837. During his forty-nine years as a professor, he taught natural science and had stints of administrative work as librarian and acting president. He was personally acquainted with every IU faculty member until at least the 1880s (he died in 1895) as well as generations of university students.

narratives interspersed. By emphasizing biography, it underlined the importance of individuals making up the academic community, forming a social institution. Wylie's book, under the descriptive title *Indiana University, Its History from 1820, When Founded, to 1890, with Biographical Sketches of Its Presidents, Professors and Graduates, and a List of Its Students from 1820 to 1887*, was long on a collective biography of the academic community and short on a descriptive history of the university.

A decade and a half later, another contribution to IU history was published, *Indiana University, 1820–1904*, edited by history professor Samuel B. Harding. It contained a historical sketch, an analysis of curriculum development, and a bibliography of publications of faculty and alumni.[10] For the first time, the intellectual contributions of the entire IU professorate, both past and present, were documented.

Nearly fifty years later, a different approach was taken in the *History of Indiana University, 1902–1937*, published in 1952.[11] Retired anatomy dean Burton Myers studied IU faculty appointments from the beginning of instruction to 1937, subdividing the chronology in half: 1824 to 1885 and 1885 to 1937. The choice of the dividing line was significant: the beginning of the administration of President David Starr Jordan, who represented a break from previous clerical leadership and the promotion of a new spirit of research. Myers wrote, "In contrast with the 60 appointments to the faculty in the first sixty-one years of the life of the University, there were 897 appointments made in the fifty-two years from 1885 to 1937."[12] The rise in the number of faculty appointed was a consequence of the growth of the student body over that 113-year span.[13]

Myers's analysis was made possible by a new method of record-keeping starting circa 1935: a cumulative collection of individual faculty data collected on single sheets of paper. These biographical data sheets contained information for each faculty member, such as name, title, years of service, birth date and birthplace, educational

[10]Harding, *Indiana University, 1820–1904*.

[11]Myers, *History of Indiana University*, 1952. Despite its title, the book had several chapters covering the entire history from 1820 to 1937.

[12]Myers, 577.

[13]Myers, *History of Indiana University*, 1952. He included photographs of active faculty in 1937 who had served twenty-five years or more—fifty-two men and women in all.

background, previous positions, marital status, and political and religious affiliations.

Mellie P. Cravens, wife of John Cravens, IU registrar and secretary to the board of trustees, worked in the Register of Graduates Office. In 1936, under her direction, a cumulative register of alumni between 1830 and 1935 was prepared.[14] Her husband, who served as President Bryan's trusted executive assistant, retired in the summer of 1936 after forty-one years of service. President Bryan, seventy-six years old, shocked the trustees by indicating in early 1937 that he wanted to retire, after thirty-five years at the helm. The trustees named Herman Wells, dean of the School of Business Administration, acting president in June 1937, giving some time to mount a proper search for a permanent replacement.[15] John Cravens died in August. Amid the flux of administrative transitions, by November the trustees authorized Wells to support the preparation of a faculty directory—a who's who of the instructional staff—for use of the board and the administration.[16] Thus, refinements in record management techniques allowed for recent data to be integrated in cumulative reports of IU's academic community.

9.2 Memorializing Faculty

Although the board of trustees had noted faculty deaths occasionally in their minutes with memorial resolutions, there was no regular policy. As the faculty grew from a small, intimate group to a larger, more heterogenous community, new president Wells suggested to the trustees that memorial resolutions be prepared for faculty upon their death. The trustees agreed with him, as noted in their 1940 minutes, but no procedure was identified to produce them.[17]

[14]Myers, pp. 479–480. Alumni records were transferred to the IU Archives in 1936. Before her marriage, Mellie had worked as a secretary for President Bryan. Myers, p. 593.

[15]See Capshew, *Herman B Wells*, Chapter 5.

[16]Indiana University Board of Trustees, "Minutes of the Board of Trustees of Indiana University, 22 November 1937–23 November 1937" (Bloomington, IN: Indiana University Archives; Indiana University Libraries Digital Collections Services, November 23, 1937), https://purl.dlib.indiana.edu/iudl/archives/iubot/1937-11-22.

[17]Indiana University Board of Trustees, "Minutes of the Board of Trustees of Indiana University, 25 March 1940–26 March 1940" (Bloomington: Indiana University Archives & Indiana University Libraries Digital Collections Services,

Wells continued to report faculty deaths at the trustees' meetings through the 1940s, but by the early 1950s, with increasing student enrollments following the war and a concomitant swelling of faculty numbers, the president instead created a necrology committee composed of seasoned faculty members. The committee was responsible for ensuring that a memorial resolution, usually written by departmental colleagues, was prepared shortly after the death of a faculty member. That was the plan, and most faculty were memorialized in this way. But a few faculty fell inadvertently through the committee's net because the faculty that had volunteered to write the resolution became too busy or forgot to complete the assignment.

The first to chair the necrology committee was F. Lee Benns (1889–1967), a member of the history faculty since 1920. A 1937 survey indicated Benns was the most highly rated instructor among both faculty and recent honors graduates. He was "known as a very demanding teacher but one widely revered."[18] When Benns retired in 1954, Dean of the Faculties Herman Briscoe wrote to John Stoner on President Wells's behalf, asking him to take on the necrologist role.[19] (Around this time, the role became known as the university necrologist.) Stoner (1902–1988), a member of the Department of Political Science since 1938, served as university necrologist for four years.[20] Turning to another member of the history department, in 1958 Wells recruited Associate Professor Chase Mooney (1913–1973) to serve.[21]

Records documenting the history of the necrology committee in the 1960s are lacking, but archival sources note that history professor Oscar Winther (1903–1970) chaired the committee starting in 1964[22] and that folklorist John Ashton (1900–1971), former dean of the graduate school, directed the committee's work until 1970.[23] From 1970 to 1973, history professor Donald Carmony (1910–2005), editor of the *Indiana Magazine of History*, chaired the committee.

March 26, 1940), https://purl.dlib.indiana.edu/iudl/archives/iubot/1940-03-25.

[18] James H. Madison, *Indiana University Department of History: Past to Present* (Bloomington: Indiana University Department of History, 2010), 8.

[19] "Faculty Necrology" (Reference file, Indiana University Archives, n.d.).

[20] Stoner retired in 1972. His colleagues memorialized him, saying, "His career spanned the transit from the insular elitism of the pre-war school with its few thousand students to the contemporary multiversity."

[21] See "MEMORIAL RESOLUTION ON THE DEATH OF CHASE C. MOONEY".

[22] See "MEMORIAL RESOLUTION FOR OSCAR OSBURN WINTHER"

[23] Ashton's faculty memorial resolution did not mention this role.

In 1973, President Ryan appointed chemistry professor Harry Day (1906–2007) to the position of university necrologist. Day, a member of the team that created the first fluoridated toothpaste in the 1950s, had been at the university since 1940 and served various administrative roles, including chemistry chair and associate dean for research and advanced studies. Aided by his longtime secretary, Elizabeth Greene (1921–2011), he conducted all aspects of his career with effectiveness and dispatch. Although he retired in 1976, at seventy years of age, Day continued as necrologist for sixteen years, until 1989. By the time he reached eighty, Day appended an appeal to be relieved of his duties to his annual necrology report.

Historical research occupied the energies of both Day and Greene into the 1990s. Day embarked on a history of chemical instruction at IU, dating back to 1837, when Theophilus Wylie was hired as a faculty member in the natural sciences.[24] Not only was chemistry a venerable subject of teaching, but the department had also grown to be the largest among the science departments at IU. In the course of his research, Day discovered the existence of Wylie's extensive personal diaries in the university archives. The diaries gave details about Wylie's activities during the greater part of the nineteenth century, including his family life and university events, often with an indication of his personal reactions. Greene laboriously transcribed the faded handwriting into typescript. Archivist Dolores Lahrman (1920–1997) and her staff assisted in translating the frequent Greek, Latin, and French phrases that Wylie used to express his meaning.

The transcription of the diaries was completed in 1987, with Greene providing a preface and Day supplying an introduction. Wylie's diaries became an invaluable source for both Bloomington and IU history of the last two-thirds of the nineteenth century. Later, staff at the IU Archives discovered some missing diaries, and Greene dutifully transcribed those too, completing the work in 1992.[25] The same year, Day published his historical chronicle, entitled *The Development of Chemistry at Indiana University, 1829–1991*.[26] Nearly seven hundred pages, it was a meticulous compendium of names, dates, and facts about every aspect of teaching and research in the discipline as it was practiced at the university.

[24]Wylie was a cousin of Andrew Wylie, the first president, who died in 1851.

[25]See archival description of Theophilus Wylie's diaries.

[26]Harry G. Day, *The Development of Chemistry at Indiana University, 1829–1991* (Bloomington: Indiana University, 1992).

In 1989, Day's importuning about a replacement yielded fruit, as President Tom Ehrlich appointed English professor Donald Gray (b. 1927) as university necrologist. Gray, a specialist in Victorian literature, joined the English faculty in 1956. He was a superb teacher, supervising dozens of Ph.D. dissertation students, and a noted editor, publishing the Norton *Pride and Prejudice* and *Alice in Wonderland* as well as serving as editor of the academic journals *College English* and *Victorian Studies.* He also edited and contributed to *The Department of English at Indiana University Bloomington, 1868–1970*, published in 1973, following the observance of the IU sesquicentennial in 1970.[27]

Gray had witnessed the university's growth and diversification for a third of a century upon his appointment and had extensive contacts in the faculty and administration. The new job meant increased exchanges with every school on the Bloomington campus plus coordinating information from other campuses from around the state. Gray was quietly effective, working with faculty colleagues as they crafted memorial sketches of their late peers, often supplying insights to their personalities and their impact on university life.

Once written, faculty memorial resolutions were read aloud at meetings of the Bloomington Faculty Council (BFC), co-chaired by the BFC president and the campus's presiding officer, first the Bloomington chancellor and more recently the Bloomington provost. In 2010, education professor Robert Arnove questioned "the process by which memorial resolutions are prepared and brought before this body" because "a number of colleagues have passed away in 2008 and 2009 and I haven't seen anything for them." Vice Provost for Faculty and Academic Affairs Thomas Gieryn explained:

> We've worked very, very hard—"we" being Don Gray, the campus necrologist and emeriti faculty members and I—have worked hard contacting deans and chairs of all the departments to provide memorial resolutions. We beg them, we give them models, we tell them it's not that onerous. It gets difficult sometimes and I noticed certainly as you did that sometimes it takes a great deal of time to find the right person to write the resolution. We encourage all colleagues who know of someone who has died who has not had a memorial resolution read

[27] Donald J. Gray, ed., *The Department of English at Indiana University Bloomington, 1868–1970* (Bloomington: Indiana University, 1973).

> to bring that to the attention of their chair so that we can reach that closure.[28]

To be sure, a few deceased faculty members escaped the necrologist's net, but this unique historical record grew year upon year, providing informed summations of faculty careers and a symbolic closure to university service.

Professor Gray soldiered on as university necrologist for decade after decade, cajoling faculty writers and editing their prose, on every campus of the university. Over time, however, as campus autonomy grew in Indianapolis and in the regionals and administrative personnel changed, the other campuses stopped sending information about faculty deaths. By the time she left office in 2011, Provost Karen Hanson suggested Gray's title be changed to IUB necrologist. In 2017, after twenty-eight years, he penned a short memo, "The IU Necrologist: Duties and Procedures," based on his experience, and submitted a request to the university administration to be relieved of this duty.[29]

Gray got his wish the following year. He was now ninety years old and in his sixty-second year of service at Indiana University. In February 2018, Provost Lauren Robel presented a verbal encomium at a regular meeting of the BFC, right after the customary reading of the latest faculty memorial resolution. She prefaced her remarks with a verse of Victorian poet laureate Alfred, Lord Tennyson, from his famous poem, *In Memoriam A.H.H.*:

> I sing to him that rests below,
> And, since the grasses round me wave,
> I take the grasses of the grave,
> And make them pipes whereon to blow.

She began her tribute to Gray by noting, "We start every meeting of the Bloomington Faculty Council with our memorial resolutions. And it is extraordinarily fitting that we do so. The resolutions are human and charming and grounding and give us a sense of our history and our colleagues, and the vast range of the interest

[28]Indiana University Bloomington Faculty Council, "Indiana University Bloomington Faculty Council Minutes, 07 September 2010" (Bloomington: Indiana University Archives & Indiana University Libraries Digital Collections Services, September 7, 2010), https://purl.dlib.indiana.edu/iudl/archives/bfc/2010-09-07.

[29]Donald J. Gray, "The IU Necrologist: Duties and Procedures" (circa 2017).

represented on this campus." She continued by introducing Gray and commending his work as the university necrologist.

Robel remarked that Gray was a leading scholar of Victorian literature, thus her choice of Tennyson's elegy, musing that his scholarship might have motivated his nearly thirty years of service as necrologist, "or perhaps it was simply his love for Indiana University and his understanding of the importance of this role." Regardless, "Don has done incredibly important work" for his university colleagues, for the campus, and for the family and friends of departed faculty members.[30]

Gray turned his files on university necrology over to the Office of the Vice Provost for Faculty and Academic Affairs during the 2017–18 academic year. Indermohan Virk, a staff member responsible for the Patten Foundation lecture series, added the role of campus necrologist to her portfolio. In her duties, she works with the leadership of BFC and colleagues of deceased faculty to craft an appropriate memorial resolution, which is read into the record during regular council meetings.

9.3 The Bicentennial Era

Amid his long service as necrologist, Gray embarked on a collateral project to collect video interviews of emeriti professors. Begun in 2005, it was a way to collect stories of faculty experiences from retired academics. Similar in concept to the oral history center, initiated in 1970 as part of the university's sesquicentennial commemoration, it gathered personal narratives of faculty careers. In 2008, it was folded into the Bicentennial Oral History Project to capture alumni recollections in advance of the 2020 institutional anniversary. Teachers and students contributed vital data to this ongoing effort. Gray expressed the rationale of the emeriti project: "What we were trying to get, I think, is a picture of what a faculty member did, how it changed and how the students changed."[31] By 2017, Gray had conducted 150 interviews and bequeathed the

[30] Indiana University Bloomington Faculty Council, "Ndiana University Bloomington Faculty Council Minutes, 06 February 2018" (Bloomington: Indiana University Archives & Indiana University Libraries Digital Collections Services, February 6, 2018), https://purl.dlib.indiana.edu/iudl/archives/bfc/2018-02-06.

[31] "Brownlee preserves stories of emeriti faculty"

project to two other emeriti professors, Bonnie Brownlee and Bruce Jaffee, both younger.[32]

The Office of the Bicentennial was created in 2016 to plan, coordinate, and implement a wide array of public events to shed light on the history of Indiana University, culminating in the institution's 200th anniversary on January 20, 2020.[33] Special attention was paid to documenting the history of students, faculty, administrators, and alumni. Staff at the Office of the Registrar helped with statistical analyses of the historical demography of the student body, providing estimates of the total number of individuals taking at least one course since the beginning of instruction in 1825 (nearly 2,000,000) and the count of graduates (approaching 1,000,000). A website featuring biographical profiles of the first 200 graduates was produced, and then coverage was extended to all degree recipients.[34] In a similar fashion, the faculty records group within the Office of the Vice Provost for Faculty and Academic Affairs provided data on the number and characteristics of instructional staff since classes began in 1825. Because of historical changes in the definition of faculty as well as incomplete records, they could only give a ballpark estimate, which was near 50,000. In contrast, because of the smaller numbers of trustees and officers, the administration has proven easier to document its historical demography. The Office of the Bicentennial chose to continue a long-running series of volumes of biographical sketches that stretched back to Theophilus Wylie's 1890 IU history. The result was *Trustees and Officers of Indiana University, Volume III: 1982–2018*, with a team of five editors and numerous contributors. The historical total of trustees and officers was about 650 individuals.[35]

[32]See also *Indiana University Bicentennial Final Report* (Bloomington: Indiana University, 2020), 30–31.

[33]A good overview is provided in the *Indiana University Bicentennial Final Report.*

[34]The Degree Compendium and The First 200

[35]Linda Fariss Keith Buckley Derek F. DiMatteo and Colleen Pauwels, eds., *Trustees and Officers of Indiana University, Volume III: 1982–2018* (Bloomington: Indiana University, 2019). The first historical list is found in Wylie, *Indiana University, Its History from 1820, When Founded, to 1890, with Biographical Sketches of Its Presidents, Professor and Graduates, and a List of Its Students from 1820 to 1887*; earlier volumes were Myers, *Trustees and Officers of Indiana University 1820–1950*, 1951 and Eleanor Roehr, *Trustees and Officers of Indiana University, 1950 to 1982* (Bloomington: Indiana University, 1983).

As a human institution, it remains important to document the members of the academic community and their activities. The first history of Indiana University, published in 1890, was a successful attempt to reconstruct the names and careers of individual members of the bodies of students, faculty, and administrators of the institution's first seven decades in the face of incomplete historical data. By 1900, the office of the registrar was established and had devised a system to track each student who matriculated and those who graduated. As enrollments grew, the number of graduates increased, and the alumni association established a collateral tracking system as it underwent professionalization in the first quarter of the twentieth century.[36] By 1935, administrators had rationalized faculty recordkeeping, facilitating administrative reporting and historical documentation. Although the media and techniques of recordkeeping have changed over time, maintaining accurate and complete records of each member of the academic community continues to be a core aspect of IU's identity and makes possible historical analysis, reflection, and celebration.

[36] See Shirley, *The Indiana University Alumni Association.*

10 The Resurrection of Wylie House

Figure 14: Wylie House. Back row, l-r: Andrew Wylie, Margaret Wylie, Rebecca Wylie, Theophilus Wylie, Lizzie Breckenridge, Lillian Hershey, and Herman Wells. Front row: Wylie children.

> I was always interested in anything that was a living reminder of the antiquity of the University.
>
> —Herman B Wells, Interview

What is the most significant surviving physical artifact from the early history of Indiana University? A handful of early diplomas, handwritten letters, and published materials form a sparse but invaluable documentary record. No physical trace remains of the university's first campus building—only an Indiana state historical marker stands on the site where IU began as the Indiana State Seminary in the 1820s. One possible candidate is the 1843 book *The New Purchase; or, Seven and a Half Years in the Far West*, which offers the first extended narrative about IU, written by its inaugural professor, Baynard Hall.

In terms of material culture as well as on programmatic grounds, a strong case can be made for the Wylie House, built in 1835 by the first IU president, Andrew Wylie, as a residence for his large family. Purchased by the university in 1947, it started functioning as a museum twenty years later but did not employ its first curator until 1983. Now, as the Wylie House Museum, it plays a central role in IU's history and heritage activities.

When the house was built in 1835, the institution was known as Indiana College, and classes had been offered for a decade. Wylie had been in office for seven years, and student enrollment had reached forty. Located two blocks from campus, at Second and Lincoln Streets, the house was one of the finest in the area. Built of brick in the Georgian style, the house sat on a crest of land, surrounded by twenty acres, including cultivated gardens, tree plots, and outbuildings.

President Wylie guided the institution for twenty-two years until a woodchopping accident led to his death by infection in 1851. The house remained in his immediate family until 1859, when it was sold to Professor Theophilus A. Wylie, a half-cousin of Andrew Wylie, who also had a large family. That Wylie family stayed in the home for over fifty years, a period that encompassed the Civil War to the Great War. In 1915, the house was sold to IU political science professor Amos S. Hershey and his wife, Lillian S. Hershey. They owned the house for over thirty years, until it was sold to Indiana University in 1947. President Herman B Wells engineered its purchase, taking an important step in preserving the property and laying the groundwork for its eventual use as a historic house museum. Wells's historical sensibility had been nurtured years before, starting with his involvement with another old house in Bloomington.

10.1 Living at Woodburn House

In 1932, after a couple of years as an instructor in economics at Indiana University, Herman Wells started renting rooms at the Woodburn House, 519 North College Avenue. The young teacher, thirty years old, had an interest in antique furniture and was beginning to collect English fox-hunting prints, befitting his status as a confirmed bachelor. The landlord was IU history professor emeritus James A. Woodburn, who had been living in Ann Arbor since his retirement in 1924, the same year Wells received his Bachelor of Science degree from the School of Commerce and Finance. Woodburn, who had lived in the family house since his 1856 birth, had a keen appreciation for its long history.

The house, built in 1829, was a historic structure. In 1855, his father, also an IU professor, James W. Woodburn, purchased the entire block for $1,100 and added a second story to the house in 1858. After the death of the father James in 1865, his widow took in student boarders. Their daughter, Ida Woodburn, hosted the first official meeting of the Delta chapter of the Kappa Kappa Gamma sorority there in 1873. Local lore suggested that an infamous "bogus" underground student newspaper, *The Dagger*, was started there. Later, IU faculty members, including psychologist William Bryan and political scientist Amos Hershey, resided in the house. The son James inherited the house and raised a family there.[1]

Wells enjoyed living in the Woodburn House and its proximity to campus. He also became acquainted with another historic house in this period—the Wylie House—which was located a half dozen blocks south of the Woodburn House. In 1915, the house had passed from the Wylie family to another IU professor, Amos Hershey, and his wife, Lillian.

[1]"The Dagger: 1875–80" (Bloomington: Indiana University Archives, n.d.). Reference file, Indiana University Archives; "Delta: The Early Years"; "Woodburn House"

Amos S. Hershey, a scion of the Pennsylvania chocolate manufacturing family, joined the Indiana faculty in 1895. A specialist in international law and diplomacy, in 1914, he was the founding chair of the Department of Political Science.[2] After the First World War, President Woodrow Wilson appointed him to the US delegation to the Paris Peace Conference as a technical advisor. Lillian, a proficient singer, wed Amos in 1892. She was an active businesswoman, selling antiques and home furnishings from her residence, which she called The Old Treasure House. The Hersheys entertained often, and Wells was a frequent guest. Calling Mrs. Hershey "a delightful person," Wells recalled, "Everybody knew the Hersheys. The house was most interesting, because she just lived with her antiques. She'd sell anything she had—rugs and furniture and so forth. The house was the perfect setting for that."[3] Their friendship was fueled by a shared interest in antiques and fine furnishings. Professor Hershey retired from teaching in 1932 and died the following year. Lillian Hershey continued to live in the Wylie House and operate her antiques business.

In 1933, Wells took a leave of absence to serve the state of Indiana as it reorganized its financial institutions during the Depression. A banking wunderkind, he analyzed the banking system in Indiana and supervised a team that rewrote the state's banking laws in early 1933. The reform legislation passed under the governorship of Paul McNutt, former dean of the IU School of Law, creating a new Indiana Department of Financial Institutions. Wells served in three capacities: as secretary to the Commission on Financial Institutions, bank supervisor, and supervisor of the Division of Research and Statistics for the department. This triple role gave him great authority in regulating the state's banking system—and a comfortable salary to indulge his taste for antiques and fine furnishings.[4]

In 1935, Wells moved from teaching to administration when he was appointed dean of the IU School of Business Administration by President William Bryan. He continued his meteoric administrative rise two years later, when the board of trustees selected him as

[2]Oliver P. Field, *Political Science at Indiana University, 1829–1951* (Bloomington: Bureau of Government Research, Department of Government, Indiana University, 1952).

[3]Herman B Wells, "Oral History Interview by Bonnie Williams" (Wylie House Collections, March 19, 1992).

[4]See Wells, *Being Lucky*, Chapter 4; and Capshew, *Herman B Wells*, Chapter 3.

acting president after Bryan retired after thirty-five years. Wells was in office for only a few weeks when he noticed that Lillian Hershey had put the Wylie House on the real estate market, and he began a warm correspondence with her.[5] At the August 1937 meeting of the trustee board, acting president Wells reported to the trustees that the Wylie House was for sale, listed at $30,000. Further discussion by the board was planned but apparently not memorialized.[6] Wells continued to serve as acting president for nine months, fulfilling day-to-day responsibilities as well as launching an ambitious university self-study, before being named the eleventh IU president in March 1938.[7]

10.2 Paying Tribute to Andrew Wylie

Two months later, in May 1938, the new president received a letter from Roy Quinn, an Indianapolis resident, lamenting the neglect of the first president, Andrew Wylie, on the recent Foundation Day, a celebration of the university's heritage. Ruing that he was not a "University man" despite his rearing in Bloomington, Quinn admitted, "I learned to love old I.U. and revel in its glorious past and pull for its promising future." He observed that, over the half century he had been visiting Bloomington's Rose Hill Cemetery, he had never seen a flower on Wylie's grave. He suggested, "With a band and military units and everything else needed to make such a thing a success why not lay a wreath upon the grave of the original 'forgotten man'?"[8]

In his reply, Wells agreed that the university should pay tribute to Wylie and suggested that a committee of the senior class place a wreath on his grave each Foundation Day. "This would cause students to remember Dr. Wylie," he thought, "more than any other

[5] "Hershey, Mrs. Amos Shartle" (Bloomington, IN: Indiana University Archives, n.d.). IUA/C213/B268/F.

[6] Indiana University Board of Trustees, "Minutes of the Board of Trustees of Indiana University, 09 August 1937" (Bloomington, IN: Indiana University Archives; Indiana University Libraries Digital Collections Services, August 9, 1937), https://purl.dlib.indiana.edu/iudl/archives/iubot/1937-08-09.

[7] Capshew, *Herman B Wells*, chap. 5.

[8] Roy Quinn, "Letter to Herman Wells" (Indiana University Archives, May 16, 1938). IUA/C213/B455.

action I can think of."[9] The next year, Wells oversaw an expansion of the 1939 Foundation Day commemoration, with activities not just in Bloomington but also around Indiana (Kokomo, Marion, Anderson, Terre Haute, Fort Wayne, North Vernon, Michigan City, Rushville, Muncie, Washington, Decatur, Peru, Spencer, South Bend, Evansville, and Salem) and in other states (St. Louis, St. Petersburg, Boston, Champaign, Iowa City, Denver, Grand Rapids, Louisville, Los Angeles, Milwaukee, New Haven, and Detroit).[10]

Wells wrote to Quinn again, telling him that a pilgrimage to the gravesite of Andrew Wylie was planned as part of the Foundation Day activities and inviting him to come. "These services mark the fulfillment of an idea you had a year ago this month," Wells wrote, "and I hope they may become a part of Indiana University's tradition for all the years to come."[11] Demonstrating Wells's ability to harness an unexpected suggestion into a university priority, the Wylie pilgrimage was the first stirring of a new tradition.[12]

The tradition became an annual event, continuing throughout the war years (with one exception in 1944). President emeritus Bryan was a frequent participant along with President Wells and student leaders. In 1945, the 125th anniversary of the university was celebrated at graduation ceremonies, and the commencement speaker, Ralph Cooper Hutchison, president of Washington and Jefferson College, attended the pilgrimage and laid the wreath on Wylie's grave. (Wylie had been president of both colleges sequentially before coming to IU, and in 1816, he unsuccessfully attempted to merge them.)[13] For the decade after the war, the pilgrimage remained a part of the celebration of the university's founding, known as Founders Day after 1951.[14]

---

[9]Herman B Wells, "Letter to Roy Quinn" (Indiana University Archives, May 26, 1938). IUA/C213/B455.

[10]"I.U. Founding to Be Observed by Alumni Throughout the World," *Indianapolis News*, May 2, 1939, 13.

[11]Herman B Wells, "Letter to Roy Quinn" (Indiana University Archives, May 2, 1939). IUA/C213/B455. IUA/Reference file: Foundation Day.

[12]"Inaugurating What Is Expected to Be an Annual Custom," *Indianapolis Star*, May 5, 1939, 17. Photo caption. Pictured: Albert Higdon, president of the senior class; Herman Wells; Mrs. Harry A. Axtell, granddaughter of President Wylie; Miss Madeline, great-granddaughter of President Wylie; William Bryan.

[13]Before he assumed the IU presidency, Andrew Wylie was president of both Jefferson College and Washington College, located a dozen miles apart. He attempted unsuccessfully to merge them in 1816; they were united in 1865.

[14]Pilgrimage records are spotty; no documents have surfaced for 1946 and 1948.

10.3 The Purchase of Wylie House

During the war, the director of the university library, Robert Miller, put together an ad hoc archives committee to preserve and care for documentation of the university's past.[15] The president's suite in Bryan Hall, constructed in 1936, was built with a five-floor archival unit attached, called the President's File Room. It contained a vast collection of documents generated during the thirty-five-year administration of former president Bryan as well as copies of past official catalogs, bulletins, and printed announcements and programs. Wells, aware of the need for good recordkeeping, acceded to the plan to rename the space the University Archives and put librarian Mary Craig in charge. His secretaries kept his presidential files in good order. A sign was posted in the room:

> NOTICE!
> No person shall take any paper of any sort from this room without giving a receipt therefor to the file clerk, who is made directly responsible to the Trustees of the University. This order applies to all persons, including the undersigned.
> HERMAN B WELLS

The notice humorously underscored Wells's egalitarian convictions.

After the Second World War ended in 1945, Wells kept his eye on the Wylie House and continued his correspondence with Lillian Hershey, sharing their interest in antiques and decorative objects. The president was still living in the Woodburn House and found it was well suited for entertaining and other official functions. (James Woodburn had given the house to IU in 1941, two years before his death.)[16]

Wells used the opportunity of a postwar visit by Governor Ralph Gates in 1947 to put into motion an ingenious plan. On a tour around campus and the city, Wells and Gates drove by the Wylie House. The governor was suitably impressed and urged Wells to put the funds to acquire the property on the university's 1947 budget

[15](Bloomington: Indiana University Archives, n.d.). IUA/C213/B30/F.

[16]Indiana University Board of Trustees, "Minutes of the Board of Trustees of Indiana University, 10 October 1941–11 October 1941" (Bloomington, IN: Indiana University Archives; Indiana University Libraries Digital Collections Services, October 10, 1941), https://purl.dlib.indiana.edu/iudl/archives/iubot/1941-10-10.

request.[17] The purchase went through, and Wylie House became an institutional property after 112 years of service as a family home. The terms included a provision for Mrs. Hershey to live in the house four years without paying rent or taxes. When she moved to Florida in 1951, the university took possession.[18]

University archivist Craig, who had received a Master of Library Science degree from Columbia University, turned out to be less interested in the written record than in the material culture of the past, and she soon added to her responsibilities the role of unofficial but acknowledged caretaker of the Wylie House. Both Wells and Craig were aficionados of antique furniture and historic houses, and the prospect of furnishing the Wylie House in period pieces was enticing to each. In their quest for antiques, Wells and Craig used campus storage spaces, including the attic of Wylie House, to hold accumulating treasures of furniture and other furnishings.

In October 1951, two grandchildren of Theophilus Wylie joined the trustee board for lunch: sister and brother, Mrs. Morton Bradley (née Marie Boisen), from Boston, and Mr. Anton Boisen, from Chicago. They provided valuable background information about the house and some of its former occupants. Also, family letters, receipts, and other documents were conveyed to the University Archives. Soon after, the trustees discussed four options for the Wylie House:

- Establish the house as a museum, to depict in detail how a scholar of the 1830's lived, worked, and entertained. Much of the original furniture is available, and we know exactly where it was placed.
- Restore the house as it was, or in the style of the period, with some additional comforts, and use as a guest house. It would be incorporated into either

[17] Clark, *Indiana University*, 1977, p. 150, 180–181. See also Wells, "Oral History Interview by Bonnie Williams."

[18] Indiana University Board of Trustees, "Minutes of the Board of Trustees of Indiana University, 12 June 1947–14 June 1947" (Bloomington, IN: Indiana University Archives; Indiana University Libraries Digital Collections Services, June 12–14, 1947), https://purl.dlib.indiana.edu/iudl/archives/iubot/1947-06-13; Indiana University Board of Trustees, "Minutes of the Board of Trustees of Indiana University, 30 June 1947" (Bloomington, IN: Indiana University Archives; Indiana University Libraries Digital Collections Services, June 30, 1947), https://purl.dlib.indiana.edu/iudl/archives/iubot/1947-06-30; Capshew, *Herman B Wells*, 184–85.

the Halls of Residence or the Union system. Such usage is common in other universities.
- Restore the house structurally and use it for headquarters for some group such as the Alumni Association.
- Restore the house structurally and use it as one of the home management houses.[19]

Although the board favored the guest house option, action was deferred. In 1953, with university office space at a premium, Wylie House was pressed into service as the temporary headquarters of IU Press, launched in 1950.[20] The university press office stayed in the building until 1959. Craig corresponded with another grandson, T. A. Wylie, at the end of 1954 and early 1955, sending him a Wylie family tree and exchanging other information.

10.4 Remembering Andrew Wylie

Although Wells was familiar with the first president's house and had engineered its purchase for the university, Andrew Wylie the man and his influence on IU were a mystery. In the spring of 1960, after announcing his impending retirement two years hence, Wells renewed his attention to the house associated with the original campus at Second Street and College Avenue. In support of the idea that the house should be restored to its original appearance, he further publicized the legacy of Andrew Wylie.

In November 1960, Wells gave a speech at Louisville's Filson Club, a venerable history society dedicated to Kentucky and the Ohio River valley. The speech was published in the club's history quarterly under the title "The Early History of Indiana University as Reflected in the Administration of Andrew Wylie, 1829–1851," under Wells's byline. He claimed that Wylie, almost forgotten outside of IU

[19]Indiana University Board of Trustees, "Minutes of the Board of Trustees of Indiana University, 16 November 1951" (Bloomington, IN: Indiana University Archives; Indiana University Libraries Digital Collections Services, November 16, 1951), https://purl.dlib.indiana.edu/iudl/archives/iubot/1951-11-16.

[20]Indiana University Board of Trustees, "Minutes of the Board of Trustees of Indiana University, 01 December 1952" (Bloomington, IN: Indiana University Archives; Indiana University Libraries Digital Collections Services, December 1, 1952), https://purl.dlib.indiana.edu/iudl/archives/iubot/1952-12-01; Capshew, *Herman B Wells*, 185, 203–4.

circles, was a "notably important figure in the early development of western state universities." The more he knew about Wylie, the more determined he became to bring Wylie's legacy to light.

With the aid of IU archivists and historians, Wells pieced together his narrative account from the few surviving sources, including contemporary reminiscences from peers and students, to portray Wylie's personality and career as an educator. He summed up his contributions under four categories: establishing the curriculum, promoting good student-faculty relations, serving as chief spokesman for higher education, and mounting successful defenses of the university against outside forces.[21] Wells concluded with a salute to his predecessor:

> If the Indiana University of today is an institution of immeasurable value and service to the state and nation, and I firmly believe that it is, we must revere the memory of the first president who offered the intellectual and moral leadership so vital and necessary to the University in its infant days. He gave stability in a period characterized by instability. A university is a durable institution, built on the accumulated wisdom of the past. How fortunate that our past included Andrew Wylie![22]

By the time Wells's article appeared in print in 1962, the Wylie House restoration was underway.[23]

Andrew Wylie's legacy was emerging as a touchstone for the university's past, and his home was a material embodiment of that legacy. It was a visible sign of the university's rich cultural heritage, and its curation and interpretation would provide varied ways to connect to IU's history.

10.5 Wylie House Restoration

The Edward D. James architectural firm was selected to perform the long-delayed renovation of the Wylie residence and produced a

[21]Capshew, *Herman B Wells*, 121–22.

[22]Capshew, *Herman B Wells*, 126.

[23]Herman G. [sic] Wells, "The Early History of Indiana University as Reflected in the Administration of Andrew Wylie, 1829–1851," *Filson Club Historical Quarterly* 36 (1962): 113–27.

condition report for the university in late 1960. The project was termed a "restoration," which meant renovating the structure to resemble its original finished appearance in 1835.

Architect Edward James had experience in historic preservation and, in 1957, was appointed American Institute of Architects (AIA) preservation officer for the state of Indiana, where he coordinated the Historic American Building Survey Inventory. His younger associate, H. Roll McLaughlin, was assigned as project architect for the Wylie House restoration. In 1960, McLaughlin was appointed AIA assistant preservation officer, working under James. Later that year, McLaughlin was elected first vice president of the new Historic Landmarks Foundation of Indiana (now Indiana Landmarks), a non-profit organization formed by civic and business leaders interested in the preservation of architectural heritage.[24] Drafting plans for the Wylie House restoration, McLaughlin embarked on an important early project at the outset of his long career.[25]

McLaughlin relied on his architectural training and understanding of the principles of historic preservation to guide the project. In the fall of 1960, McLaughlin spent ten weeks in Europe studying preservation techniques and stopped by Washington, Pennsylvania, where Andrew Wylie lived prior to coming to Bloomington.[26] (Nationwide design standards were not instituted until 1966, when the National Historic Preservation Act was passed.) Motivated by a sense of original intent, he focused narrowly on the architectural creation of the house in 1835 rather than considering the entire eighty-year span during which two related, yet separate Wylie families were in residence. The goal was to restore the house to the year it was built.

The IU trustee board approved an agreement with the Edward D. James firm in January 1961, with a preliminary cost budget of $250,000, with a justification: "Because of the nature of the work, which precludes definite advance plans and specifications, this will be done on a time-card basis cost of work done."[27] In June

[24]Among the leaders of Historic Landmarks Foundation of Indiana were Eli Lilly and Herman Krannert. H. Roll McLaughlin, "HABS in Indiana, 1955–1982: Recollections," in *Historic American Buildings Survey in Indiana*, ed. T. M. Slade (Bloomington: Indiana University Press, 1983), 13–20, pp. 16–17.

[25]Preservation Development Inc., "Wylie House Historic Structure Report" (Bloomington, 2001).

[26]Preservation Development Inc., 15.

[27]Indiana University Board of Trustees, "Minutes of the Board of Trustees of Indiana University, 20 January 1961–21 January 1961" (Blooming-

1961, President Wells appointed a Committee on the Restoration of Wylie House, chaired by Joseph Franklin, longtime IU treasurer, and including archivist Mary Craig, physical plant director H. H. Brooks, librarian Cecil Byrd, landscape architect Frits Loonsten, and architect Edward James.[28]

The actual renovation work was done by IU physical plant employees, around fifteen in all, supervised by John Dixon, a master carpenter. The initial phase, lasting about a year, stabilized the foundation, rebuilt the west wall, repointed all exterior walls, rebuilt fireplace hearths, removed the roof, and removed plaster from interior walls. For the next three years, a variety of finish work occurred. A new roof, with poplar shake shingles split by physical plant employee Wally Sullivan, was installed, and copper guttering was added. Interior walls were re-lathed and replastered. In the kitchen, the floor joists were replaced and the floorboards too, with old-growth poplar flooring. The back porch, including its foundation, was removed. Wood trim was stripped and repainted, exterior doors and some windowsills were replaced, new limestone steps were installed at entrances, and most windows were reglazed with antique glass. The attic was reconstructed, with new walls, doors, stairs to the roof, and a roof access hatch with copper hinges. The main staircase was carefully disassembled, stripped of paint, reassembled, and repainted.[29]

As the restoration project continued, in 1962, the university got a new president, Elvis J. Stahr, and Herman Wells moved into the role of university chancellor, a new senior administrative post. The traditional pilgrimage to Wylie's grave in Rose Hill Cemetery on Founders Day went on, now led by President Stahr and joined regularly by Wells.

10.6 Wylie House Museum

Indiana University issued a press release announcing the opening of the museum to the public in October 1965. It fell to the university

ton, IN: Indiana University Archives; Indiana University Libraries Digital Collections Services, January 20–21, 1961), https://purl.dlib.indiana.edu/iudl/archives/iubot/1961-01-20.

[28] Preservation Development Inc., "Wylie House Historic Structure Report," 13–14.

[29] Preservation Development Inc., 14–15.

archivist, Mary Craig, to keep the place running. With no additional staff and little interpretation, by default the museum focused on the building itself in its renovated state. After the initial flurry of publicity, the museum was open by appointment. Craig continued to acquire period furnishings, and those that were not put on display immediately were consigned to storage at the university. There was little attempt to curate the history of the house as successive families lived there. There was, however, a trove of documents slowly gathering in the archives, through occasional gifts and the rediscovery of materials already in the archives that had been poorly cataloged previously.

Preceding the 1967 pilgrimage to Wylie's gravesite, President Stahr led a special Founders Day ceremony to commemorate the centennial of the admission of women to IU. A total of six women received honorary degrees. Then Stahr invited the audience to join him and Wells for

> a pilgrimage to the grave and then to the house of Andrew Wylie, first president of Indiana University. Wylie House was purchased for the University at the express request of Governor Ralph Gates, who instructed that it be restored to its original form. The necessity of collecting funds for the renovation and the time required to do the actual work postponed the opening until two years ago. Since then, increasing numbers of students, parents, school children, and others have toured this home of so much historical significance to Indiana University and to the State. I should add, Wylie House gives some *continuing reality* to our annual Founders' Day reminder that ours is a pioneer university.

Charter bus transportation was available from the Indiana Memorial Union.[30]

During the 1970 IU sesquicentennial year, records indicate that an application for nomination of the Wylie House to the National Register of Historic Places was begun by IU staff but not completed.[31] In 1972, Chancellor Wells bought a neighboring house as a real estate investment to protect Wylie House and help buffer possible future

[30]Elvis Stahr, "Founders' Day Ceremonial" (Indiana University Archives, May 3, 1967), http://fedora.dlib.indiana.edu/fedora/get/iudl:2078062/OVERVIEW. IUA/C75.

[31]Preservation Development Inc., "Wylie House Historic Structure Report," 16.

development.[32] In 1976, the United States bicentennial brought renewed attention to local landmarks, including several historic structures in Bloomington connected to the university. A flurry of successful listings on the National Register of Historic Places was completed, including the Monroe County Courthouse (1976) and the Carnegie Library (1978).[33] Three properties with strong links to IU were listed: the Wylie House (1977), Seminary Square Park (1977), and the Old Crescent (1980).[34] Coincidentally, Mary Craig retired in 1977, but she remained active. In 1978, the home next door was purchased by the university, dubbed the Wylie House Annex, and provided office space and additional storage.[35]

In the third volume of Thomas Clark's massive sesquicentennial history of IU, he mentioned the Wylie House in passing, calling it an "institutional shrine" to the university's past and a "memorial of 'Andrew the First.' "[36] The vision that animated the restoration of the house's architectural glory in the 1960s had dissipated in the 1970s, and Wylie House remained an architectural relic, impassively witnessing the passing years.

10.7 Curatorial Beginnings

The annual pilgrimage to Andrew Wylie's gravesite and to the Wylie House had continued, with President John Ryan leading the party in 1983. The home, Ryan noted, "was a mansion almost beyond comprehension" in its day.[37] That year, Bonnie Williams was hired as the first curator of Wylie House. With determination and energy,

[32]The address was 215 E. Second Street. Indiana University Board of Trustees, "Minutes of the Board of Trustees of Indiana University, 22 September 1972" (Bloomington, IN: Indiana University Archives; Indiana University Libraries Digital Collections Services, September 22, 1972), https://purl.dlib.indiana.edu/iudl/archives/iubot/1972-09-22.

[33]Dana D'Esopo, co-chair of the Historic Preservation Subcommittee filled out the courthouse form; Bruce Tone and Dana D'Esopo, Save the Library Committee, filled out the library form.

[34]Donald Carmony, IU professor of history and editor of the Indiana Magazine of History, and H. Roll McLaughlin, restoration architect, filled out the form for the Wylie House; Mary Alice Gray of the Bloomington/Monroe County Bicentennial Commission for Seminary Square; and Daniel F. Harrington of the IU Heritage Committee for the Old Crescent.

[35]Preservation Development Inc., "Wylie House Historic Structure Report," 21.

[36]Clark, *Indiana University*, 1977, 181, 512.

[37]Indiana University Board of Trustees, "Minutes of the Board of Trustees of Indiana University, 09 April 1983" (Bloomington, IN: Indiana University

Williams launched into making the house more than an architectural relic.

Williams, who was the only staff member at the Wylie House, did have a small group of volunteers who helped with research and visitor relations and interpretation. For the first few years, the house had limited public hours, and, in her words, "interpretation was confined to standard third-person tours describing the collection and giving some historical background about the Wylie family and early Indiana University."[38]

In 1991, one volunteer, who had worked previously as a first-person interpreter at another historic site, was eager to try first-person techniques at the Wylie House. Williams was skeptical about whether there was enough research into the Wylie family and their daily life to support the creation of a living-history character, as well as how to deal with certain anachronistic features of the house, such as electrical outlets and a security system.

After more reading and discussion, however, Williams was willing to try it. Using a "my time / your time" approach, Williams was inspired to create a first-person "ghost interpretation." The idea was that the character worked "in the context of a recreated past but could call on a knowledge of past and future events as needed to help explain the story to visitors."[39] Williams, dressed in the style of the 1840s, greeted fourth graders who were on a field trip to the historic house:

> Good morning and welcome to all of you! Mrs. Williams, who looks after Wylie House, told me she was expecting a group of young visitors this morning. She thought you might enjoy it if I showed you the house and told you a little about what it was like when I was a girl here. I said I'd be most pleased to do so. I enjoy talking about old times. Of course, 150 years is a long time to remember back! But I will say, my memory has always been sharp. My name is Elizabeth Wylie. You may call me Miss Wylie. Andrew Wylie was my Papy, and this is

Archives; Indiana University Libraries Digital Collections Services, April 9, 1983), https://purl.dlib.indiana.edu/iudl/archives/iubot/1983-04-09.

[38]Bonnie Williams, "Playing in the Stream of History: A Flexible Approach to First-Person Interpretation," *Association for Living Historical Farms and Agricultural Museums Proceedings* 14 (1996): 255–61.

[39]Williams, 256.

> the home I grew up in many, many years ago. Oh, my dears, what memories.... Let's go into the parlor where we can sit and visit for a spell.[40]

Williams explained the rationale behind the approach: "Instead of transporting visitors back in time and pretending it is the 1840s, I bring someone from the 1840s into the present—a 'ghost,' so to speak."[41]

By playing a ghost, the interpreter had access to knowledge about the past as well as the present, providing flexibility in answering questions about the house or its furnishings. Even obvious anachronisms, such as the motion detectors for the security system, could be explained. The ghost of Miss Wylie answered when a schoolchild pointed out the small plastic box with a blinking red light in the corner of a room:

> You know, I studied on that for the longest time. It certainly wasn't here when I was a girl. Finally I asked Mrs. Williams and she told me it was a burglar alarm! I told her that when I was a girl, our "burglar alarm" was our dog! Well, in those days there was always someone in the house, and nowadays that's not so, and we don't have a dog here anymore to protect the house. So I suppose it is a good idea to have one of these new burglar alarms, just to be on the safe side.[42]

Williams admitted that the ghost approach necessitated a lot of background research to be able to respond to visitors' observations and to answer questions, but in the end, "we talk about what we do know."[43] At the end of the group tour, Williams came out of character: "As you know, I am not really a ghost. I am an historian. It's my job to learn about the past and to share what I've learned with you. And I have found that sometimes the best way to do that is to pretend, like we did today. I enjoyed sharing and learning with you! Do you like studying history this way? Maybe someday some of you will become historians, and you may even do work like

---

[40]"Playing in the Stream of History.", p. 255. See also Stacy Flora Roth, Past into Present: Effective Techniques for First-Person Historical Interpretation (Chapel Hill: University of North Carolina Press, 1988), where Williams's technique is discussed on page 17.

[41]255.

[42]258.

[43]259.

this!"[44] Both children and adults responded well to this conclusion, which gave the tour a sense of closure and provided the opportunity to ask questions about the museum.

Williams used and refined her ghost interpretation at the Wylie House for nearly a decade for visitor tours. She also practiced a form of historical reenactment, where a small group would get into character as various members of the Wylie family and read their nineteenth-century letters to each other.

In the 1990s, some house features needed additional remediation. In 1994, the trustee board officially renamed the facility the Wylie House Museum, to better reflect its function.[45] In 1995, a wheelchair ramp was installed, which required excavation on the north side. Some artifacts were found, mostly bits of broken china, and cleaned and cataloged. Another conservation assessment survey was completed in 1995.

In 1995, volunteer researcher Elaine Herold, aided by curator Williams, published a compilation of 163 letters exchanged by the members of the Andrew Wylie family. The project was made possible by an Indiana Heritage Research Grant from the Indiana Historical Society and the Indiana Humanities Council. Under the title *Affectionately Yours: The Andrew Wylie Family Letters, 1828 to 1859*, the book gives glimpses of the mid-nineteenth-century Hoosier life of the first family of IU.[46] The letters reveal information about travel, weather, and academic life, as well as family drama and emotion about courtship and marriage, sickness and death. By showing the rich texture of day-to-day living, the collection of letters humanizes the Wylie family as they faced the perennial challenges of life.

An eighteenth-century fortepiano surfaced in IU storage in 1997, having lain there for decades. Curator Williams and the Wylie House Museum volunteers were excited, thinking that it might be the one that Andrew Wylie brought to Bloomington in 1829. Despite extensive research, the fortepiano's provenance was murky.

[44] 258.

[45] Indiana University Board of Trustees, "Minutes of the Board of Trustees of Indiana University, 24 September 1994" (Bloomington, IN: Indiana University Archives; Indiana University Libraries Digital Collections Services, September 24, 1994), https://purl.dlib.indiana.edu/iudl/archives/iubot/1994-09-24.

[46] Bonnie Williams and Elaine Herold, eds., *Affectionately Yours: The Andrew Wylie Family Letters, 1828 to 1859* (Bloomington: Indiana University Wylie House Museum, 1995).

It likely belonged to the Wylies but could not be proven conclusively. In any event, plans were made to restore the instrument, built in 1795 by the Broadwood Company in England. Local harpsichord craftsman Theodore Robertson rebuilt the instrument. Based on a bibliography of the Wylies' own sheet music, musicians searched the Lilly Library for appropriate period music "that represents what the Wylie family would likely have experienced." In 2001, an audio recording, *Wylie House Music from the Parlor*, was produced, played on the Broadwood fortepiano and featuring two pianists and two vocalists.[47]

With funds provided by state and federal grants, Williams started preparing a bibliography of Andrew Wylie with the aid of stalwart volunteers. Published in November 2000, *Andrew Wylie: A Bibliography* was edited by Diane Chaudemanche and Elaine Herold. It contained an annotated list of seventy-three primary, secondary, and tertiary sources, plus a short list of artifacts associated with Wylie, including the house.[48]

10.8 Jo Burgess and the Education Center

Jo Burgess, former head of Preservation Services at IU Libraries, became the director of the Wylie House Museum at the beginning of the 2000–01 academic year.[49] She had a knack for physical artifacts and an aesthetic that was historically informed. In her first year, a consultant produced a thorough analysis of the house's history and current state of preservation.[50] The *Wylie House Historic Structure Report* made sober reading, with several serious threats to the house's historical fabric identified. Next door, the Wylie House Annex had had substantial structural issues ever since it was acquired that made it nearly impossible to control environmental conditions.

[47]"Wylie House Music from the Parlor," 2001. Audio recording; liner notes by Sophia Grace Travis.

[48]Diane Chaudemanche and Elaine Herold, eds., *Andrew Wylie: A Bibliography*, 2000, http://hdl.handle.net/2022/20329.

[49]Indiana University Board of Trustees, "Minutes of the Board of Trustees of Indiana University, 15 September 2000" (Bloomington, IN: Indiana University Archives; Indiana University Libraries Digital Collections Services, September 15, 2000), https://purl.dlib.indiana.edu/iudl/archives/iubot/2000-09-15.

[50]Preservation Development Inc., "Wylie House Historic Structure Report."

In her first years, Burgess had the white walls decorated with historically appropriate colors, embellished by artful stencil work. She compiled an index to the family letters contained in *Affectionately Yours* and published a second edition in 2002. After that, an unexpected trove of more letters was acquired by the Wylie House Museum, consisting of several hundred from the Theophilus Wylie family and another one hundred letters from the Andrew Wylie family. Several letters found their way into the third edition of the book, published in 2011.[51]

Burgess made concerted efforts to expand educational programming. In summer 2005, she hired a full-time curator of education—Bridget Edwards—who had a doctorate in anthropology.[52]

Aided by the dean of university libraries Suzanne Thorin, Edwards got on the radar of the university administration in 2006, when the trustees heard a brief presentation by Vice President Clapacs on the idea of adding an education center to the museum facilities.[53] In 2008, the education center project was approved, and in 2009, contracts were let to design and build the education center.[54] In May 2010, the trustees approved the naming of the new facility after a descendant of Theophilus Wylie, the Morton C. Bradley Jr. Education Center.[55] Personnel changes ensued, starting with

---

[51] Jo Burgess, ed., *Affectionately Yours: The Andrew Wylie Family Letters*, I: 1828–1859, II: 1860–1918 vols. (Bloomington: Wylie House Museum, 2011). Volume I: https://scholarworks.iu.edu/dspace/items/4323e65e-8053-4624-a19c-cec3c14205f0; Volume II: https://scholarworks.iu.edu/dspace/items/4c56273e-06d6-427e-a533-769e9cf5504e.

[52] Edwards served from July 2005 to September 2011.

[53] Indiana University Board of Trustees, "Minutes of the Board of Trustees of Indiana University, 09 June 2006" (Bloomington, IN: Indiana University Archives; Indiana University Libraries Digital Collections Services, June 9, 2006), https://purl.dlib.indiana.edu/iudl/archives/iubot/2006-06-09.

[54] Indiana University Board of Trustees, "Minutes of the Board of Trustees of Indiana University, 15 August 2008" (Bloomington, IN: Indiana University Archives; Indiana University Libraries Digital Collections Services, August 15, 2008), https://purl.dlib.indiana.edu/iudl/archives/iubot/2008-08-15; Indiana University Board of Trustees, "Minutes of the Board of Trustees of Indiana University, 14 August 2009" (Bloomington, IN: Indiana University Archives; Indiana University Libraries Digital Collections Services, August 14, 2009), https://purl.dlib.indiana.edu/iudl/archives/iubot/2009-08-14.

[55] Indiana University Board of Trustees, "Minutes of the Board of Trustees of Indiana University, 07 May 2010" (Bloomington, IN: Indiana University Archives; Indiana University Libraries Digital Collections Services, May 7, 2010), https://purl.dlib.indiana.edu/iudl/archives/iubot/2010-05-07.

the departure of education curator Edwards in 2011, followed by the retirement of director Burgess in 2012.[56]

10.9 The Recent Past

When Burgess retired in 2012, librarian Carey Beam became the next museum director, carrying on the tradition of engagement with both the Bloomington community and the larger communities related to nineteenth-century American history and culture. In the *Wylie House Museum Handbook* of 2016–17, a guide for staff and volunteers, the basic mission of interpreting the early history of IU and Bloomington remained the same but was elaborated in the following way:

> The mission of the Wylie House Museum is to preserve, collect, and study the house, its artifacts, documents, and landscape, and through them to interpret with the public the early history and culture of Indiana University and the town of Bloomington. We seek to engage the visitor in an experience of history which is stimulating, thoughtful, and enjoyable; which is factually accurate and respectful of the period and people we interpret; and which excites an interest in and appreciation of domestic history, the heritage of Indiana University and Bloomington, and the visitor's own personal history.[57]

The mission statement also emphasized the ongoing historical research program involving the museum's buildings, collections, landscape, and archives, noting that all of it is part of the university's teaching and research mission.

[56]Indiana University Board of Trustees, "Minutes of the Board of Trustees of Indiana University, 07 December 2012" (Bloomington, IN: Indiana University Archives; Indiana University Libraries Digital Collections Services, December 7, 2012), https://purl.dlib.indiana.edu/iudl/archives/iubot/2012-12-07.

[57]Wylie House Museum, Indiana University Libraries, "Wylie House Museum Handbook" (2016–2017), 3.

10.10 Connecting to the Past

At the gala sesquicentennial dinner in 1970, University Chancellor Wells paid tribute to his presidential predecessors. He talked about the "rich store of anecdotes and recollections about the early life of the university" possessed by President Bryan, who had lived in Bloomington for ninety-five years and had been associated with the university during his entire adult life. Bryan knew friends of the first president, Andrew Wylie. And the first president, so it was alleged, had met George Washington when he was a boy. Wells continued the story, smiling, "It was my later good fortune to share with Dr. Bryan remembrances of things past. They became so much a part of me that I find myself occasionally reminiscing about George Washington." The audience roared with laughter.[58]

Wells was using humor to convey a serious point about the human need for connection to the past. Appreciating those who came before, whether in our families, communities, or institutions, is a vital part of our common heritage. In his ninetieth year, Wells reflected on this during an interview with Bonnie Williams, the first curator of the Wylie House, saying, "I was always interested in anything that was a living reminder of the antiquity of the University."[59] He became acquainted with the Wylie House in the early 1930s. When he became president later in the decade, he set his sights on acquiring the house for the university, which took him ten years. It was another decade and a half before the house received an architectural restoration. During the sesquicentennial era, as historian Clark noted, it was an "institutional shrine." Exquisitely restored to its architectural glory, it was a relic admired from afar, but with tenuous connections to the ongoing life of the university. In the 1980s, interpretative programs and cultural research on the home and its inhabitants reengaged the Wylie House with its local context. Renewed financial and programmatic investments by the university after 2000 had ensured the welfare of the Wylie House Museum during IU's bicentennial era. Throughout his long life, Herman Wells played a catalytic role in the resurrection of Wylie House, the most significant artifact relating to the early history of Indiana University.

[58] *The Vision of Herman B Wells*, Documentary film, 1993, 47:15–20.
[59] Wells, "Oral History Interview by Bonnie Williams."

Coda

> It has been said that history itself is a dialogue in the present with the past about the future.
>
> —Douglass Adair, *Fame and the Founding Fathers*

Figure 15: Postcard of the Sunken Gardens. The old Dunn Quarry on Third Street near Hawthorne Drive was converted into a rock garden in 1928 to serve the recreational needs of the campus. Known by students as the "passion pit," it was demolished to make way for the Jordan Hall greenhouse (now Biology Hall). **Copyright holder unknown. Image from the IU Archives.**

Spring Break 2020: A New Watershed?

Figure 16: Sample Gates

> A watershed is a marvelous thing to consider: This process of rain falling, streams flowing, and oceans evaporating causes every molecule of water to make the complete trip once every two million years. The surface is carved into watersheds—kind of familial branching, a chart of relationship, and a definition of place. The watershed is the first and last nation, whose boundaries, though subtly shifting, are unarguable. Races of birds, subspecies of trees, and types of hats or rain gear go by the watershed. The watershed gives us a home, and a place to go upstream, downstream, or across in.... Watershed consciousness...is not just environmentalism...but a move toward a profound citizenship in both the natural and the social worlds. If the ground can be our common ground, we can begin to talk to each other (human and non-human) once again.
>
> —Gary Snyder, "Coming into the Watershed"

Indiana University entered new institutional terrain in March 2020 around spring break with the arrival of a global pandemic. Tentative plans to extend spring break another week were soon revised as the magnitude of the public health crisis became apparent. As the Indiana government issued directives for all state residents to shelter in place, IU campuses around the state were closed and classes moved to online learning delivered via the internet. Commencement ceremonies were canceled, and the year-long commemoration of the IU bicentennial ceased three months from its scheduled conclusion on June 30. At this writing, four years later, the university has weathered this public health crisis. A vaccination for COVID-19 was developed in record time, in-person classes resumed, and social life returned, albeit to a new normal.

What this means for American higher education more generally is still too early to tell, but some think it represents a transition to a new "watershed" in our history. Literally, a watershed is a land area where precipitation eventually flows into a body of water, usually a river, lake, or ocean. So, the boundaries of a watershed are high points on the land, like hilltops, ridges, or mountain crests. The Continental Divide provided by the Rocky Mountains is an example of a large-scale watershed boundary. Rainfall on the eastern side of the country flows into the Atlantic Ocean; on the western side, the Pacific Ocean. On a much smaller scale, the IU campus is bisected by a ridge, running near Tenth Street, separating the land into two larger watersheds. On the north side of campus, Griffy Creek and Cascades Creek drain into the West Fork of the White River. On the south side, Clear Creek and Jackson Creek drain into the East Fork of the White River. Both are the main tributaries of the Wabash River. More than a third of the campus is served by the Jordan River (renamed Campus River), which becomes part of Clear Creek once it leaves campus.

Metaphorically, watersheds have rich connotations. Used to denote a significant point of division or transition between two phases or conditions, it can be applied to historical cases and used as a basis for historical periodization. Dramatic change characterizes the movement into a new watershed, as "before" and "after" acquire a new relevance.

I suggest that Indiana University has operated in four historic watersheds in the last two hundred years and is on the verge of a fifth. The establishment of the institution in 1820 can be seen as the watershed instauration, with a landscape of unique opportunities, resources, and challenges. Located on Seminary Square, part of the original congressional land grant that endowed the school, classes started in 1825, and the college produced its first four graduates in 1830. The movement from seminary to college to university, the curriculum based on classical languages, and the financial and political challenges for the survival of a tiny institution were all part of the institutional landscape of the early days. That first watershed ended abruptly after a third of a century when the College Building burned down in 1854.

That almost killed the university. But the town of Bloomington and the small body of alumni rallied to provide financial and moral support, and the institution rebuilt. Amid rebuilding, the institution's sole fiscal allocation—the small University Fund endowment—was threatened by legal maneuvering in 1855, but Governor Joseph A. Wright pressed the legislature to restore the endowment, narrowly avoiding disaster for the university. Wright happened to be among the students who attended when the seminary first opened, although he never graduated.

Stronger due to overcoming critical challenges to its very existence, IU went on for the next three decades, growing slowly in a time when higher education had little relevance to the civic life of the state's residents. The institutional landscape of this period saw the Civil War, admission of women and African Americans as students, and the protracted campaign to receive designation as a federal land-grant university under the 1862 Morrill Act, which was unsuccessful. Instead, IU gained a sibling state university—Purdue University in West Lafayette—as well as a permanent rival.

This second watershed was upended by another campus fire, in 1883. The newer of the two main buildings—Science Hall—was destroyed. Unlike in 1854, it did not threaten the university's continued existence, although it was a hard blow. By that time, the university had acquired enough institutional momentum to carry it through. It prompted the board of trustees to make a fateful decision to move the campus across town, to a patch of farm woodlot known as Dunn's Woods. In 1885, the campus acquired a new leader, President David Starr Jordan, a research scientist with a national reputation. Focused on investigation as the basis for teaching as well as research, his administration modernized the curriculum, instituted the elective system, and reorganized the faculty into departments. The university's aspirations were elevated as it became involved in national dialogues about higher education, research, and the role of universities in America.

For over a half century, IU operated in this environment. It grew steadily, through the turn of the twentieth century, the First World War, and the Great Depression of the 1930s, much of it under the leadership of William Lowe Bryan, another research scientist and the protégé of Jordan. It was not until the advent of the Second World War and its aftermath that IU entered another watershed.

Starting in 1945, the postwar landscape for American higher education was changed significantly as the federal government subsidized college education for military veterans through the GI Bill and invested heavily in research and development as an important basis for national security. This "golden age" of rising enrollments and ample funding lasted until the early 1970s when the political and social environment changed. In the next two decades, American higher education reached the status of a "mature industry," as one observer noted, as competition for students, funding, and reputation became even more pronounced.[60]

[60]Arthur Levine, "How the Academic Profession Is Changing," *Daedalus* 126, no. 4 (1997): 1–20; "Higher Education Becomes a Mature Industry," *About Campus: Enriching the Student Learning Experience* 2, no. 3 (1997): 31–32, https://doi.org/10.1177/108648229700200.

In the early years of the twenty-first century, the major features of the post–World War II watershed were still in place, although buffeted by ceaseless political winds as American society and culture underwent change. While still serving the education and knowledge needs of the state of Indiana, this long-lasting institutional watershed was becoming increasingly globalized, and student tuition and private philanthropy assumed greater importance in the university's budget as state legislative support slowly dwindled.

Looking back over the two-hundred-plus-year history of Indiana University from the present, one can generalize some broad themes. IU has grown into a multifaceted educational enterprise with a myriad of connections to local communities, the Hoosier state, the nation, and the world. Its education, research, and service missions grew out of the flagship campus in Bloomington during its first century. In the second century, the university extended its programs statewide and developed physical campuses in several Hoosier communities. As a human institution, IU remains in constant flux, responding internally to cultural imperatives of teaching and learning as well as reacting to the myriad external demands placed on it.

In keeping with the focus of this book on how the university was shaped by its history and physical environment, watershed periods provide a way to examine large-scale changes. There is no question that 2020 will go down in IU's history as a significant year, perhaps marking a new watershed. But the meaning of that year to the history of Indiana University is still being written.

Campus Expansion Map (1885–2020)

Figure 17: Static version of the IU campus footprint map (1885–2020), based on official campus maps, from twenty acres at the beginning to nearly 2,000 acres at present. The interactive version is available in the HTML edition.

Acknowledgments

Figure 18: Boy with bicycle at Jordan River

A scrawny boy, aged nine, pedaled his twenty-inch red Schwinn bicycle up Woodlawn Avenue from Bryan Park to the Indiana University campus, looking for adventure. The warm spring air was full of mysterious promise. Accompanied by a friend who lived across the street on Maxwell Lane and one of his brothers, the boys knew that winding paths through the woods, immense gray buildings, and running water would await them. Once on campus grounds, anticipation gave way to delight in the present moment—riding endlessly on interconnected walkways, catching goldfish in the creek left discarded from fraternity parties, searching for a drinking fountain in the cavernous Union building. The waking reverie lasted until the lengthening shadows brought them back to the hunger in their bellies and to the relief of their homes. In the spring and summer of 1964, that boy was introduced to the wonders of university life by the physical environment of the campus, where he was able to engage all of his senses, six blocks away from his home. Still innocent of the ways of place-making, the names Maxwell and Bryan held no connotations. The boy's name was Jimmy Capshew, and he has lived in the university's sheltering shadow since.

This book was a long time in the making, delayed by the global pandemic. Along the way, I received assistance from many people, most notably from the excellent staff of the University Archives at Indiana University Bloomington. I am grateful to my colleagues Dina Kellams, Kristin Leaman, Carrie Schwier, Mary Mellon, Molly Wittenberg, Brad Cook, and Amanda Rindler.

In 2015, I was drawn into the organization and then operation of the IU Office of the Bicentennial under its mastermind, Kelly Kish, whose administrative acumen is matched only by her prodigious intellect. She always asked the hard questions, but I could count on her for unflagging support. The staff of the Bicentennial Office, including Bre Anne Kusz, Jeremy Hackerd, Sarah Jacobi, Angel Nathan, Sarah Reynolds, Rafal Swiatkowski, and Brittany Terwilliger, buoyed my efforts at every turn.

I made presentations to several audiences, both local and national, about the research on which this book is based, including the Monroe County History Club, the IU Alumni Association's Mini

University, the Friends of the Monroe County Public Library, and the History of Education Society.

Several persons facilitated access to documents and shared relevant information, including Anita Bracalente, Jonah Busch, Greg Buse, Carey Champion, Terry Clapacs, Michael Chitwood, Bridget Edwards, Harry Ford, Deborah Lemon, Richard McClelland, Sarah Mincey, David Parkhurst, Eileen Savage, and Indermohan Virk.

The people who read drafts of chapters occupy a high niche in my personal pantheon: Bre Anne Kusz, Roger Beckman, Jonah Busch, Duncan Campbell, Carey Champion, Michael Chitwood, Harry Ford, Donald J. Gray, Jeremy Hackerd, Sarah Mincey, Michael Nelson, Laura Plummer, Sarah Reynolds, Eric Sandweiss, Edith Sarra, Curt Simic, Andrea Singer, and John Summerlot. It was a pleasure working with illustrator Joe Lee, whom I first met two decades ago.

When the time came to publish this research, Diane Dallis-Comentale, Ruth Lilly Dean of University Libraries, suggested I try the new publishing service provided by the Department of Scholarly Communication. Adam Mazel, Digital Publishing Librarian, was an excellent guide and an effective colleague in creating my first "born digital" book. The interactive map was made possible through the innovative efforts of Theresa Quill, Map and Spatial Data librarian.

A special thanks goes to Michael McRobbie, University Chancellor and President Emeritus, who had faith in planning for the university's future by a thorough understanding of its past.

Halloween 2024

Bibliography

Bloomington Telephone 7, no. 46 (March 29, 1884): 1.
Indiana Student, April 1, 1898, 53.
Indiana Student, April 6, 1901, 12.
Arbutus, June 1906, 388–90.
Indiana Daily Student, November 15, 1999.
Bloomington: Indiana University Archives, n.d. IUA/C213/B30/F.
"About Ivy L. Chamness," n.d. https://honorsandawards.iu.edu/awards/honoree/2297.html.
Abram, David. *The Spell of the Sensuous: Perception and Language in a More-Than-Human World.* New York: Vintage, 1996.
Adair, Douglass. *Fame and the Founding Fathers: Essays by Douglass Adair.* Edited by Trevor Colburn. New York: W. W. Norton & Company, 1974.
Addis, Alfred. "Latin Grammars." *The Literary and Theological Review* 6, no. 21 (1839): 59–66.
Albert, Barb. "I.U. Group Launches Battle to Rescue Beloved Woods." *Indianapolis Star*, February 12, 1982, 22.
"Alumni Council Meetings." *Indiana University Alumni Quarterly* 6, no. 3 (July 1919): 392–94.
"Alumni Notes by Classes: 1906." *Indiana University Alumni Quarterly* 24, no. 1 (1937): 74.
"Balls and Strikes: A Story." *Arbutus*, 1899, 174–79.
Banta, D. D. *A Historical Sketch of Johnson County, Indiana.* Chicago: J.H. Beers & Co., 1881.
Banta, David D. "History of Indiana University I: The Seminary Period (1820–1828)." *Indiana University Alumni Quarterly* 1, no. 1 (1914): 3–24.
Banta, David D. "History of Indiana University: II: From Seminary to College (1826–1829)." *Indiana University Alumni Quarterly* 1, no. 2 (1914): 142–65.
Banta, David D. "History of Indiana University: III: The New Departure (1829–1833)." *Indiana University Alumni Quarterly* 1, no. 3 (1914): 272–92.

Banta, David D. "History of Indiana University: IV. The 'Faculty War' of 1832." *Indiana University Alumni Quarterly* 1, no. 4 (1914): 369–86.

Banta, David D. "History of Indiana University: V: From College to University (1833–1838)." *Indiana University Alumni Quarterly* 2, no. 1 (1915): 5–17.

Banta, David D. "History of Indiana University: VI: Perils from Sectarian Controversies and the Constitutional Convention (1838–1850)." *Indiana University Alumni Quarterly* 2, no. 2 (1915): 99–110.

Banta, David D. "Letter to James Woodburn." Indiana University Archives, February 9, 1889.

Banta, David D. *Indiana Student* 9, no. 7 (May 1883): 166–67.

Benson, Olof. "Description of the Plan of Improvement of University Park." Indiana University Archives/C77/B1, 1884.

Bernstein, Leonard. "Letter to David F. Parkhurst," February 13, 1982. David F. Parkhurst files.

Bischoff, Sue. "Nelson Pleased by Turnout, Originality." *Indiana Daily Student*, n.d.

Blanchard, Charles, ed. *Counties of Morgan, Monroe, and Brown, Indiana: Historical and Biographical.* Chicago: F.A. Battey & Co., 1884.

Blanck, Jacob. *Bibliography of American Literature.* Vol. 3. New Haven: Yale University Press, 1959.

Bracalente, Anita. "Indiana University's Woodland Campus." *View* 12 (2012): 25–27.

Brichford, Maynard. *Journal of the Illinois State Historical Society (1908–1984)* 64, no. 3 (1971): 355–56. http://www.jstor.org/stable/40190803.

Brichford, Maynard. *Journal of the Illinois State Historical Society (1908–1984)* 68, no. 3 (1975): 297–99. http://www.jstor.org/stable/40191173.

Brogan, Dan. "Plager's Contempt on Compromise Out of Character for Law Profession." *Indiana Daily Student*, February 19, 1982.

Brown, William M., and Michael W. Hamburger. "Organizing for Sustainability." In *Enhancing Sustainability Campuswide*, edited by Bruce A. Jacobs and Jillian Kinzie, 83–96. New Directions for Student Services 137. Wiley, 2012.

Bryan, William. "Letter to George Kessler." Indiana University Archives C286/B150/F Kessler, George, May 25, 1916.

Bryan, William Lowe. “Letter to James A. Woodburn.” Indiana University Archives, June 17, 1929. IUA/C83/B3/F Publications, Galleys, & Transcripts.

Bryan, William Lowe. “Letter to James A. Woodburn.” Indiana University Archives, November 17, 1934. IUA/C83/B3/F Publications, Galleys, & Transcripts.

Buley, R. Carlyle. *The Old Northwest: Pioneer Period, 1815–1840.* Vol. 2. Bloomington: Indiana University Press, 1950.

Bunnage, JoAnn C. “Barbara Shalucha and the Development of Hilltop Garden and Nature Center: The Cultivation of a Community Treasure,” 1999.

Burgess, Jo, ed. *Affectionately Yours: The Andrew Wylie Family Letters.* I: 1828–1859, II: 1860–1918 vols. Bloomington: Wylie House Museum, 2011. Volume I: https://scholarworks.iu.edu/dspace/items/4323e65e-8053-4624-a19c-cec3c14205f0; Volume II: https://scholarworks.iu.edu/dspace/items/4c56273e-06d6-427e-a533-769e9cf5504e.

Busch, Jonah M. “The Protect Griffy Alliance and the Golf War: Collective Action at Its Finest,” April 28, 2000. Seminar Paper, Indiana University.

Caldwell, Lynton K. “Environment: A New Focus for Public Policy?” *Public Administration Review* 23 (1963): 132–39.

Caldwell, Lynton Keith. “Foreword: A Sense of Place.” In *The Natural Heritage of Indiana*, edited by Marion C. Jackson, xv–xvi. Bloomington: Indiana University Press, 1997.

Campbell, Matthew. “Letter to David Banta.” Indiana University Archives/C112/B1, December 25, 1882.

“Campus Improvements Due to Prof. Mottier.” *Indiana Daily Student*, February 5, 1904, 1.

Capshew, James H. *Herman B Wells: The Promise of the American University.* Bloomington; Indianapolis: Indiana University Press; Indiana Historical Society Press, 2012.

Capshew, James H. “Indiana University as the ‘Mother of College Presidents’: Herman B Wells as Inheritor, Exemplar, and Agent.” Bloomington: IU Institute for Advanced Study, 2011. https://hdl.handle.net/2022/14123.

Capshew, James H. “IU Country Club?” *Herald-Times*, September 4, 1999.

Capshew, James H. “Memo University Seal.” Reference file: University Seal. Indiana University Archives, March 1, 2019.

Capshew, James H. "New Light on an Old Story: The Secret of the Faculty War." *200: The Bicentennial Magazine* 1, no. 1 (2018): 6–8.

Capshew, James H. "Nicklaus Course Raises Questions." Editorial. *Herald-Times*, September 8, 1999.

Capshew, James H. "The Campus as a Pedagogical Agent: Herman Wells, Cultural Entrepreneurship, and the Benton Murals." *Indiana Magazine of History* 105, no. 2 (2009): 179–97. https://www.jstor.org/stable/27792978.

Carleton, Emma. "About the New Purchase." *Indianapolis News*, May 16, 1902.

Carmichael, Hoagy. *The Stardust Road.* 1946. Reprint, New York: Greenwood Press, 1969.

Carmichael, Hoagy, and Stephen Longstreet. *Sometimes I Wonder: The Story of Hoagy Carmichael.* New York: Farrer, Straus; Giroux, 1965.

Carr, Edward Hallett. *What Is History?* New York: Knopf, 1961.

Cassidy, Frederic G., ed. *Dictionary of American Regional English.* Cambridge, MA: Belknap Press of Harvard University Press, 1985.

Center on Education Policy. "Public Schools and the Original Federal Land Grant Program: A Background Paper from the Center on Education Policy." Washington, 2011-04. https://eric.ed.gov/?id=ED518388.

Chamness, Ivy. "Letter to Alumni Council." Indiana University Archives, March 22, 1919. IUA/C286/B54.

Chamness, Ivy. "Letter to Herman B Wells." Indiana University Archives, 1938. IUA/C213/B118.

Chamness, Ivy. "Letter to James A. Woodburn." Indiana University Archives, November 30, 1940. IUA/C83/B4/F Testimonial Banquet/Correspondence.

Chamness, Ivy. "Letter to Mrs. C. J. Sembower." Indiana University Archives, June 3, 1935. IUA/C84/B1/F Edited Manuscripts-Alumni Quarterly.

Chamness, Ivy. "Letter to William Lowe Bryan." Indiana University Archives, June 18, 1919. IUA/C286/B54.

Chamness, Ivy. "Letter to William Lowe Bryan." Indiana University Archives, May 11, 1920. IUA/C286/B54.

Chamness, Ivy L. "Another College President." *IU Alumni Quarterly* 10 (1923): 512.

Chamness, Ivy L. "Another College President." *IU Alumni Quarterly* 25 (1938): 59.

Chamness, Ivy L., ed. *Indiana University, 1820–1920: Centennial Memorial Volume.* Bloomington: Indiana University, 1921.

Chamness, Ivy L. "Indiana University in Earlier Days: I. As Reflected in Commencement and Exhibition Programs." *Indiana University Alumni Quarterly* 16, no. 1 (1929): 33–45.

Chamness, Ivy L. "Indiana University in Earlier Days: II. As Reflected in Early Issues of the *Indiana Student.*" *Indiana University Alumni Quarterly* 16, no. 2 (1929): 199–221.

Chamness, Ivy L. "Indiana University—Mother of College Presidents." *Educational Issues* 2, no. 8 (1921): 28–29.

Chamness, Ivy L. "Indiana University—Mother of College Presidents." *Indiana University Alumni Quarterly* 9 (1922): 46–49.

Chamness, Ivy L. "IUA/C84/B1/f Edited Manuscripts-Myers." Bloomington, IN: Indiana University Archives, n.d.

Chamness, Ivy L. "More College Presidents." *IU Alumni Quarterly* 10 (1923): 334.

Chamness, Ivy L. "The First 125 Years." *Indiana Alumni Magazine* 7, no. 9 (1945): 11–14.

Chamness, Ivy Leone. "A Study of Editorial Matters in the Catalogs of the Members of the National Association of State Universities." Indiana University, 1928. Master's thesis, Indiana University.

Chamness, Ivy Leone. "Alumni Notes by Classes." Edited by Ivy Leone Chamness. *Indiana University Alumni Quarterly* 2, no. 2 (April 1915): 207.

Chamness, Ivy Leone. "Indiana University in Earlier Days: III. As Reflected in the Issues of the *Indiana Student* in the Nineties." *Indiana University Alumni Quarterly* 17, no. 1 (1930): 22–38.

Chamness, Ivy Leone. "Indiana University in Earlier Days: IV. As Reflected in Issues of the *Indiana Student* in the Nineties." *Indiana University Alumni Quarterly* 18, no. 2 (1931): 156–71.

Chamness, Ivy Leone. "Indiana University in Earlier Days: V. As Reflected in Historical Material Recently Given to the Institution." *Indiana University Alumni Quarterly* 18, no. 1 (1931): 16–29.

Chamness, Ivy Leone. "Indiana University in Earlier Days: VI. As Reflected in Official Publications." *Indiana University Alumni Quarterly* 20, no. 2 (1933): 159–68.

Chamness, Ivy Leone. "Indiana University in Earlier Days: VII. As Reflected in Official Publications." *Indiana University Alumni Quarterly* 21, no. 2 (1934): 34–47.

Chapman, M. Perry. *American Places: In Search of the Twenty-First Century Campus.* Westport, CT: Praeger, 2006.

"Charles H. Hays." *Indiana University Alumni Quarterly* 24 (1937): 511–12.

"Charles H. Hays." *Indiana Alumni Magazine* 19, no. 7 (1957): 1.

Chaudemanche, Diane, and Elaine Herold, eds. *Andrew Wylie: A Bibliography*, 2000. http://hdl.handle.net/2022/20329.

Clapacs, J. Terry. *Indiana University Bloomington: America's Legacy Campus.* Bloomington: Indiana University Press, 2017.

Clark, Thomas D. *Indiana University: Midwestern Pioneer.* 4 vols. Bloomington: Indiana University Press, 1970/1977.

Clark, Thomas D. *Indiana University: Midwestern Pioneer: Volume I: The Early Years.* 4 vols. Bloomington: Indiana University Press, 1970.

Clark, Thomas D. *Indiana University: Midwestern Pioneer: Volume II: In Mid-Passage.* 4 vols. Bloomington: Indiana University Press, 1973.

Clark, Thomas D. *Indiana University: Midwestern Pioneer: Volume III: Years of Fulfillment.* 4 vols. Bloomington: Indiana University Press, 1977.

Cokinos, Christopher. "Bernstein Note Indicates Support for 'Save the Woods'." *Indiana Daily Student*, February 19, 1982.

Cokinos, Christopher. "Law Addition Sparks Dispute over Woods." *Indiana Daily Student*, January 19, 1982.

Cokinos, Christopher. "Law School Addition Plans to Be Resubmitted." *Indiana Daily Student*, 1982-02-11.

Cokinos, Christopher. "Law School Expansion Inquiry Buried." *Indiana Daily Student*, March 31, 1982.

Cokinos, Christopher. "Law School Expansion May Incapacitate Observatory." *Indiana Daily Student*, January 21, 1982, 1.

Cokinos, Christopher. "New Addition Plan Would Save Woods." *Indiana Daily Student*, April 2, 1982.

Cokinos, Christopher. "Ryan Requests Look at Options for Law School." *Indiana Daily Student*, February 25, 1982.

Cokinos, Christopher. "Save the Woods Group Organizing to Protect Old Crescent." *Indiana Daily Student*, February 10, 1982, 3.

Cokinos, Christopher. "State to Determine If Law Applies to IU Expansion." *Indiana Daily Student*, March 12, 1982.

Cokinos, Christopher. "Wells: University to Develop Campus Natural-Areas Policy." *Indiana Daily Student*, April 30, 1982, 2.

Cokinos, Christopher, and Barbara Toman. "Trustees to Hear Law Expansion Opposition." *Indiana Daily Student*, March 5, 1982.
"Commencement, 1938." *Indiana University Alumni Quarterly* 25, no. 3 (1938): 298–337.
"Conversations about the Bloomington Campus: It Isn't Easy Being Green (But Planning Ahead Helps)." *The College* 16, no. 2 (1992): 8–11.
Conway, Thomas G. "Finding America's History." *Journal of the Illinois State Historical Society* 97, no. 2 (2004): 92–106.
Council for Environmental Stewardship. "Annual Report," 1998–1999.
Council for Environmental Stewardship. "Annual Report," 2001–2002.
Council for Environmental Stewardship. "Annual Report," 2002–2003.
Counts, Will, James H. Madison, and Scott Russell Sanders. *Bloomington Past and Present.* Bloomington: Indiana University Press, 2002.
Cravens, J. W. "History of University Land Purchases." *Indiana University Alumni Quarterly* 2, no. 2 (1915): 156–59.
Cravens, John W. "Buildings on the Old and New Campuses of Indiana University: I. The Old Seminary Building." *Indiana University Alumni Quarterly* 9, no. 1 (1922): 1–11.
Cravens, John W. "Buildings on the Old and New Campuses of Indiana University: II: Six of the Buildings on the Old Campus." *Indiana University Alumni Quarterly* 9, no. 2 (1922): 156–64.
Cravens, John W. "Buildings on the Old and New Campuses of Indiana University: III. Buildings on the New Campus and Elsewhere in Monroe County." *Indiana University Alumni Quarterly* 9, no. 3 (1922): 303–20.
Cravens, John W. "The Trustees of Indiana University." *Indiana University Alumni Quarterly* 14 (1927): 465–83.
Cumings, E. R. "The Geological Conditions of Municipal Water Supply in the Driftless Area of Southern Indiana." *Proceedings of the Indiana Academy of Science* 21 (1911): 111–46. https://journals.indianapolis.iu.edu/index.php/ias/article/view/14025.
Curti, Merle. *The American Historical Review* 80, no. 3 (1975): 518–19. https://doi.org/10.2307/1850710.
Curti, Merle. *The American Historical Review* 83, no. 4 (1978): 1101. https://doi.org/10.2307/1867836.

Cusack, Nick. "First IU Sustainability Director Named." *Indiana Daily Student*, February 19, 2009.
Day, Harry G. *The Development of Chemistry at Indiana University, 1829–1991.* Bloomington: Indiana University, 1992.
"Death of Eugene Kerr." *Indiana University Alumni Quarterly* 11, no. 4 (1924): 543–44.
"Discover Ruins of Seminary Building." *Indiana Daily Student*, January 18, 1922, 3.
Dreiser, Theodore. *A Hoosier Holiday.* New York: John Lane Company, 1916.
"Drinking Fountain at I.U." *Indiana Daily Student*, March 9, 1912.
Edmondson, Frank K. "Daniel Kirkwood—'Dean of American Astronomers'." *Mercury* 29, no. 3 (2000): 27–33.
Ehman, Lee. "The Dunn Name, but Not the Spirit." *Monroe County Historian* 3 (August 2010): 10–11.
Ehrmann, Bess V. *The Missing Chapter in the Life of Abraham Lincoln.* Chicago: Walter M. Hill, 1938.
Ellis, Edith Hennel. "The Trees on the I.U. Campus." *Indiana University Alumni Quarterly* 16, no. 3 (1929): 328–31.
"Environmental Action Day April 22 Schedule of Activities." *Indiana Daily Student*, April 22, 1970.
Environmental Law Society. "Position Statement on the Proposed Law School Addition," February 24, 1982. David F. Parkhurst files.
Erekson, Keith A. *Everybody's History: Indiana's Lincoln Inquiry and the Quest to Reclaim a President's Past.* Amherst: University of Massachusetts Press, 2012.
Esarey, Logan. *History of Indiana.* Indianapolis: W. K. Stewart Co., 1915.
"Faculty Necrology." Reference file, Indiana University Archives, n.d.
Fancher, John. "IU Law School Addition Will Not Harm Trees." *Herald-Telephone*, March 7, 1982, 1.
Fancher, John. "IU Trustees OK Law School Addition." *Herald-Telephone* 15, no. 15 (December 6, 1981): 1, 8.
Fancher, John. "Law School Addition OK'd." *Herald-Telephone*, April 4, 1982.
Fancher, John. "Law School Addition Still Up in the Air." *Herald-Telephone*, March 6, 1982, 1.
Fancher, John. "Law School Plan That Saves Woods Moves Ahead." *Herald-Telephone*, April 3, 1982.

Ferguson, Jenny. "Working to Save the Woods, Ryan Makes His Feeling Heard." *Indiana Daily Student*, March 1, 1982. For the Opinion Board.

Ferries, Ken, and Linda Herman. "Woodstock, 4-H Flavor I.U. Environmental Fair." *Indiana Daily Student*, April 23, 1970.

Field, Oliver P. *Political Science at Indiana University, 1829–1951.* Bloomington: Bureau of Government Research, Department of Government, Indiana University, 1952.

"Football Men Wore Mustaches When He Came to University." *Indiana Daily Student* 50, no. 56 (December 3, 1921): 2.

Franklin, J. A. "Letter to Thomas D. Brock." Indiana University Archives/C268/B13/F Committee, Natural Areas, July 21, 1966.

Frey, Juliet, ed. "Islands of Green and Serenity: The Courtyards of Indiana University." Bloomington: Indiana University Publications, 1987.

Fuchs, Ralph F. "Letter to the Editor." *Herald-Telephone*, March 2, 1982, 8.

Gabbay, Sue Davis. "Letter to Brad Cook." Indiana University Archives/Reference file: B+G Sunken Gardens, March 2013.

Gaines, Thomas A. *The Campus as a Work of Art.* Westport, CT: Praeger, 1991.

Garton, Daisy. "Letter to Trustees of Indiana University, President Myles Brand, and Members of the Higher Education Commission," January 12, 2000.

Goodwin, Clarence L. "The *Indiana Student* and Student Life in the Early Eighties." *Indiana University Alumni Quarterly* 17, no. 1 (1930): 146–58.

Graham, Patricia Albjerg. *Indiana Magazine of History* 70, no. 2 (1974): 180–82. http://www.jstor.org/stable/27789965.

Gray, Donald J., ed. *The Department of English at Indiana University Bloomington, 1868–1970.* Bloomington: Indiana University, 1973.

Gray, Donald J. "The IU Necrologist: Duties and Procedures," circa 2017.

"Greening the IMU: Eco-Charrette Report." Bloomington: Indiana University, February 23, 2010.

Hackerd, Jeremy L. “The Complex History of the Date Classes Began at the State Seminary of Indiana.” Indianapolis: Indiana Historical Bureau, June 30, 2008. Background Report on the State Historical Marker ("State Seminary of Indiana" marker) for Seminary Square, Bloomington, Indiana State Historical Marker Program.
Hall, Baynard Rush. *Exercises, Analytical and Synthetical; Arranged for the New and Compendious Latin Grammar.* Bedford: Harrison Hall, 1836.
Hall, Baynard Rush. *Frank Freeman's Barber Shop.* New York: Scribner, 1852.
Hall, Baynard Rush. “Letter to John Nunemacher,” May 13, 1855.
Hall, Baynard Rush. *Teaching, a Science: The Teacher an Artist.* New York: Baker; Scribner, 1848.
Hall, Baynard Rush. *The New Purchase; or, Early Years in the Far West.* 2nd ed. New Albany, IN: Jno. R. Nunemacher, 1855.
Hall, Baynard Rush (Robert Carlton, pseud.). *The New Purchase, or, Seven and a Half Years in the Far West.* Edited by J. A. Woodburn. 1843. Reprint, Princeton University Press, 1916.
Hall, Baynard Rush, Donald F. Carmony, and Herman J. Viola. “The New Purchase: Or, Seven and a Half Years in the Far West.” *Indiana Magazine of History* 62, no. 2 (1966): 101–20.
Hamburger, Michael. “Editorial.” *Herald-Times*, November 30, 1999.
Hamilton, Lee. “The Popularity of the Environmental Issue.” Indiana University Archives/Lee H. Hamilton Congressional Papers, 1965–1998/MPP2B142/Folder 18, Speech Book 16, Q., April 22, 1970.
Harding, Samuel Bannister, ed. *Indiana University, 1820–1904.* Bloomington: Indiana University, 1904.
Harrison, Robert Pogue. *Gardens: An Essay on the Human Condition.* University of Chicago Press, 2008.
Hart, James D. 5th ed. New York: Oxford University Press, 1983.
Herold, Don. *College Humor*, November 1929, 130–31.
“Hershey, Mrs. Amos Shartle.” Bloomington, IN: Indiana University Archives, n.d. IUA/C213/B268/F.
Hewett, W. T. *Cornell University: A History.* Vol. 1. New York: University Publishing Society, 1905.
Hight, Kate M. “Reminiscences.” *Indiana University Alumni Quarterly* 24, no. 4 (1937): 455–60.

Hoeveler, J. David. "Higher Education in the Midwest: Community and Culture [Reviewed Volumes One and Two]." *History of Education Quarterly* 14, no. 3 (1974): 391–402. https://doi.org/10.2307/367940.

Hollis, Daniel W. *The Journal of American History* 58, no. 1 (1971): 201–2. https://doi.org/10.2307/1890153.

Hollis, Daniel W. *The Journal of American History* 61, no. 2 (1974): 515–16. https://doi.org/10.2307/1904023.

Hollis, Daniel W. *The Journal of American History* 65, no. 3 (1978): 836–37. https://doi.org/10.2307/1901512.

Hooker, Lisa. "RHA Votes to Ask the Trustees to 'Save the Trees'." *Indiana Daily Student*, February 18, 1982.

Horn, David. "Golf Course Opponents Jam Benefit Concert." *Herald-Times*, January 17, 2000.

Hubach, Robert R. "Nineteenth-Century Literary Visitors to the Hoosier State: A Chapter in American Cultural History." *Indiana Magazine of History* 45 (1949): 39–50.

Hunt, Ralph. "Enlightening Situation? Well House Wattage Encourages Conversation Rather Than Action." *Indiana Daily Student*, November 1, 1961.

"Ideas Concerning Campus Plans Change Considerably with Time." *Indiana Daily Student* 41, no. 98 (February 11, 1916): 3.

Iglehart, John E. "Correspondence Between Lincoln Historians and This Society." In *Proceedings of the Southwestern Indiana Historical Society*, 63–88. Bulletin No. 18. Indianapolis: Indiana Historical Commission; Wm. B. Burford, 1923. https://hdl.handle.net/2027/inu.32000001722687.

"In Memoriam: William A. Rawles, '84, Robert A. Ogg, '72, William T. Patten, '93; and Necrology List." *Indiana University Alumni Quarterly* 23, no. 3 (1936): 303–13.

"Inaugurating What Is Expected to Be an Annual Custom." *Indianapolis Star*, May 5, 1939, 17. Photo caption.

Indiana University. "Annual Catalogue of the Indiana University for the Academical Year 1885–86." Bloomington: Indiana University, 1886.

Indiana University. "IU Trustees Approve 'Official Year' of University's First Classes." Indiana University Archives, March 7, 1987. News Release.

Indiana University Archives. "Finding Aid, Collection 286, Box 54." Bloomington, IN: Indiana University, n.d. IUA/C286/B54.

Indiana University Archives. "Reference File: Class Gifts." Bloomington: Indiana University; Unpublished archival material, n.d.

Indiana University Bloomington Faculty Council. "Indiana University Bloomington Faculty Council Minutes, 02 February 1982." Bloomington: Indiana University Archives & Indiana University Libraries Digital Collections Services, February 2, 1982. https://purl.dlib.indiana.edu/iudl/archives/bfc/1982-02-02.

Indiana University Bloomington Faculty Council. "Indiana University Bloomington Faculty Council Minutes, 07 September 2010." Bloomington: Indiana University Archives & Indiana University Libraries Digital Collections Services, September 7, 2010. https://purl.dlib.indiana.edu/iudl/archives/bfc/2010-09-07.

Indiana University Bloomington Faculty Council. "Ndiana University Bloomington Faculty Council Minutes, 06 February 2018." Bloomington: Indiana University Archives & Indiana University Libraries Digital Collections Services, February 6, 2018. https://purl.dlib.indiana.edu/iudl/archives/bfc/2018-02-06.

Indiana University Board of Trustees. "Minutes of the Board of Trustees of Indiana University, 01 December 1952." Bloomington, IN: Indiana University Archives; Indiana University Libraries Digital Collections Services, December 1, 1952. https://purl.dlib.indiana.edu/iudl/archives/iubot/1952-12-01.

Indiana University Board of Trustees. "Minutes of the Board of Trustees of Indiana University, 01 June 1888–07 June 1888." Bloomington, IN: Indiana University Archives; Indiana University Libraries Digital Collections Services, June 2, 1888. https://purl.dlib.indiana.edu/iudl/archives/iubot/1888-06-01.

Indiana University Board of Trustees. "Minutes of the Board of Trustees of Indiana University, 01 November 1996." Bloomington: Indiana University Archives & Indiana University Libraries Digital Collections Services, November 1, 1996. https://purl.dlib.indiana.edu/iudl/archives/iubot/1996-11-01.

Indiana University Board of Trustees. "Minutes of the Board of Trustees of Indiana University, 01 October 1948–02 October 1948." Bloomington: Indiana University Archives & Indiana University Libraries Digital Collections Services, October 1, 1948. https://purl.dlib.indiana.edu/iudl/archives/iubot/1948-10-01.

Indiana University Board of Trustees. "Minutes of the Board of Trustees of Indiana University, 02 February 1980." Bloomington: Indiana University Archives & Indiana University Libraries Digital Collections Services, February 2, 1980. https://purl.dlib.indiana.edu/iudl/archives/iubot/1980-02-02.

Indiana University Board of Trustees. "Minutes of the Board of Trustees of Indiana University, 03 April 1982." Bloomington: Indiana University Archives & Indiana University Libraries Digital Collections Services, April 3, 1982. https://purl.dlib.indiana.edu/iudl/archives/iubot/1982-04-03.

Indiana University Board of Trustees. "Minutes of the Board of Trustees of Indiana University, 03 June 1885–10 June 1885." Bloomington: Indiana University Archives & Indiana University Libraries Digital Collections Services, June 10, 1885. https://purl.dlib.indiana.edu/iudl/archives/iubot/1885-06-03.

Indiana University Board of Trustees. "Minutes of the Board of Trustees of Indiana University, 03 March 1981." Bloomington: Indiana University Archives & Indiana University Libraries Digital Collections Services, March 7, 1980. https://purl.dlib.indiana.edu/iudl/archives/iubot/1981-03-07.

Indiana University Board of Trustees. "Minutes of the Board of Trustees of Indiana University, 03 November 1938–04 November 1938." Bloomington: Indiana University Archives & Indiana University Libraries Digital Collections Services, November 3, 1938. https://purl.dlib.indiana.edu/iudl/archives/iubot/1938-11-03.

Indiana University Board of Trustees. "Minutes of the Board of Trustees of Indiana University, 03 September 1902–15 September 1902." Bloomington: Indiana University Archives & Indiana University Libraries Digital Collections Services, September 6, 1902. https://purl.dlib.indiana.edu/iudl/archives/iubot/1902-09-03.

Indiana University Board of Trustees. "Minutes of the Board of Trustees of Indiana University, 04 April 1935." Bloomington: Indiana University Archives & Indiana University Libraries Digital Collections Services, April 4, 1935. https://purl.dlib.indiana.edu/iudl/archives/iubot/1935-04-04.

Indiana University Board of Trustees. "Minutes of the Board of Trustees of Indiana University, 04 June 1884–11 June 1884." Bloomington: Indiana University Archives & Indiana University Libraries Digital Collections Services, June 7, 1884. https://purl.dlib.indiana.edu/iudl/archives/iubot/1884-06-04.

Indiana University Board of Trustees. "Minutes of the Board of Trustees of Indiana University, 04 March 1884–25 March 1884." Bloomington: Indiana University Archives & Indiana University Libraries Digital Collections Services, March 25, 1884. https://purl.dlib.indiana.edu/iudl/archives/iubot/1884-03-04.

Indiana University Board of Trustees. "Minutes of the Board of Trustees of Indiana University, 04 March 1935." Bloomington: Indiana University Archives & Indiana University Libraries Digital Collections Services, March 4, 1935. https://purl.dlib.indiana.edu/iudl/archives/iubot/1935-03-04.

Indiana University Board of Trustees. "Minutes of the Board of Trustees of Indiana University, 04 May 2001." Bloomington: Indiana University Archives & Indiana University Libraries Digital Collections Services, May 4, 2001. https://purl.dlib.indiana.edu/iudl/archives/iubot/2001-05-04.

Indiana University Board of Trustees. "Minutes of the Board of Trustees of Indiana University, 04 November 1897–06 November 1897." Bloomington: Indiana University Archives & Indiana University Libraries Digital Collections Services, November 5, 1897. https://purl.dlib.indiana.edu/iudl/archives/iubot/1897-11-04.

Indiana University Board of Trustees. "Minutes of the Board of Trustees of Indiana University, 05 December 1981." Bloomington: Indiana University Archives & Indiana University Libraries Digital Collections Services, December 5, 1980. https://purl.dlib.indiana.edu/iudl/archives/iubot/1981-12-05.

Indiana University Board of Trustees. "Minutes of the Board of Trustees of Indiana University, 05 December 2014." Bloomington: Indiana University Archives & Indiana University Libraries Digital Collections Services, December 5, 2014. https://purl.dlib.indiana.edu/iudl/archives/iubot/2014-12-05.

Indiana University Board of Trustees. "Minutes of the Board of Trustees of Indiana University, 05 November 1885–11 November 1885." Bloomington, IN: Indiana University Archives; Indiana University Libraries Digital Collections Services, November 11, 1885. https://purl.dlib.indiana.edu/iudl/archives/iubot/1885-11-05.

Indiana University Board of Trustees. "Minutes of the Board of Trustees of Indiana University, 05 October 2017–06 October 2017." Bloomington: Indiana University Archives & Indiana University Libraries Digital Collections Services, October 5, 2019. https://purl.dlib.indiana.edu/iudl/archives/iubot/2017-10-05.

Indiana University Board of Trustees. "Minutes of the Board of Trustees of Indiana University, 06 March 1982." Bloomington: Indiana University Archives & Indiana University Libraries Digital Collections Services, March 6, 1982. https://purl.dlib.indiana.edu/iudl/archives/iubot/1982-03-06.

Indiana University Board of Trustees. "Minutes of the Board of Trustees of Indiana University, 06 November 1884–11 November 1884." Bloomington: Indiana University Archives & Indiana University Libraries Digital Collections Services, November 7, 1884. https://purl.dlib.indiana.edu/iudl/archives/iubot/1884-11-07.

Indiana University Board of Trustees. "Minutes of the Board of Trustees of Indiana University, 07 December 2012." Bloomington, IN: Indiana University Archives; Indiana University Libraries Digital Collections Services, December 7, 2012. https://purl.dlib.indiana.edu/iudl/archives/iubot/2012-12-07.

Indiana University Board of Trustees. "Minutes of the Board of Trustees of Indiana University, 07 March 1987." Bloomington: Indiana University Archives & Indiana University Libraries Digital Collections Services, March 7, 1987. https://purl.dlib.indiana.edu/iudl/archives/iubot/1987-03-07.

Indiana University Board of Trustees. "Minutes of the Board of Trustees of Indiana University, 07 May 2010." Bloomington, IN: Indiana University Archives; Indiana University Libraries Digital Collections Services, May 7, 2010. https://purl.dlib.indiana.edu/iudl/archives/iubot/2010-05-07.

Indiana University Board of Trustees. "Minutes of the Board of Trustees of Indiana University, 09 April 1983." Bloomington, IN: Indiana University Archives; Indiana University Libraries Digital Collections Services, April 9, 1983. https://purl.dlib.indiana.edu/iudl/archives/iubot/1983-04-09.

Indiana University Board of Trustees. "Minutes of the Board of Trustees of Indiana University, 09 August 1937." Bloomington, IN: Indiana University Archives; Indiana University Libraries Digital Collections Services, August 9, 1937. https://purl.dlib.indiana.edu/iudl/archives/iubot/1937-08-09.

Indiana University Board of Trustees. "Minutes of the Board of Trustees of Indiana University, 09 June 2006." Bloomington, IN: Indiana University Archives; Indiana University Libraries Digital Collections Services, June 9, 2006. https://purl.dlib.indiana.edu/iudl/archives/iubot/2006-06-09.

Indiana University Board of Trustees. "Minutes of the Board of Trustees of Indiana University, 09 May 1980." Bloomington: Indiana University Archives & Indiana University Libraries Digital Collections Services, May 9, 1980. https://purl.dlib.indiana.edu/iudl/archives/iubot/1980-05-09.

Indiana University Board of Trustees. "Minutes of the Board of Trustees of Indiana University, 10 October 1941–11 October 1941." Bloomington, IN: Indiana University Archives; Indiana University Libraries Digital Collections Services, October 10, 1941. https://purl.dlib.indiana.edu/iudl/archives/iubot/1941-10-10.

Indiana University Board of Trustees. "Minutes of the Board of Trustees of Indiana University, 11 June 1891–17 June 1891." Bloomington: Indiana University Archives & Indiana University Libraries Digital Collections Services, June 16, 1891. https://purl.dlib.indiana.edu/iudl/archives/iubot/1891-06-11.

Indiana University Board of Trustees. "Minutes of the Board of Trustees of Indiana University, 12 June 1947–14 June 1947." Bloomington, IN: Indiana University Archives; Indiana University Libraries Digital Collections Services, June 12–14, 1947. https://purl.dlib.indiana.edu/iudl/archives/iubot/1947-06-13.

Indiana University Board of Trustees. "Minutes of the Board of Trustees of Indiana University, 12 June 1953." Bloomington, IN: Indiana University Archives; Indiana University Libraries Digital Collections Services, June 12, 1953. https://purl.dlib.indiana.edu/iudl/archives/iubot/1953-06-12.

Indiana University Board of Trustees. "Minutes of the Board of Trustees of Indiana University, 12 September 1947–13 September 1947." Bloomington: Indiana University Archives & Indiana University Libraries Digital Collections Services, September 12, 1947. https://purl.dlib.indiana.edu/iudl/archives/iubot/1947-09-12.

Indiana University Board of Trustees. "Minutes of the Board of Trustees of Indiana University, 13 March 1925–14 March 1925." Bloomington: Indiana University Archives & Indiana University Libraries Digital Collections Services, March 14, 1925. https://purl.dlib.indiana.edu/iudl/archives/iubot/1925-03-13.

Indiana University Board of Trustees. "Minutes of the Board of Trustees of Indiana University, 14 August 2009." Bloomington, IN: Indiana University Archives; Indiana University Libraries Digital Collections Services, August 14, 2009. https://purl.dlib.indiana.edu/iudl/archives/iubot/2009-08-14.

Indiana University Board of Trustees. "Minutes of the Board of Trustees of Indiana University, 14 July 1961–15 July 1961." Bloomington: Indiana University Archives & Indiana University Libraries Digital Collections Services, July 14, 1961. https://purl.dlib.indiana.edu/iudl/archives/iubot/1961-07-14.

Indiana University Board of Trustees. "Minutes of the Board of Trustees of Indiana University, 14 June 2019." Bloomington: Indiana University Archives & Indiana University Libraries Digital Collections Services, June 14, 2019. https://purl.dlib.indiana.edu/iudl/archives/iubot/2019-06-14.

Indiana University Board of Trustees. "Minutes of the Board of Trustees of Indiana University, 15 August 2008." Bloomington, IN: Indiana University Archives; Indiana University Libraries Digital Collections Services, August 15, 2008. https://purl.dlib.indiana.edu/iudl/archives/iubot/2008-08-15.

Indiana University Board of Trustees. "Minutes of the Board of Trustees of Indiana University, 15 February 1838." Bloomington: Indiana University Archives & Indiana University Libraries Digital Collections Services, February 15, 1838. https://purl.dlib.indiana.edu/iudl/archives/iubot/1838-02-15.

Indiana University Board of Trustees. "Minutes of the Board of Trustees of Indiana University, 15 September 2000." Bloomington, IN: Indiana University Archives; Indiana University Libraries Digital Collections Services, September 15, 2000. https://purl.dlib.indiana.edu/iudl/archives/iubot/2000-09-15.

Indiana University Board of Trustees. "Minutes of the Board of Trustees of Indiana University, 16 December 1884–19 December 1884." Bloomington: Indiana University Archives & Indiana University Libraries Digital Collections Services, December 1884. https://purl.dlib.indiana.edu/iudl/archives/iubot/1884-12-16.

Indiana University Board of Trustees. "Minutes of the Board of Trustees of Indiana University, 16 June 1904–22 June 1904." Bloomington: Indiana University Archives & Indiana University Libraries Digital Collections Services, June 22, 1904. https://purl.dlib.indiana.edu/iudl/archives/iubot/1904-06-16.

Indiana University Board of Trustees. "Minutes of the Board of Trustees of Indiana University, 16 November 1898–18 November 1898." Bloomington: Indiana University Archives & Indiana University Libraries Digital Collections Services, November 18, 1898. https://purl.dlib.indiana.edu/iudl/archives/iubot/1898-11-16.

Indiana University Board of Trustees. "Minutes of the Board of Trustees of Indiana University, 16 November 1951." Bloomington, IN: Indiana University Archives; Indiana University Libraries Digital Collections Services, November 16, 1951. https://purl.dlib.indiana.edu/iudl/archives/iubot/1951-11-16.

Indiana University Board of Trustees. "Minutes of the Board of Trustees of Indiana University, 17 February 1950." Bloomington: Indiana University Archives & Indiana University Libraries Digital Collections Services, February 17, 1950. https://purl.dlib.indiana.edu/iudl/archives/iubot/1950-02-17.

Indiana University Board of Trustees. "Minutes of the Board of Trustees of Indiana University, 17 March 1950." Bloomington: Indiana University Archives & Indiana University Libraries Digital Collections Services, March 17, 1950. https://purl.dlib.indiana.edu/iudl/archives/iubot/1950-03-17.

Indiana University Board of Trustees. "Minutes of the Board of Trustees of Indiana University, 19 December 1943." Bloomington: Indiana University Archives & Indiana University Libraries Digital Collections Services, December 19, 1943. https://purl.dlib.indiana.edu/iudl/archives/iubot/1943-12-19.

Indiana University Board of Trustees. "Minutes of the Board of Trustees of Indiana University, 19 January 1950." Bloomington: Indiana University Archives & Indiana University Libraries Digital Collections Services, January 19, 1950. https://purl.dlib.indiana.edu/iudl/archives/iubot/1950-01-19.

Indiana University Board of Trustees. "Minutes of the Board of Trustees of Indiana University, 19 July 1841–24 July 1841." Bloomington: Indiana University Archives & Indiana University Libraries Digital Collections Services, July 21, 1841. https://purl.dlib.indiana.edu/iudl/archives/iubot/1841-07-19.

Indiana University Board of Trustees. "Minutes of the Board of Trustees of Indiana University, 19 June 1908–23 June 1908." Bloomington: Indiana University Archives & Indiana University Libraries Digital Collections Services, June 22, 1908. https://purl.dlib.indiana.edu/iudl/archives/iubot/1908-06-19.

Indiana University Board of Trustees. "Minutes of the Board of Trustees of Indiana University, 19 May 1950." Bloomington: Indiana University Archives & Indiana University Libraries Digital Collections Services, May 19, 1950. https://purl.dlib.indiana.edu/iudl/archives/iubot/1950-05-19.

Indiana University Board of Trustees. "Minutes of the Board of Trustees of Indiana University, 20 January 1961–21 January 1961." Bloomington, IN: Indiana University Archives; Indiana University Libraries Digital Collections Services, January 20–21, 1961. https://purl.dlib.indiana.edu/iudl/archives/iubot/1961-01-20.

Indiana University Board of Trustees. "Minutes of the Board of Trustees of Indiana University, 20 March 1894–23 March 1894." Bloomington: Indiana University Archives & Indiana University Libraries Digital Collections Services, March 22, 1894. https://purl.dlib.indiana.edu/iudl/archives/iubot/1894-03-20.

Indiana University Board of Trustees. "Minutes of the Board of Trustees of Indiana University, 21 October 1949–22 October 1949." Bloomington: Indiana University Archives & Indiana University Libraries Digital Collections Services, October 21, 1949. https://purl.dlib.indiana.edu/iudl/archives/iubot/1949-10-21.

Indiana University Board of Trustees. "Minutes of the Board of Trustees of Indiana University, 22 June 1942–23 June 1942." Bloomington: Indiana University Archives & Indiana University Libraries Digital Collections Services, June 23, 1942. https://purl.dlib.indiana.edu/iudl/archives/iubot/1942-06-22.

Indiana University Board of Trustees. "Minutes of the Board of Trustees of Indiana University, 22 November 1937–23 November 1937." Bloomington, IN: Indiana University Archives; Indiana University Libraries Digital Collections Services, November 23, 1937. https://purl.dlib.indiana.edu/iudl/archives/iubot/1937-11-22.

Indiana University Board of Trustees. "Minutes of the Board of Trustees of Indiana University, 22 September 1947." Bloomington: Indiana University Archives & Indiana University Libraries Digital Collections Services, September 22, 1947. https://purl.dlib.indiana.edu/iudl/archives/iubot/1947-09-22.

Indiana University Board of Trustees. "Minutes of the Board of Trustees of Indiana University, 22 September 1972." Bloomington, IN: Indiana University Archives; Indiana University Libraries Digital Collections Services, September 22, 1972. https://purl.dlib.indiana.edu/iudl/archives/iubot/1972-09-22.

Indiana University Board of Trustees. "Minutes of the Board of Trustees of Indiana University, 23 March 1899–25 March 18997." Bloomington: Indiana University Archives & Indiana University Libraries Digital Collections Services, March 25, 1899. https://purl.dlib.indiana.edu/iudl/archives/iubot/1899-03-23.

Indiana University Board of Trustees. "Minutes of the Board of Trustees of Indiana University, 24 March 1902–25 March 1902." Bloomington: Indiana University Archives & Indiana University Libraries Digital Collections Services, March 25, 1902. https://purl.dlib.indiana.edu/iudl/archives/iubot/1902-03-24.

Indiana University Board of Trustees. "Minutes of the Board of Trustees of Indiana University, 24 September 1838–27 September 1838." Bloomington: Indiana University Archives & Indiana University Libraries Digital Collections Services, September 27, 1838. https://purl.dlib.indiana.edu/iudl/archives/iubot/1838-09-24.

Indiana University Board of Trustees. "Minutes of the Board of Trustees of Indiana University, 24 September 1994." Bloomington, IN: Indiana University Archives; Indiana University Libraries Digital Collections Services, September 24, 1994. https://purl.dlib.indiana.edu/iudl/archives/iubot/1994-09-24.

Indiana University Board of Trustees. "Minutes of the Board of Trustees of Indiana University, 25 March 1940–26 March 1940." Bloomington: Indiana University Archives & Indiana University Libraries Digital Collections Services, March 25, 1940. https://purl.dlib.indiana.edu/iudl/archives/iubot/1940-03-25.

Indiana University Board of Trustees. "Minutes of the Board of Trustees of Indiana University, 25 March 1940–26 March 1940." Bloomington: Indiana University Archives & Indiana University Libraries Digital Collections Services, March 26, 1940. https://purl.dlib.indiana.edu/iudl/archives/iubot/1940-03-25.

Indiana University Board of Trustees. "Minutes of the Board of Trustees of Indiana University, 25 September 1941–27 September 1941." Bloomington: Indiana University Archives & Indiana University Libraries Digital Collections Services, September 27, 1941. https://purl.dlib.indiana.edu/iudl/archives/iubot/1941-09-25.

Indiana University Board of Trustees. "Minutes of the Board of Trustees of Indiana University, 27 June 1997." Bloomington: Indiana University Archives & Indiana University Libraries Digital Collections Services, July 27, 1997. https://purl.dlib.indiana.edu/iudl/archives/iubot/1997-06-27.

Indiana University Board of Trustees. "Minutes of the Board of Trustees of Indiana University, 28 January 1944–30 January 1944." Bloomington: Indiana University Archives & Indiana University Libraries Digital Collections Services, January 28, 1944. https://purl.dlib.indiana.edu/iudl/archives/iubot/1944-01-28.

Indiana University Board of Trustees. "Minutes of the Board of Trustees of Indiana University, 30 June 1947." Bloomington, IN: Indiana University Archives; Indiana University Libraries Digital Collections Services, June 30, 1947. https://purl.dlib.indiana.edu/iudl/archives/iubot/1947-06-30.

Indiana University Board of Trustees. "Minutes of the Board of Trustees of Indiana University, 30 May 1941–02 June 1941." Bloomington: Indiana University Archives & Indiana University Libraries Digital Collections Services, May 31, 1941. https://purl.dlib.indiana.edu/iudl/archives/iubot/1941-05-30.

Indiana University Board of Trustees. "Minutes of the Board of Trustees of Indiana University, 31 May 1963–03 June 1963." Bloomington: Indiana University Archives & Indiana University Libraries Digital Collections Services, May 31, 1963. https://purl.dlib.indiana.edu/iudl/archives/iubot/1963-05-31.

"I.U. Founding to Be Observed by Alumni Throughout the World." *Indianapolis News*, May 2, 1939, 13.

IU Office of Sustainability. "Office of Sustainability 2020 Vision," 2010.

IU Task Force on Campus Sustainability. "Campus Sustainability Report." Bloomington: Indiana University, January 7, 2008.

"IUA/C239/B3 All-University Committee on Names." Bloomington, IN: Indiana University Archives, n.d.

"Ivy Chamness to Edit Quarterly." *Indiana University Alumni Quarterly* 8 (1921): 331–32.

Jacobs, Bruce A., and Jillian Kinzie. "Editors' Notes." In *Enhancing Sustainability Campuswide*, edited by Bruce A. Jacobs and Jillian Kinzie, 1–6. New Directions for Student Services 137. Wiley, 2012.

Jordan, David Starr. *Days of a Man, Being Memories of a Naturalist, Teacher, and Minor Prophet of Democracy.* Vol. 1. 2 vols. Yonkers-on-Hudson, NY: World Book Company, 1922.

Jordan, David Starr. "Letter to Lemuel Moss," October 7, 1883. IUA/C73/B1/F Jordan, David Starr.

Keith, B. D., B. T. Hill, and M. R. Johnson. "Indiana University Campus Limestone Tour." Digital Information. Indiana Geological Survey, 2015. https://legacy.igws.indiana.edu/bookstore/details.cfm?Pub_-Num=DI02.

Keith, Brian D. "Follow the Limestone: A Walking Tour of Indiana University." 2009. Reprint, Bloomington: Originally published June 2009 by Indiana Geological Survey; Bloomington/Monroe County Convention; Visitors Bureau; republished July 2013 by Indiana Geological Survey; Visit Bloomington; current edition published July 2018 by Indiana Geological; Water Survey; Visit Bloomington, July 2018.

Keith Buckley, Linda Fariss, Derek F. DiMatteo, and Colleen Pauwels, eds. *Trustees and Officers of Indiana University, Volume III: 1982–2018.* Bloomington: Indiana University, 2019.

Knepper, George W. *Indiana Magazine of History* 75, no. 1 (1979): 95–96. http://www.jstor.org/stable/27790359.

Krause, Carrol. *Showers Brothers Furniture Company: The Shared Fortunes of a Family, a City, and a University.* Bloomington: Indiana University Press, 2012.

Lahrman, Dolores M., and Delbert C. Miller. *The History of Mitchell Hall, 1885–1986.* Bloomington: Indiana University Archives, 1987.

Lesnick, Gavin. "Campus Icon Retains History, Myth from 1868." *Indiana Daily Student*, September 13, 2005. https://www.idsnews.com/article/2005/09/campus-icon-retains-history-myth-from-1868.

Levell, Frank H. "Report of the Alumni Secretary." *Indiana University Alumni Quarterly* 8 (1921): 323.

Levine, Arthur. "Higher Education Becomes a Mature Industry." *About Campus: Enriching the Student Learning Experience* 2, no. 3 (1997): 31–32. https://doi.org/10.1177/108648229700200.

Levine, Arthur. "How the Academic Profession Is Changing." *Daedalus* 126, no. 4 (1997): 1–20.

"'Local' column." *Indiana Student*, May 26, 1896, 29.

Louis, Kenneth Gros. "Remarks at the Sample Gates and Plaza Dedication." Bloomington, IN: Indiana University Archives, June 13, 1987. John Ryan Speeches, Indiana University Archives/C45.

Lyon, Robert E. "The History of Chemistry at Indiana University, 1829–1931." *Indiana University News-Letter* 19, no. 3 (March 1931).

Madison, James H. *Hoosiers: A New History of Indiana.* Bloomington: Indiana University Press; Indiana Historical Society Press, 2014.

Madison, James H. *Indiana University Department of History: Past to Present.* Bloomington: Indiana University Department of History, 2010.

McCaslin, William, and D. D. Banta. *History of Johnson County, Indiana.* Chicago: Brant & Fuller, 1888.

McLaughlin, H. Roll. "HABS in Indiana, 1955–1982: Recollections." In *Historic American Buildings Survey in Indiana*, edited by T. M. Slade, 13–20. Bloomington: Indiana University Press, 1983.

McMains, Howard F. "The Indiana Seminary Charter of 1820." *Indiana Magazine of History* 106 (2010): 356–80.

"Meeting in Woodburn Room, June 4, 1936," June 4, 1936. Folder: Publications, Galleys & Transcripts, IUA/C83/B3/F, Indiana University Archives.

Merriman, Jerry. "How Should We Grow?" *Herald-Times*, November 10, 1999. Letter to the Editor.

Morrison, Sarah Parke. "Some Sidelights of Fifty Years Ago." *Indiana University Alumni Quarterly* 6, no. 3 (July 1919): 529–35.

Mottier, David. “Letter to Joseph Pierce.” Indiana University Archives C174/B31/F Mottier, David, February 13, 1896.
Mottier, David. “Letter to William Bryan.” Indiana University Archives C174/B31/F Mottier, David, November 5, 1902.
Mottier, David, and Ulysses S. Hanna. “Suggestions on the Improvement of the East Campus.” Indiana University Archives C174/B31/F Mottier, David, November 10, 1913. Report to IU Board of Trustees.
Murray, Agnes M. “Early Literary Developments in Indiana.” *Indiana Magazine of History* 36 (1940): 327–33.
Myers, Burton D. “Letter to Herman B Wells.” Indiana University Archives, April 1, 1941. IUA/C213/B404/F Myers, Dean B. D.
Myers, Burton Dorr. *History of Indiana University: Volume II, 1902–1937, The Bryan Administration.* Edited by Burton D. Myers and Ivy L. Chamness. Bloomington: Indiana University, 1952.
Myers, Burton Dorr. *The History of Medical Education in Indiana.* Bloomington: Indiana University Press, 1956.
Myers, Burton Dorr. *Trustees and Officers of Indiana University 1820–1950.* Edited by Ivy L. Chamness and Burton D. Myers. Bloomington: Indiana University, 1951.
Nave, Erin, and Kara Saige. “Golf Course Cancelled.” *Indiana Daily Student*, January 18, 2000.
Nolan, James. “Indiana University History.” *Courier-Journal*, January 17, 1971.
“Obituary: Baynard Rust [*sic*] Hall.” *New York Times*, January 27, 1863, 5.
Office of the Bicentennial. “Indiana University Bicentennial Final Report.” Bloomington: Indiana University, 2020. https://wayback.archive-it.org/219/20240413230003/https://200.iu.edu/doc/IU-bicentennial-final.pdf.
Olmsted, Olmsted, and Eliot. “Letter to Joseph Swain.” Indiana University Archives C174/B32/F Olmsted, Olmsted, and Eliot—Campus Plan 1896, December 8, 1896.
Ostrom, Elinor. *Governing the Commons: The Evolution of Institutions for Collective Action.* New York: Cambridge University Press, 1990.
Parkhurst, David F. “Letter to Kenneth Gros Louis,” January 18, 1982. David F. Parkhurst files.
Parkhurst, David F. “Letter to Leonard Bernstein,” February 7, 1982. David F. Parkhurst files.

Patton, John B. "Location to the Natural Areas Committee," June 30, 1982. David F. Parkhurst files, University Archives, Indiana University.

Pearce, John Ed. "The Middle Years of Indiana University: A Review." *Courier-Journal*, November 18, 1973.

Pering, Cornelius. "The Pering Letters of 1833." *Indiana University Alumni Quarterly*, no. 20 (1933): 409–28.

Plager, Sheldon J. "Letter to Alumni and Friends of the University and the Law School Community," April 8, 1982.

Plager, Sheldon J. "The Woods and the Law School Institution Addition," February 1, 1982. Memo to Law School Student Body and Staff. David F. Parkhurst files, University Archives, Indiana University.

Pope, Alexander. *An Epistle to the Right Honourable Richard Earl of Burlington*. London: L. Gilliver, 1731.

Preservation Development Inc. "Wylie House Historic Structure Report." Bloomington, 2001.

"Professors Take Divergent Views on Building Site." *Indiana Daily Student*, March 28, 1935, 1, 3.

"Program for the Rededication Ceremony for Indiana University's Owen Hall and Wylie Hall, October 18, 1985." Bloomington: University Printing Services, 1985.

Pyle, Ernie. "It's in the Air." *Indiana Daily Student*, September 5, 1922, 4.

Quinn, Roy. "Letter to Herman Wells." Indiana University Archives, May 16, 1938. IUA/C213/B455.

Relph, Edward. *Place and Placelessness*. London: Pion Limited, 1976.

Reschke, Michael. "IU Building Wave to Keep Going in 2018." *Herald-Times*, December 25, 2017. https://www.heraldtimesonline.com/story/news/local/2017/12/26/iu-building-wave-to-keep-going-in-2018/117591668/.

Reynolds, Heather, Eduardo Brondizio, and Jennifer Robinson, eds. *Teaching Environmental Literacy: Across Campus and Across the Curriculum*. Bloomington: Indiana University Press, 2010.

Richardson, Dixie Kline. *Baynard Rush Hall: His Story*. Indianapolis: Dixie Kline Richardson, 2009.

Riddle, Ward G. "Letter to Burton D. Myers." Indiana University Archives, April 21, 1942. IUA/C213/B404.

Ringenberg, William C. *History: Reviews of New Books* 6 (1978): 148.

Roberts, Sam. "Leon G. Billings, Architect of Clean Air and Clean Water Acts, Dies at 78." *New York Times*, November 17, 2016.
Roehr, Eleanor. *Trustees and Officers of Indiana University, 1950 to 1982*. Bloomington: Indiana University, 1983.
Roosevelt, Theodore. "Straightout Americanism." *Indiana University Alumni Quarterly* 5, no. 3 (July 1918): 295–307.
Ross, John M. "Letter to Herman B Wells," April 27, 1982. David F. Parkhurst files.
Rothblatt, Sheldon. "A Note on the 'Integrity' of the University." In *Aurora Torealis: Studies in the History of Science and Ideas in Honor of Tore Frängsmyr*, edited by Marco Beretta, Karl Grandin, and Svante Lindqvist, 277–98. Sagamore Beach, MA: Science History Publications, 2008.
Roznowski, Tom. "The Trees Grew First: IU's Woodland Campus." *The Ryder*, April 2017, 24–25.
Ryan, John. "Letter to David F. Parkhurst," April 30, 1982. David F. Parkhurst files.
Ryan, John W. "Charge to the Class," May 8, 1982. Indiana University commencement location, Indiana University Archives/C45/John Ryan Speeches.
Ryan, John W. "Remarks at the Sample Gates and Plaza Dedication." Bloomington, IN, June 13, 1987. John Ryan Speeches, Indiana University Archives/C45.
Sandweiss, Eric. "Personal Communication to the Author," June 7, 2024.
Save the Woods. "Save the IU Crescent Forest." *Real Times* 6, no. 6 (February 19, 1982): 2. Originally circulated as "An Open Letter to Indiana University Alumni," February 11, 1982. David F. Parkhurst files, University Archives, Indiana University.
Schlechtweg, Harold. "Environmental Day Activities Listed." *Indiana Daily Student*, April 20, 1970.
Schlechtweg, Harold. "Nelson Outlines Proposals to End National Pollution." *Indiana Daily Student*, April 23, 1970.
Schuyler, David. "Frederick Law Olmsted and the Origins of Modern Campus Design." *Planning for Higher Education* 25, no. 2 (1996–1997): 1–10.
Scott, Bob. "The Revolution Is Here, Escape in Dunn Meadow." *Indiana Daily Student*, April 20, 1970.
S[enour], F. C. "A Novel of Indiana University." *The Vagabond* 2, no. 3 (March 1925): 51–52.

Shamon, Marvin. "The Traditions of Indiana University." Indiana University Archives/Reference file: Buildings—Bloomington Campus Well House, Rose., c1935?

Shirley, Janet Carter. *The Indiana University Alumni Association: One Hundred and Fifty Years, 1854–2004*. Bloomington: Indiana University Alumni Association, 2004.

Shively, George. *Initiation*. New York: Harcourt, Brace; Company, 1925.

Shively, George J., ed. *Record of S.S.U. 585*. New Haven: Brick Row Book Shop, 1920.

Slatalla, Michelle. "How the Trees Were Saved, Law Addition Flap Is Finally Over." *Indiana Daily Student*, April 8, 1982. For the Opinion Board.

SmithGroupJJR. "Indiana University Bloomington Campus Master Plan," March 2010.

Snyder, Gary. "Coming in to the Watershed: Biological and Cultural Diversity in the California Habitat." *Chicago Review* 39, no. 3/4 (1993): 75–86. https://doi.org/10.2307/25305721.

Solberg, Winton U. *Indiana Magazine of History* 67, no. 3 (1971): 268–69. http://www.jstor.org/stable/27789750.

Stahr, Elvis. "Founders' Day Ceremonial." Indiana University Archives, May 3, 1967. http://fedora.dlib.indiana.edu/fedora/get/iudl:2078062/OVERVIEW. IUA/C75.

Stoner, Richard B. "Form Letter," April 26, 1982. David F. Parkhurst files.

Sudhalter, Richard M. *Stardust Melody: The Life and Music of Hoagy Carmichael*. New York: Oxford University Press, 2002.

Tandy, Jeannette Reed. "Pro-Slavery Propaganda in American Fiction of the Fifties." *South Atlantic Quarterly* 21.1, no. 1 (January 1, 1922): 41–50. https://doi.org/10.1215/00382876-21-1-41.

Tandy, Jeannette Reed. "Pro-Slavery Propaganda in American Fiction of the Fifties." *South Atlantic Quarterly* 21.2, no. 2 (April 1, 1922): 170–78. https://doi.org/10.1215/00382876-21-2-170.

"The 1915 Commencement." *Indiana University Alumni Quarterly* 2, no. 3 (1915): 278–92.

"The Centennial Commencement." *Indiana University Alumni Quarterly* 7 (1920): 370–418.

"The Dagger: 1875–80." Bloomington: Indiana University Archives, n.d. Reference file, Indiana University Archives.

"The Decline of Campustry." *Daily Student*, November 11, 1903.

"The Guardian: Origins of the EPA." *EPA Historical Publication-1*, Spring 1992.

"The New Purchase or Seven and Half Years in the Far West." *Indiana Magazine of History*, n.d. unsigned review of Hall, *The New Purchase* (1916).

"The Old Crescent." NRHP Inventory-Nomination Form; United States Department of the Interior: Heritage Conservation and Recreation Service, 1980.

The Vision of Herman B Wells. Documentary film, 1993.

Toman, Barbara, and Christopher Cokinos. "Trustees Approve Addition Plan." *Indiana Daily Student*, April 5, 1982.

Toman, Barbara, and Christopher Cokinos. "Trustees Will Re-Evaluate Plan." *Indiana Daily Student*, March 8, 1982, 1, 5.

Towne, Steven E. "Indiana University During the Civil War." *200: The Bicentennial Magazine* 1, no. 2 (2018): 18–19.

Trouillot, Michel-Rolph. *Silencing the Past: Power and the Production of History.* Boston: Beacon Press, 1995.

Turner, F. J. "The Significance of History." *Wisconsin Journal of Education and Midland School Journal* 21, no. 10/11 (October–November 1891): 230–34, 253–56.

Ulrich, Rudolph. "Letter to Joseph Swain." Indiana University Archives C174/B44, May 1899.

Vico, Giambattista. *The New Science of Giambattista Vico: Unabridged Translation of the Third Edition (1744) with the Addition of the "Practic of the New Science".* Translated by Thomas Goddard Bergin and Max Harold Fisch. Ithaca, NY: Cornell University Press, 1984.

Visher, Stephen S. "Water Supply Problems of Bloomington, Indiana," *Proceedings of the Indiana Academy of Science* 66 (1956): 188–91.

Weatherwax, Paul. "Familiar Trees Greet Returning Alumni." *The Review*, May 1960, 12–18.

Weatherwax, Paul. *The Woodland Campus of Indiana University.* Bloomington: Indiana University, 1966.

Weisenburger, Francis P. *Indiana Magazine of History* 74, no. 4 (1978): 367–68. http://www.jstor.org/stable/27790338.

"Well-House Innovation." *Daily Student*, October 15, 1907.

Wells, Herman B. *Being Lucky: Reflections and Reminiscences.* Bloomington: Indiana University Press, 1980.

Wells, Herman B. "Letter to Burton D. Myers." Indiana University Archives, July 18, 1941. IUA/C213/B404.

Wells, Herman B. "Letter to Roy Quinn." Indiana University Archives, May 26, 1938. IUA/C213/B455.

Wells, Herman B. "Letter to Roy Quinn." Indiana University Archives, May 2, 1939. IUA/C213/B455. IUA/Reference file: Foundation Day.

Wells, Herman B. "Oral History Interview by Bonnie Williams." Wylie House Collections, March 19, 1992.

Wells, Herman B. "Letter to Dolores Lahrman." Indiana University Archives, May 13, 1987.

Wells, Herman B. "Letter to John Ryan." Indiana University Archives, April 7, 1987.

Wells, Herman B. "Letter to Paul Weatherwax." Lilly institution/LMC 2283/B4/F Wells, Herman B., August 22, 1961.

Wells, Herman G. [sic]. "The Early History of Indiana University as Reflected in the Administration of Andrew Wylie, 1829–1851." *Filson Club Historical Quarterly* 36 (1962): 113–27.

Williams, Bonnie. "Playing in the Stream of History: A Flexible Approach to First-Person Interpretation." *Association for Living Historical Farms and Agricultural Museums Proceedings* 14 (1996): 255–61.

Williams, Bonnie, and Elaine Herold, eds. *Affectionately Yours: The Andrew Wylie Family Letters, 1828 to 1859.* Bloomington: Indiana University Wylie House Museum, 1995.

Woodburn, James A. "Baynard Rush Hall." In *Dictionary of American Biography*, 1936.

Woodburn, James A. *History of Indiana University: Volume I, 1820–1902.* Bloomington: Indiana University, 1940.

Woodburn, James A. "Letter to William Lowe Bryan." Indiana University Archives, February 28, 1935. IUA/C83/B3/F Publications, Galleys, & Transcripts.

Woodburn, James A. "Local Life and Color in the New Purchase." *Indiana Magazine of History* 9, no. 4 (1913): 215–33.

Woodburn, James A. "Presentation of the *History of Indiana University*, Volume I at the Woodburn Testimonial Dinner." Indiana University Archives, n.d. IUA/C83/B4/F Woodburn, James.

Woodburn, James A. "Sketches from the University's History I: College Men and College Life about 1850." *Indiana University Alumni Quarterly* 2 (1915): 249–69.

Woodburn, James A. "Sketches from the University's History II: College Men and College Life About 1850 (Continued)." *Indiana University Alumni Quarterly* 2 (1915): 409–27.
Woodburn, James A. "Sketches from the University's History III: Faculty and Curriculum about 1850." *Indiana University Alumni Quarterly* 3 (1916): 20–37.
Woodburn, James A. "Sketches from the University's History IV: Daniel Read, Professor of Ancient Languages, 1843–1856." *Indiana University Alumni Quarterly* 3 (1916): 127–48.
Woodburn, James A. "Sketches from the University's History V: Death of President Wylie: A Year of President Ryors and Election of Dr. Daily: Death and Services of Dr. David H. Maxwell." *Indiana University Alumni Quarterly* 3 (1916): 347–59.
Woodburn, James A. "Sketches from the University's History VI: The Vincennes Suit and the Fire." *Indiana University Alumni Quarterly* 3 (1916): 489–500.
Woodburn, James A. "Sketches from the University's History VII: Dark Days after the Fire: Courage in Adversity." *Indiana University Alumni Quarterly* 4 (1917): 1–11.
Woodburn, James A. "Sketches from the University's History VIII: The Board of Trustees Sixty Years Ago; Student Reminiscences." *Indiana University Alumni Quarterly* 4 (1917): 117–28.
Woodburn, James Albert. "Higher Education in Indiana." Edited by Herbert B. Adams. Bureau of Education, Circular of Information No. 1, 1891: Contributions to American Educational History. Washington: Government Publishing Office, 1891.
Woodburn, James Albert. "The New Purchase." In *Proceedings of the Tenth Annual Meeting of the Ohio Valley Historical Association*, edited by Harlow Lindley, 6:43–54. 1. Indiana Historical Society Publications, 1916.
"Work of the Alumni Council." *Indiana University Alumni Quarterly* 3, no. 3 (July 1916): 397–405.
Wright, Mike. "Critics Flock to Golf Forum." *Herald-Times*, December 1, 1999.
Wright, Mike. "Golf Course Alternative Offered." *Herald-Times*, January 14, 2000, A1, A9.
Wright, Mike. "Golf Course Opponents Dress Like Fish, Trees." *Herald-Times*, 1999-11-13.

Wright, Mike. "Group Behind New IU Golf Course Includes Alumni, Development Firm." *Herald-Times*, November 30, 1999.

Wright, Mike. "Issues Raised about Golf Course's Impact." *Herald-Times*, October 13, 1999.

Wright, Mike. "IU Delays Action on a New Golf Course." *Herald-Times*, December 2, 1999.

Wright, Mike. "IU Students, Staff to Have Golf Access." *Herald-Times*, November 10, 1999.

Wright, Mike. "Trustees Want Public Input on Golf Course." *Herald-Times*, 1999-11-24.

Wylie House Museum, Indiana University Libraries. "Wylie House Museum Handbook," 2016–2017.

"Wylie House Music from the Parlor," 2001. Audio recording; liner notes by Sophia Grace Travis.

Wylie, Theophilus. "Diary Entry." Indiana University Archives, June 28, 1857.

Wylie, Theophilus. "Diary Entry." Indiana University Archives, September 6, 1885.

Wylie, Theophilus. "Letter to Judge Andrew Wylie," July 18, 1881. IUA/C202/B5/F Letters relating to history.

Wylie, Theophilus A. *Indiana University, Its History from 1820, When Founded, to 1890, with Biographical Sketches of Its Presidents, Professor and Graduates, and a List of Its Students from 1820 to 1887.* Indianapolis: Wm. B. Burford, 1890.

www.ingramcontent.com/pod-product-compliance
Lightning Source LLC
LaVergne TN
LVHW100518110826
845146LV00002B/684

* 9 7 9 8 2 1 8 7 9 4 0 8 8 *